D1806867

Maker Education Meets Technology Education

International Technology Education Studies

Series Editor

Marc J. de Vries (*Delft University of Technology, The Netherlands*)

Editorial Board

John R. Dakers (*Delft University of Technology, The Netherlands*)
Jonas Hallström (*Linköping University, Sweden*)
Philip Reed (*Old Dominion University, USA*)

VOLUME 19

The titles published in this series are listed at *brill.com/ites*

Maker Education Meets Technology Education

Reflections on Good Practices

Edited by

Remke M. Klapwijk, Jianjun Gu, Qiuyue Yang and
Marc J. de Vries

BRILL

LEIDEN | BOSTON

Cover illustration: Photograph by Science Hub Delft University of Technology

All chapters in this book have undergone peer review.

The Library of Congress Cataloging-in-Publication Data is available online at https://catalog.loc.gov

Typeface for the Latin, Greek, and Cyrillic scripts: "Brill". See and download: brill.com/brill-typeface.

ISSN 1879-8748
ISBN 978-90-04-68189-7 (paperback)
ISBN 978-90-04-68190-3 (hardback)
ISBN 978-90-04-68191-0 (e-book)

Copyright 2023 by Koninklijke Brill NV, Leiden, The Netherlands.
Koninklijke Brill NV incorporates the imprints Brill, Brill Nijhoff, Brill Hotei, Brill Schöningh, Brill Fink, Brill mentis, Vandenhoeck & Ruprecht, Böhlau, V&R unipress and Wageningen Academic.
All rights reserved. No part of this publication may be reproduced, translated, stored in a retrieval system, or transmitted in any form or by any means, electronic, mechanical, photocopying, recording or otherwise, without prior written permission from the publisher. Requests for re-use and/or translations must be addressed to Koninklijke Brill NV via brill.com or copyright.com.

This book is printed on acid-free paper and produced in a sustainable manner.

Printed by Printforce, United Kingdom

Contents

PART 3
Thematic Reflections

Preface

Maker Education and Technology Education share common interests yet often operate independently. In this book they have been brought together. We have collected a set of good practices in maker activities and some colleagues reflected on this set, each from a different thematic point of view.

We want to thank all chapter authors for their writing. We also want to thank our co-editors from China who worked with us to get good examples from China and also an interesting view on what happens in their country in terms of Maker Education and Technology Education.

We hope that this book will be instrumental in bringing together Maker Education and Technology Education practices. It is our belief that a closer connection between the two can be beneficial for both. That in turn will be beneficial for pupils and students, and are they not the ones we want to serve in the end?

Marc de Vries and Remke Klapwijk
Delft University of Technology

Figures and Tables

Figures

Tables

Notes on Contributors

HildaRuth Beaumont (formerly known as David Barlex)
has worked in education for some 50 years and for most of that time was known as David Barlex. David became an acknowledged leader in design & technology education, curriculum design and curriculum materials development. Recently he has identified disruptive technologies relevant to the school curriculum and ways in which young people may be engaged with these. His most recent publication with Frank Banks Teaching STEM in the secondary school was very well received with a second edition being published in 2020. Since 2021, David has found that he is much, much happier and at ease with himself if dressed and presenting as female. Hence, he is now living full time as HildaRuth and continuing with both academic writing and consultancy under the name of HildaRuth Beaumont.

Bert Bredeweg
is professor of science education at the Amsterdam University of Applied Sciences and an associate professor at University of Amsterdam. His research interest focusses on the use of artificial intelligence in education and addresses several themes including interactive knowledge representations, computational thinking and learning analytics. At the Applied University Bredeweg leads the Smart Education lab.

Jeffrey Buckley
is a Lecturer in Research Pedagogy in Technological University of the Shannon: Midlands Midwest, Ireland. He received his PhD in 2018 from KTH Royal Institute of Technology, Sweden, where he examined the role of spatial ability in technology education. His research interests primarily relate to learning, assessment, and research methods in technology and engineering education, and he is currently Associate Editor for the *International Journal of Technology and Design Education.*

Marc J. de Vries
is professor of Science Education and professor of Christian Philosophy of Technology at Delft University of Technology, the Netherlands. He is the editor-in-chief of the *International Journal of Technology and Design Education* and series editor of the *International Technology Education Studies* book series. He wrote a monograph *Teaching about Technology* that introduces philosophy of technology for technology educators. He is the coordinator of the international conference series Pupils' Attitudes Towards Technology.

Christian Dindler

is associate professor of participatory interaction design at the Department of Digital Design and Information Studies at Aarhus University. In his research, Christian focuses on the ethics of designing digital technology and the effects that interaction design processes have on individuals and organisations. He has engaged with these issues in several ways, including studies of how participants experience taking part in design, how ethics is dealt with in design, and how children can be empowered to critically and constructively engage with digital technology. In his research practice, Christian works in close collaboration with private and public partners to develop knowledge and solutions that are grounded in practice and provide value for the partners involved.

Nathan Eskue

is an aerospace engineering professor at TU Delft, specializing in AI, robotics, manufacturing, project/business management, and rapid iteration prototyping. He holds degrees in business information systems, marketing, operations management, an MBA, and a masters of Data Science from Columbia University. Nathan has spoken at over 60 international conferences on AI, aerospace/defence, quantum, and other technical topics. He's worked for NASA, Raytheon, Northrop Grumman, and other aerospace organizations for over twenty years, with experience in product development, project management, supply chain, manufacturing, and AI architecture.

Wendy Fox-Turnbull

is an Associate Professor at the University of Waikato who is Deputy Head of School for Te Kura Toi Tangata School of Education. This Trimester she is Acting Head of School. She is the editor of *Australasian Journal of Technology Education*, on the Editorial Board of *International Journal of Work Integrated Learning* and co-editor *European Journal of STEM Education*. Wendy was chair of the Technology Education New Zealand (TENZ Council) from 2006 to 2018, and has convened two TENZ conferences: TENZ 2005 and TENZ/ICTE 2017 and one International Technology Research conference (PATT) in 2013. Research special interests include authentic learning in technology education, the place of women in technology related careers, the role and nature of effective conversations in learning and teaching and learning approaches for the 21st Century. Wendy is a registered and certified primary teacher.

Mathieu Gielen

is an Assistant Professor in "design for children's play" at Delft University of Technology and director of the Play Well Lab, where students, academics and external partners collaborate to build knowledge on child-centered design for children's playful wellbeing. His work focuses on advancing opportunities for free play through design, and participatory methods for inclusion of children's perspectives in design. He participated in the research and development project that produced "Your Turn", a series of primary school projects and tools for co-design with children.

Jianjun Gu

is Doctor of Education, Distinguished Professor of Changjiang Scholars Program of the Ministry of Education, National Cultural Famous Scholar and Outstanding Talent, Director of K-12 Technology and Engineering Education Center, Director of STEM Education Research Institute and Director of the International Technology and Engineering Educators Association (ITEEA) China Center. Chief Investigator of Labor and Technology Curriculum Guidelines for Compulsory Education, Head of Committee of Technology Curriculum Standards for Senior High Schools, Head of Committee of General Technology Curriculum Standards for Senior High Schools, Head of Committee of Labor and Technology Curriculum Standards for Compulsory Education, Chief Investigator of Primary and Secondary Technology and Engineering Curriculum Guidelines, as well as the Vice President of China Education Equipment Association.

Katrine Holm Kanstrup

works as chief advisor at Center for Computational Thinking & Design at Aarhus University, Denmark. She leads teacher and school leader programs on technology comprehension. She founded FabLab Spinderihallerne that offered the first "FabAcademy" in Denmark. Katrine Holm Kanstrup led a school district program that built makerspaces at 12 schools and six high schools, and she co-founded the FabLab@SCHOOLdk school district alliance, teacher community, and conference. She led 15 public, private, and research partnerships to invent more playful educational and cultural services in co-creation with children and integrating emerging technology.

Rolf Hut

studied Applied Physics in Delft. He got his PhD in environmental sciences (hydrology). During his PhD he became as a "MacGyver" scientist who creates measurement devices from household appliances and materials. Through this work he started teaching maker education courses at Delft, most notably "design engineering for physics students", the topic of Chapter 9 of this book.

Ole Sejer Iversen

Professor in Interaction Design and director of Center for Computational Thinking & Design at Aarhus University, Denmark. Professor Iversen was one of the founders of the European Fablearn (MakeEd) conference series and chair of the committee of experts developing the national Danish curriculum for Technology Comprehension in K-9 appointed by the Minister of Education in Denmark. Ole Sejer Iversen is associate editor of the *International Journal of Child-Computer Interaction* and a long-term member of the steering committee of the Interaction Design & Children and the Participatory Design conference series.

Kaiju Kangas

is an assistant professor of technology education, in the Faculty of Educational Sciences at the University of Helsinki, Finland. Her research focuses on maker-centred learning in the context of design, craft, and technology education, from the pre-primary and comprehensive levels of education to pre- and in-service teacher education. Recently, she has been involved in research focusing on "Generation AI" maker education to develop educational initiatives on teaching AI and data agency to novice learners.

Remke M. Klapwijk

is a researcher in Delft University of Technology on the Pedagogy of Design and Technology Education and co-founder of the Delft Science Hub in which primary schools, teacher educators, engineers and designers cooperate. Her research interests relate primarily to design thinking, creativity, formative assessment, prototyping and spatial thinking. She co-developed the toolbox Make Design Learning Visible, a formative assessment tool and developed various (in-service) teacher resources and trainings. Together with Peter Troxler she chaired the First Dutch Fablearn Conference in 2018.

Hyuksoo Kwon

is a professor of integrative STEM education/Technology Education at Kongju National University, Republic of Korea. He is a writer for multiple textbooks (e.g. Science, Technology, Engineering from middle school to high school) in South Korea. His research interests are technology teachers, makerspaces, integrative STEM education, and K-12 Engineering. He has conducted several projects (STEM program development, National School Makerspace project, and Textbook Policy) supported and funded by Korean government. Together with Korean Technology and Engineering Teachers' Association, he has conducted cultural movement for improving the public perception toward technology and engineering education.

Suneel Madahar

is a teacher of design at the International School Delft, in The Netherlands. He gained a degree in Pharmacology from King's College London, but realized education and teaching was his true passion. Starting his teaching career as a Biology and Science teacher, Suneel has managed also teach mathematics, philosophy and computer studies. At the turn of the century, he was asked to teach Design and since then has become a fierce advocate of not only teaching design, but to instill the love of design and its importance in trying to solve the world's problems using the principles of design.

Varpu Mehto

is a doctoral researcher at the Faculty of Educational Sciences, University of Helsinki. Her dissertation focuses on the dynamic role of materiality in learning-by-making, and aims to foster relational, embedded, and embodied learning through practices of craft. Recently she has also been involved in a research project exploring shifting nature-culture relations and collective atmospheres in everyday life of children.

Álvaro Núñez-Solís

has a Master's degree in Manufacturing Systems Sciences and studied Industrial and Systems Engineering (ITESM Querétaro). He leads the Obsolete Products Management System based on a Collaborative Circular Economy that helps companies reduce, reuse and/or recycle their obsolete products (computers, laptops, tablets, smartphones, robotic assembly lines, etc.) Author of the books "Ser Emprendedor Antes de los 30s" (Being an entrepreneur before the 30s) and "No Nos Queda de Otra: 10 Razones Por Qué Emprender" (We do not have another option!: 10 Reasons Why undertake). He is also an International speaker on "Circular Economy Entrepreneurship and Electronic Waste Recycling" (www.alvaronunez.mx).

James Otieno Jowi

is the Principal Education Officer of the East African Community (EAC) responsible for the coordination and development of regional education policies and frameworks for the seven EAC countries. He is also a Senior Lecturer of Comparative Education at the School of Education, Moi University, Kenya. He is also the founder of Sustainable Rural Initiatives (SRI) rural community based NGO transforming lives of rural communities in western Kenya. He holds a PhD in

Higher Education Studies from University of Twente, a Masters in Comparative and International Education, University of Oslo, a Master of Philosophy in Linguistics and Bachelor of Education degree from Moi University, Kenya.

Monique Pijls

is senior lecturer at the Amsterdam University of Applied Sciences. Her interests in research and educational design cover maker education, reasoning with multiple representations, collaborative learning, and the integration of art, science and technology in education. She developed the Minor Maker Education.

Freek Pols

studied applied physics at Delft University of Technology. He worked for ten years as a secondary school physics teacher. He gave several workshops, including *Arduino* and *teaching inquiry*. In 2019 he started working as the first-year lab course coordinator at the Applied Physics program at the University of Technology, Delft. In 2023 he finished his PhD study *"Development of a teaching-learning sequence for scientific inquiry through argumentation in secondary physics education"*. His research focusses on teaching scientific inquiry at Pre-University and first-year university level.

Elwin Savelsbergh

is a professor of Curriculum Development at the Utrecht University of Applied Sciences and an associate professor at Utrecht University. Key themes in his research program are: (technological) literacy, education for sustainable development, citizenship, and pedagogical content knowledge.

Miroslava Silva-Ordaz

is a primary and design teacher at the International School of Delft, she also works as liaison with the Science Hub TU Delft on educational projects focused on Science, Technology and Sustainability. She holds a PhD in Educational Technology and has over 20 years of experience working in education as a teacher, consultant, and face to face/online international trainer. During her professional career, she gained experience working for non-profit organisations for international schools at the primary and secondary, as well as in higher education as a researcher, facilitator and consultant. She really likes working with different age groups and especially children as they are natural explorers.

Annemiek G. C. van Boeijen

graduated in 1990 as a designer and worked as such in international projects. Since 2000 she works for the department Human Centered Design, Delft

University of Technology. Social themes, such as sustainability, inclusiveness and migration demand her attention. In 2015 she defended her thesis *Crossing Cultural Chasms – Towards a Culture-Conscious Approach to Design*. Her research is focused on the role of culture in design processes, developing methods geared to support designers in cultivating a culture-sensitive approach. She is initiator and co-editor of the *Delft Design Guide* and author of *Culture Sensitive Design: A Guide to Culture in Practice*.

Gerald van Dijk

is a senior lecturer and researcher at the University of Applied Sciences Utrecht. His research interests include design and maker education, language sensitive STEM education, education for sustainable development (ESD) and teacher education. Furthermore, he is frequently involved in reforming technology curricula at a national level in The Netherlands, primarily for general secondary education.

Tom van Eijck

is lecturer at the Amsterdam University of Applied Sciences, in the field of science education. His research interest is science education, maker education and technology in education. He currently works on a research project about interactive knowledge representations that stimulate reasoning in primary science education.

Maarten Van Mechelen

is a Senior Researcher at LEGO Education where he leads the research strategy for project teams from conception to launch and ensures products have a measurable impact on the intended learner outcomes. He has a PhD in Child-Computer Interaction and previously held academic positions at the Center for Computational Thinking and Design at Aarhus University, the Faculty of Industrial Design Engineering at Delft University of Technology, and the Meaningful Interactions Lab at KU Leuven. Maarten is a Steering Committee Member of the FabLearn Europe/MakeEd conference series, and an Associated Editor of the *International Journal of Child-Computer Interaction*.

Marie-Louise Wagner

is a research assistant and centre coordinator at Center for Computational Thinking & Design at Aarhus University, Denmark. Marie-Louise has developed and implemented a range of workshops and courses that focus on digital fabrication, design processes and making in an education context. She was project manager on the elective subject in Technology Comprehension in

Danish primary schools, which was a trial project in collaboration with the Ministry of Education in Denmark. She has done in-service teacher training, participated in research dissemination and helped municipalities with the establishment of makerspaces across Denmark.

Marten B. Westerhof
is a Marie Skłodowska-Curie PhD Fellow at Technological University Dublin. His research focuses on the development of children's spatial ability through educational maker activities. He is an external researcher at Waag, an applied research institution in Amsterdam, to develop spatial maker activities and professional development for maker educators. His main research interests are spatial ability, learning through design, maker education, and pedagogy. For his MSc thesis in design at Delft University of Technology he developed a toolkit for organising playful design education workshops through a co-design process with Sustainable Rural Initiatives, a non-profit organisation in Western Kenya.

P. John Williams
is Professor of Education and the Director of Graduate Research in the School of Education at Curtin University. His current research interests include STEM, mentoring beginning teachers, Pedagogical Content Knowledge and electronic assessment of performance. He regularly presents at international and national conferences, consults on Technology Education in a number of countries, and is a longstanding member of eight professional associations. He is the series editor of the Springer Contemporary Issues in Technology Education and is on the editorial board of six professional journals. He has authored or contributed to over 250 publications, and is elected to the International Technology and Engineering Education Association's Academy of Fellows for prominence in the profession.

Qiuyue Yang
is Doctor of Education, researcher Hubei University of Technology on the Vocational and Technology Education. Her research interests relate primarily to technical literacy, STEAM education, technical design thinking, creativity, formative assessment, vocational and technical ability development. As a core member, she participated in the Technical Literacy Assessment Research among primary school, secondary school and college students under the Humanities and Social Sciences project of the Ministry of Education. She has attended the ICTE and the International Technology and Engineering Educators Association (ITEEA) to give presentations.

PART 1

The Rise of Maker Education across the World

∵

CHAPTER 1

Introduction

Remke Klapwijk and Marc de Vries

Abstract

The value given to learning by making has swung like a pendulum back and forth through history. Recently, the idea that learning by making is important has gained momentum through the Maker Movement. The new movement is attractive as it revalues making and it's possibilities to learn a variety of skills as well as scientific concepts through making in informal as well as formal contexts. Its signature pedagogies, including a playful approach, focus on collaboration and celebration of learning through productive mistakes may provide new opportunities and inspiration for Technology Education. To explore this, this book provides two types of chapters. The first type is case study chapters. These chapters are descriptions of a certain practice with a focus on the particular features of that practice and not so much a thematic comparison with other practices or with theory. That happens in the second type of chapters. In those chapters the authors have used the case studies to reflect on different themes associated with Maker Education in relation with Technology Education.

Keywords

maker education – maker movement – educational value of making – constructionism – relation with design and technology education

1   Learning from the Maker Movement

The rise of the Maker Movement – a community of hobbyists, tinkerers, engineers, hackers, and artists who creatively design and build projects for both playful and useful ends (Martin, 2015, p. 30) provides new opportunities and inspiration for Technology Education as well as a number of challenges. Currently no books have been published on this theme while the Maker Movement has been maturing, improving practices, opening up new makerspaces and the maker space pedagogies and strategies have entered formal schooling. In addition, academic publications on Maker Education and empirical investigations

© KONINKLIJKE BRILL NV, LEIDEN, 2023 | DOI:10.1163/9789004681910_001

have been on the rise in recent years (Mersand, 2021; Rouse & Rouse Gillespie, 2022; Schad & Jones, 2019).

Although there have been interactions between researchers, innovators and teachers operating in the field of Technology Education and those in the Maker Movement, these fields have been developed along separate, social and academic lines. Technology education, as part of foundational education, vocational education or higher education, has a long history, whereas the Maker Movement started at the beginning of the 21st century and is a new shoot in the educational field.

In this book the two fields will meet. They have many elements in common, they are both focused on the material world and the agency of learners is an important element in both traditions. The purpose of this book is to understand and analyze the kind of informal and formal educational activities that take place under the umbrella of the Maker Movement and then relate this to the field of Technology education in a way that helps to uncover what researchers, innovators and teachers in this field can learn from the principles, ideas and practices that are central to the Maker Movement and vice versa.

In this Introduction, Section 2 describes the rise of Maker Education and in Section 3 we analyze the social trends and reasons that made it come to life and spread across countries and continents. Signature pedagogical ideas of the maker movement including learning through experience and tinkering, constructivism and social learning are described in Section 4. This section also focuses on the educational value: what do you learn through making? Section 5 relates the rise of Maker Education to the already present Technology Education and aspects of sustainability are discussed in Section 6. The set-up of the book with its case studies and thematic chapters is explained in the last section.

2   The Rise of Maker Education

Making things is at the core of humanity. Young children will make things during play; for example, they may build a shelter using bed sheets and a standing lamp. Working with materials is present in all societies, whether we prepare meals, make clothing, renovate spaces or repair bikes. However, due to changes in modern technology, making has been removed from house-holds and everyday life, to industries. It is no longer possible or necessary to repair products, and quite often households prefer to buy ready-made products instead of making these themselves. Making as such is not on the rise.

However, the idea that learning by making is important has gained momentum through the Maker Movement that started in the United States of America.

It is hard to say exactly where and when the movement started, but many consider the Americans Seymour Papert and Cynthia Solomon as initiators of the Maker Movement. Both were working as computer scientists in a time where computers were not common at all. During and after the second world war, computers have been invented and in the sixties most companies and households did not own any computers. Although two Dutch teenagers Kees Koster and Lambert Meertens, tried to build their own computer in the early sixties, at that time hardly anybody expected that citizens would be able to build and program a computer due to its cost and complexity. Ken Olson, president and founder of Digital Equipment Corporation, a manufacturer of computers said: "There is no reason for people to wish to have a computer at home" (Rooijendijk, 2010).

Computer scientists Papert and Solomon who worked at the Massachusetts Institute of Technology, did not share this public opinion and developed a vision in which children would actively make things with computers via programming. In 1968, Papert (2005, reprinted from 1980) writes in *Teaching Children Thinking* about his concerns that computers will be used in schools for the dumbest part of learning, namely rote learning. Therefore, Papert and Solomon, the latter also working as a computer teacher in elementary and secondary schools, start advocating an active, creative role for children and list lots of possible educative projects that can be done with a computer such as controlling puppets, making movies, programming and composing music. With this vision in mind, Papert, Solomon and partners developed the first programming language for children, called Logo, that features a Turtle. To this very day, later versions of Logo, including Scratch are among the most popular programming environments for children.

They were true visionaries at that time describing a school computation laboratory in which children could invent, build and experiment with computers (Martinez & Stager, 2013; Papert & Solomon, 1971). Papert and Solomon envision computers children could experiment with:

> In our image of a school computation laboratory, an important role is played by numerous 'control ports' which allow any student to plug any device into the computer.... The laboratory will have a supply of motors, solenoids, relays, sense devices of various kinds etc. Using them, the students will be able to invent and build an endless variety of cybernetic systems. (1971, p. 39)

An interesting element in their approach is the combination of digital and physical making, an element which is also present in the current maker movement.

Although computers were extremely expensive for an average household, many people – especially teenagers and twenties – started to build computers and make code in the sixties. Around 1975 the first kit to build your own computer – Altair was launched and was a huge success. Newsletters and magazines were launched, and the hobbyists computer builders and programmers met in clubs, in shops and organized meetings in many countries across Europe, the USA and elsewhere. It was possible to build relatively cheap and good computers and these hobbyist and tinkerers would write code that was personally relevant for them. For example, in 1984, a Dutch teacher Lucie Blom convinced her schoolboard to buy a computer for use in school and – as hardly any Dutch educational software was available – she wrote many educative software including programs that would learn children to learn to count (Anonymous, 1984, 13 September). When it was no longer possible to make computers that could compete with the ones from the store – many of the components became very small and could no longer be joined manually – the building and making of computers by hobbyists decreased.

Another important moment that can be considered as initiating the maker movement is a course called "How to make almost anything" at the MIT Media lab in the early 2000s given by professor Neil Gershenfeld. Students with different backgrounds and disciplines joined the course and learned to use digital tools to make and express themselves. Gershenfield was surprised that these inventions were not only highly personal, but were executed by students working alone, when in a corporate context such products would be the work of teams (Martinez & Stager, 2013, p. 24). He noticed the emergence of a collaborative culture that emerged during classes in his own fab lab. Until today, the course has been running and resulting products are documented and shared through website presentations.

A few years later, Gershenfeld reached out to new target groups including underserved youth in inner-city communities by providing a portable lab with making equipment that could be transported to various locations (Blikstein, 2018; Gershenfeld, 2005). Through the lab ordinary people could make things using digital tools such as a 3D-printer or a laser cutter.

This portable lab is the predecessor of the thousands of fab labs and other Makerspaces around the world today. At first the fab labs grew slowly and were mainly concentrated in the United States and Europe. This changed when Dough Dougherty launched Make Magazine in 2005 and organized a Maker Fair in 2006 in the San Francisco area that attracted tens of thousands of people, as the fairs of the computer builders had done in the past. It turned out that many hobbyists, tinkerers, engineers, hackers, and artists where creatively designing and building projects – using digital and non-digital technologies – and through the Make Magazine and Make Fairs a community was born. More and more countries established fab labs and makerspaces, e.g. in 2007 the first Fab-Lab in the Netherlands was founded. Sharing of ideas is stimulated in the maker movement. In order to use the free facilities, each project has to be documented and shared in a way that another fab lab user could make it or use it as inspiration for a new product. Websites such as Makezine[1] or Instructables[2] show a great many of inspiring artefacts such as lamps, art and even jewels in the form of chemical molecules that can be made using the fab lab tools.

The maker movement was at this point mainly thriving outside educational institutes, at home and in informal contexts. It was not until 2008, that digital fabrication places and the accompanying pedagogical ideas reached K-12 schools. Paulo Blikstein of Stanford University started working with K-12 schools in Brazil and in the United States to create pedagogies and fab labs that could be used in schools (Blikstein, 2008). Digital fabrication is in his eyes a way to create artefacts that have an attractive appearance and would inspire children to make things that they were personally interested in. He also wanted to bring more agency to students and sees the FabLab as a disruptive place in schools, where students could safely make, build and share their inventions. Blikstein also established a world-wide network of educators. The first FabLab@School conference in 2011 was visited by many K-12 educators from around the world and many became involved in developing and implementing the FabLabs and Makerspaces in their own schools, see for example Chapter 2 on the rise of maker education in China and Chapter 3 about Denmark. Around 2013, commercial organizations jumped on and started programs that further increased the momentum of making and coding in K-12 education (Blikstein, 2018).

In ten years' time, a network of educators was established. In accordance with the open and sharing culture of the maker spaces, educators and researchers in many countries, share their educational ideas. In the FabLearn Fellow program, experienced educators in formal and informal learning spaces are brought together to contribute to research on making and makerspaces. In the 2020–2022 cohort, educators from Brazil, China, Denmark, Hong Kong, Italy, India, Iran, Israel, Jordan, Kenya, Peru, Puerto Rico, Senegal, Thailand, Togo, the United Kingdom, and the United States were involved (Fablearn website,[3]). A meta-review from 2021 included empirical studies from over 26 countries with all continents represented (Mersand, 2021). The ideals and ideas of the maker movement have spread quickly. A visitor of the first Dutch Fablearn conference noticed an enthusiastic vibe and a willingness and openness to listen to each other's "educational experiments". The culture of tinkering in the FabLabs has influenced the educators and researchers and created a willingness to let "1000 flowers grow". Many researchers report that there is a huge diversity among the pedagogic and didactic approaches in maker spaces, also maker spaces have been founded by different stakeholders including libraries, science centra, companies, local governments and schools.

This short history of the maker movement shows that maker education – unlike technology education – started outside the educational institutes. All initiatives emphasize the active use of digital and other technologies to make, build and create. Making is considered as fun, and tinkering as something that supports people to learn and to express themselves. Interaction with other makers is essential for novices as well as experienced makers and the "public" act of sharing work in progress leads to learning. Free choice and activities that are personal important for the maker are especially advocated. An important credo is that everybody is a maker, can join the worldwide community of makers which values an open culture. In the Netherlands, the maker movement uses a broad definition of making and includes lots of activities that are traditionally seen as female, such as knitting and making jam. Although the movement officially wants to include everybody, this is a complicated issue. Researchers such as (Vossoughi, Hooper, & Escudé, 2016) have shown that the maker movement in the USA is heavenly influenced by white, middle-class ideas of making and is led by people with leisure time, technical knowledge and resources to make (Barton, Tan, & Greenberg, 2017, p. 5). While these researchers (Rose, 2005; Vossoughi, Hooper, & Escudé, 2016) appreciate the attention of the Maker Movement for making, they argue that making is not just fun but a necessity for working class and immigrant families:

> Working-class folks have not had the luxury of discovering making and tinkering: they've been doing it all their lives to survive – and creating exchange networks to facilitate it. Somebody across the street or down the road is a mechanic, or is wise about home remedies, or does tile work, and you can swap your own skills and services for that expertise. (Rose, 2014, p. XXV)

The same necessity to make is present among immigrant families leading to forms of creativity and reinvention that are embodied in the everyday life of immigrant families. For example, Vossoughi et al. (2016) point to the Haitian writer Edwidge Danticat (Danticat, 2013, August 27) who describes the story of her mother that highlights the historical conditions that necessitated creativity: "If you can't afford clothes, but you can make them – make them. You have to work with what you have, especially if you don't have a lot of money. You use creativity, and you use imagination" (Danticat, 2013, para. 8). Quite often, ingenuity in making is born in tight circumstances. In this spirit, it is important to understand that making practices are present in diverse forms in all communities and instead of bringing making as a new activity from outside, inquiries are needed into existing forms of making in nondominant communities (Vossoughi et al., 2016). Creating environments in which participants share stories about familiar practices (use of sewing machines, baking, kite making and home repairs) can support new ways of noticing the scientific, artistic and creative ways of everyday activities and helping participants to realize the intellectual complexity and knowledge they and their families possess as well as how these may be expanded and connected to academic knowledge (Vosshoughi et al., 2016; Blikstein, 2008).

Blikstein aims at empowerment and increased self-esteem by augmenting the familiar practices of building and making with computational tools and scientific reasoning. Blikstein (2013, p. 7) states:

> Especially in low-income schools, students would often tell me that they used to 'make' and build things with their parents and friends, and often had jobs in garages, construction companies, or carpentry shops. However that experience was disconnected from their school life, since they did not see a link between the intellectual work in the classroom and the manual labor in the wood shop. Because of bias inherit within the educational system their own forms of engineering and tinkering, stripped down of any form of mathematical of scientific content, were looked down upon by society and by themselves.

3   Reasons behind the Rise of Maker Education

Although specific people have considerably influenced the rise of the maker movement and maker education, a number of cultural and historic reasons may explain why the making movement has spread the last fifteen years across the world.

The first reason may seem a bit contradictory at first sight. Due to industrialization as well as emancipation, making things yourself has become less prevalent in many societies. Many products are nowadays made in a manner that they are not repairable anymore.[4] Especially in households in western societies, less and less people are engaged in making, e.g. clothes are bought and many households no longer use sewing machines. As a result, a great many children lack the opportunity to learn to make things at home. In other words, the value of making has been rediscovered. Vossoughi et al. (2016) however make it clear that for working class families, making has never been away and it is not a luxury, but an economic necessity.

The idea that everybody is a maker and that making is part of our identity as humans is a reaction to this as it revalues making. Many of those who are in power and make decisions on education, whether for their own children or for their school or nation, see the value of making in learning and want to recreate and revive making as this will lead to engagement, fun and educative opportunities for the next generation. This kind of reasoning is for example present in talks and books by Astrid Poot, one of the key figures in the Dutch maker Movement.

The second reason for the rise of maker education has to do with the social acceptance of the ideas of progressive, experience-based constructivist education (Blikstein, 2018). In many of the talks and popular books by advocates of the making movement, maker education is compared with traditional learning through books and instruction. In the field of educational research and practice, one can see two different streams, on the one hand the instructionalists and on the other hand the constructivists. This division goes back till the end of the 18th century when in Switzerland, Johann Pestalozzi started to experiment with what we would call nowadays learning through experience and construction of knowledge. Maker education is placed in this tradition and seen as constructivist containing the promise of learning through experience and self-regulated learners that acquirer higher order skills through personal relevant projects in disruptive yet safe places. This is in line with what many policymakers, companies, parents as well as scholars want for children, they want more emphasis on learning by doing as well as nurturing skills such as creative thinking and problem solving as they are essential in our current, ever changing society and workplaces. Innovation and solving social problems are considered important, and young people should get the opportunity to embark on this early on. This is reflected in curriculum goals present in for example the US Next Generation Science Standards or in the Dutch Curriculum. Many curricula place a stronger emphasis on problem solving, creative thinking, scientific practices, and give design, engineering and making a more central place in the K-12 curriculum.

Another, third reason is related to the attractiveness and status of digital, innovative technologies for children, parents and teachers. In combination with highlighting the value of the more traditional tools of hammers and sewing machines, and the idea that everybody is a maker, it is possible for a lot of people to identify with the maker movement. As shown in the case study on the Amsterdam Maker Spaces of the Libraries, parents as well as children are attracted. In addition, the dramatic reduction of cost in Digital Fabrication

Technologies has given Maker education momentum (Martinez & Stager, 2013; Blikstein, 2018).

Finally, the fact that the maker movement started mainly outside the educational systems may have supported its development. Educational systems are hard to change, as policy makers may want changes, early adopters inside the system may want changes, but in practice there is a lot of resistance and educational systems tend to change slowly. However, in the case of the maker movement, the makers were already there, but became visible through the fairs and magazines and gained momentum, visibility and more status. As the movement growth was first mainly in the non-formal context of households, followed by more informal settings such as in the public maker spaces and supported by universities, it was possible to experiment with and create spaces that fostered new teaching and learning approaches and to put new ideals about learning into practice. In these small, informal spaces, it was shown that a different kind of approach to education was possible and success stories that were happening in many places were being shared. Quite often, as innovation theory has shown, innovations are developed by small companies and not within the big, existing companies. So, the fact that the early innovators could work and innovate outside the formal educational contexts through working with partners such as local municipalities, companies, libraries and museums who provided money as well as time helped to shape new pedagogies around formal and informal maker education. This in turn inspired K-12 schools as we can derive from the meta-review by Rouse and Gillespie Rouse (2022).

4   Educational Value: What Do You Learn through Making?

In this section, key pedagogic ideas/concepts of the maker movement are described as well as the kind of social and cognitive learning outcomes it wants to achieve. We will also give insights into educational reformers who emphasized the value of making.

4.1   *Educational Reformers Valuing Materiality*
For a long time, making and materiality was absent in formal education. Schools would focus on literacy and learning math. This changed when the Swiss Johann Pestalozzi (1746–1827) who – inspired by the French Philosopher Rousseau – entered the scene. He focused on educating the poor and discovered that the use of objects from the child's environment eased the learning of math and language: "Long before the spelling-book comes on, children might be made acquainted with those objects, of which they are to learn the names,

either by their being exhibited to them in reality, or represented by good models and drawings" (Pestalozzi cited in Biber, 1831, p. 175). Pestalozzi emphasized that every aspect of the child's life contributed to the formation of their personality, character, and capacity to reason. His educational methods were child-centered and based on individual differences, sense perception, and the student's self-activity. He was allowed to teach in the town of Stans where his approach was evaluated as very successful by school authorities who praised him for his progress. In eight months, he had not only taught children of five and six years of age to read perfectly, but also to write, draw and understand arithmetic. Pestalozzi's method was used by the primary school that Albert Einstein attended. Einstein said of his education at Aarau, "It made me clearly realize how much superior an education based on free action and personal responsibility is to one relying on outward authority" (Isaacson, 2007, p. 65).

Friedrich Fröbel (1782–1852) was a student from Pestalozzi and a reformers who followed Pestalozzi in his attention for child-centered pedagogies and emphasis on personal experiences and materiality. Fröbel created the concept of kindergarten and manufactured playing materials for preschool children as he recognized the importance of the activity of the child in learning. He also introduced the concept of "free work" (Freiarbeit) into pedagogy and established the "game" as the typical form that life took in childhood and stressed the educational value of games and play. Activities in the first kindergarten included singing, dancing, gardening, and self-directed play with the Fröbel materials. Both Fröbel and Pestalozzi combine materiality with a child-centered pedagogy in which children learned through playful, self-driven activities.

In the same century in Finland, Uno Cygnaeus initated handicraft-based education in 1865 called Sloyd. In Sloyd, there is an emphasis on working with a variety of materials including woodwork, metalwork and textiles and creating personally designed products. Sloyd spread around many countries and is compulsory in Finnish, Danish, Swedish and Norwegian schools. Nowadays, these countries are still among the frontrunners in design and technology education and have added digital technologies to the range of materials used in primary and secondary education.

A little later, in Italy Maria Montessori (1870–1952) promoted learning through every day activities, such as caring for the school environment and setting a table to have lunch together. She also developed specific, tangible materials that could be used to learn math and other subjects. "The hand is the chief teacher of the child" was an important credo. Usually, children work independently or in small groups; however, by observing others they also learn and become engaged in new activities. The materials provide concrete experience but move the child towards the abstract.

The American philosopher, psychologist and educational reformer John Dewey (1859–1952) and the French philosopher and psychologist, Jean Piaget (1869–1980) are also often mentioned as inspirational for the maker movement (Blikstein, 2013, 2018; Martinez & Stager, 2013). Both Dewey and Piaget emphasized the fact that children construct knowledge and that they need personal, concrete, high quality experiences in order to understand more abstract concepts. Education will fail if one begins with language instead of beginning with real and material action (Piaget, 1976). This view is known as constructivism, as people construct knowledge from experience and through social interaction. Papert, mentioned earlier as one of the fathers of the maker movement, worked together with Piaget and coined the term constructionism:

> Constructionism – the N word as opposed to the V word – share constructivism's connotation of learning as "building knowledge structures" irrespective of the circumstances of learning. It then adds the idea that this happens especially felicitously in a context where a learner is consciously engaged in constructing a public entity. (Papert, 1991, p. 1)

Martinez and Stager see an analogy between John Dewey's ideas about the spiral process of knowledge creation and iterative design processes applied in maker education (2013, p. 14). According to Dewey, educators need to recognize what surroundings are conducive to having experiences that lead to growth, this includes utilizing both physical and social surroundings so they contribute to valuable experiences (Dewey, 1938, p. 40).

4.2   *Key Principles in Maker-Centered Education*

Making is not new in education, it is present in art, engineering, design and technology education, home economics, maker education, disciplines that are all maker-centered.

What exactly is making? There are several conceptions present in the context of the maker movement (Martin, 2015, p. 30). Martin uses these definitions to develop the following encompassing working definition of

> making as a class of activities focused on designing, building, modifying, and/or repurposing material objects, for playful or useful ends, oriented toward making a "product" of some sort that can be used, interacted with, or demonstrated. Making often involves traditional craft and hobby techniques (e.g., sewing, woodworking, etc.), and it often involves the use of digital technologies, either for manufacture (e.g., laser cutters, CNC machines, 3D printers) or within the design (e.g., microcontrollers, LEDS). (p. 31)

This definition shows that the actual construction and building using all sorts of materials are key processes, however, other related processes such as designing and repurposing objects are also important. Other processes that are often mentioned are tinkering, playful experimenting with materials to discover how things work through experience, thinking – including imagining what one wants to make and thinking about something before or after doing, e.g. what happens to this material when I heat it – and engineering – applying and extracting technological and scientific principles while making (Martinez & Stager, 2013). So all the processes around making are often included in the context of the maker movement, in other fields like design and engineering, making is seen as a sub process that is an essential element embedded in the overall design and engineering processes. Making also refers to different domains, including amongst others digital fabrication, ICT, wood, metal, electronics, food and textiles. Almost all products are in the form of physical artefacts, except for the ICT technologies as they yield products such as devices, programs, codes or are used for information and communication processes.

Researchers and educators in the field of design and technology education and those involve in maker movement initiatives, stress the importance of agency of the learner. Allowing learners to make something related to their personal interest will usually lead to strong, intrinsic motivation (Martin, 2015). Authentic projects and design challenges related to the learners interest and surroundings are thought to have a similar effect. Although evidence exists, not all learners become necessarily motivated through authentic design and make projects, e.g. in a case study on informal learning Martin tells the story about Victor who finds it difficult to start a personal project. Even when Victor is encouraged to follow personal interests, he does not become engaged in making. At some point, his makerspace coaches discover that Victor really likes to help other learners with their projects. Victors gets engaged, not through personal interests in a specific topic or through tinkering on his own with the materials, but through social relations and his motivation to help others (Martin & Betser, 2020).

An important question is on how to introduce the art of making and its related processes such as tinkering and designing to novices. A strong point of informal communities is the mix of learners present. Coaches and participants that have gained expertise in certain making techniques, materials as well as ways of working, are important in "initiating" novices. By observing, watching, joining and following discussions and tinkering of the more experienced participants, novices will learn about sound making practices, become engaged and develop their maker capability. Martin and Betser (2020) describe how a novice participant in a maker place observes a mentor taking apart a sensor, follows the explanations given through gesturing and talking on the functions of different parts and then comes up with the idea to take a game controller apart. Disassembling the game controller gave this novice learner the capability to engage with another group of children present in the maker space and used his expertise to propose and explain an idea to improve their design.

Learners may also bring personal experience to making, e.g. during a summer camp a girl named Kristen started spontaneously sketching during a design project, while another participant who had prior experience in engineering and making through his family, applied a strategy of comparing his teams non-working wind turbine with a working wind turbine from another team. By comparing the spatial configurations, the team was able to get the wind turbine running (Ramey & Uttal, 2017). Making, designing, tinkering and related processes are learned through noticing the strategies and artefacts of other participants.

Besides open approaches were novices start making through engagement with other learners, there are various other ways to engage learners in designing, tinkering and making to novices. In design and technology education, teams are often given a design challenge or problem. Educators may start with a very broad topic, like Blikstein (2008) who did a project on electricity safety during a two-week project with students in Brazil or with a very specific challenge, e.g. develop a floating device that can carry as much marbles as possible (Looijenga, Klapwijk, & de Vries, 2015). The design challenge can be defined by the coaches and educators or by the participants. In the context of the maker movement, the design or problem solving task can be just for fun, while in design and technology educations the idea is to develop relevant and potential useful designs.

A third approach to start making is by "playing" and tinkering with a specific material or technology. This approach is often present in art education and aims at understanding the possibilities of the materials, e.g. what will happen when I heat this material. This playful approach, starting from the materials and curiosity, helps to discover and extend possibilities as a stepping stone towards innovative functional products or art. The approach is also found in digital fabrication and ICT; as these technologies change quickly, there is no common knowledge how to use them best and these are discovered by novices through creative tinkering.

Learning how to use certain technologies or materials can also entail that experts give instructions, demonstrations, step-by-step tasks or construction kits. This approach is often present in vocational education and in Sloyd but also in informal contexts such as maker spaces. For example, children may make a puzzle or tissue box to learn to work with the laser printer and then move on to design a more personal object. In the maker movement, but also in other traditions, the step of becoming an expert in a technology is considered a first step towards personal, creative fabrication.

All these approaches are used in maker education, art, engineering or design and technology education. Nevertheless, the maker movement approach has unique features. Learning is especially done through self-directed tinkering and experimenting, learners will discover what works and what does not work. In this process, learners need support from knowledgeable others but also act as knowledgeable others. Learning is thus a material and social process. Especially in informal makerspaces participants may meet participants from different age-groups and with different expertise's. The social aspect of learning is thought to be strong in maker contexts because – due to materiality – artefacts can be shared. The visibility and tangibility of the artefacts make it easier to learn together, both during the design and make process as well as afterwards.

The maker movement's focus on tinkering in a safe environment with social interaction with no strict hierarchies – a mentor may learn from the tinkering and thinking of novices – and just-in-time explanations are signature pedagogies. In addition, giving (exciting) materials and technologies without a lot of instruction or specific curriculum goals is advised, learners should be allowed to use their intellect to make something but also extend their own intelligence (Stager & Martinez, 2013).

Martin (2015) summarizes this maker mindset or signature pedagogic approach as follows:
1. Playful. Play, fun and interest are at the heart of making.
2. Asset- and growth-oriented. Makers are free to focus their activities where they want to and a "growth-mindset" is stimulated. The emphasis is on what they can do and what they can learn.
3. Failure-positive. Failure is perceived as something should not be avoided, but even celebrated. The process of becoming stuck and then "unstuck" is at the heart of tinkering (Pretich et al., 2013).
4. Collaborative. Sharing, collaboration and helping others who do other projects is embraced.

Some authors have critiqued the focus on playfulness and fun, they argue that this is very much an elite point of view, as making is an economic necessity for many makers, e.g. the working class and immigrants. In design and technology education, there is also more focus on the fact that material artefacts have a social function and are needed for food, for shelter, for environmental protections, etc.

4.3   *What Do They Learn from Making?*

An important goal of maker-centered education is to get learners acquainted with the practices prevalent in engineering and designing. Through embodied learning, learners will engage in problem solving and conjecturing about possible solutions (Blikstein, 2013, 2018). By making prototypes, tinkering or more formal testing the learners will get feedback on their imagined solutions from the materials. These materials can be seen as "educators" and will become part of the social discourse. It is just not possible to practice many of the key ways of working in design and engineering without embodied learning.

Making, especially when combined with designing and experimenting, can contribute to the learning of scientific and technological concepts and rules. Although these concepts never dictate a solution, they often guide the search for a solution and may point in a specific, promising direction (Kroes, 1995) or help to reflect on the tinkering, models and prototypes made and explain how they work or why do not work. For example, learners may develop understanding of some of the key concepts in design and engineering, e.g. form-function thinking, system thinking or experience firsthand how triangular connections add strength to constructions.

Applying scientific concepts and reasoning is also part of maker projects, through tinkering and designing learners may understand these in a deeper way than just from textbooks. Stammes (2021), in a study on making and designing toothpaste and thermos challenges in the context of chemistry education showed that pupils and teachers talked about concepts such as structure-property relationships, chemical mechanisms, differences between conducting and isolating materials applying them in their sketches, prototypes and experiments. However, as tinkering and designing can be done in a trial-and-error way, learners may develop working solutions without a real understanding of the scientific concepts behind them, especially when concepts are "hidden", because many scientific phenomena are invisible, such as the bonding of molecules.

Meta-reviews on maker-centered education also indicate that concept learning does take place through making (Shad & Jones, 2019; Shersand, 2021; Rouse & Rouse Gillespie, 2022). Especially e-textile projects have been extensively studied (Buechley, 2006; Buechley & Hill, 2010; Kafai, Fields, & Searle, 2014; Litts, Kafai, Lui, Walker, & Widman, 2017; Tofel-Grehl et al., 2017). E-textiles, perhaps emerged as the first-ever female dominated computing field; more than 60% of e-textile designers in the world are women (Buechley, Peppler, Eisenberg, & Yasmin, 2013). Using tools such as LilyPad Arduino it becomes possible to easily sewn circuits into clothing or other textile products leading to electronically-enhanced high-end fashion and personalized products.

Conductive thread is used instead of wires, sewable LEDS instead of light bulbs and leads to increased insights of students understanding of functional loops. Prior work about concept shows that elementary school students tend to struggle with understanding circuity and typically generate linear representations rather than loop-based circuits (Osborne, 1983). These misconceptions persist with high school and college students. In a quasi-experimental study, Tofel-Grehl and colleagues (2017) compared concept-learning through an e-textile unit with a more traditionally circuit unit using breadboards with eight grade students. This study with 155 students in total did not demonstrate statistically advantages of the e-textile curriculum or of the traditional curriculum, in both conditions knowledge on concepts related to electricity and circuits improved. The e-textiles approach lead to significant gains in students perception of family, peer and teacher support for their engagement in science compared to the traditional approach. In addition, there were indications that using e-textiles has advantages over the traditional curriculum, e.g. significant gains at item level were more common in the e-textile group. Litts and colleagues (2017) report on a project in which 23 high school students aged 16 to 17 years were involved in a 15 sessions project on e-textiles. Pre- and post-testing shows that the students' ability to design functional circuits and coding increases. Through e-textiles many of the students involved have specifically learned how to connect knowledge and practices from both the computer and engineering/electronics disciplines. This e-textile project showcases that integrative learning of concepts and practices from different disciplines can be achieved through well-thought of maker projects.

Making and its related practices such as designing, engineering, coding are potentially suitable vehicles for technological and scientific concept learning. However, many researchers have argued that a discourse on these concepts should be present in order to learn. Van Breukelen, Van Meel, & De Vries (2017) noticed that only a small amount of the teacher-student interaction in design activities centered around explicating concepts in a project focusing on designing a solar power system for a model house. Only 13% of all interventions concerned, to a greater or lesser extent, direct explication of underlying science. Furthermore, the design challenge lacked sufficient de- and recontextualization of addressed concepts according to the involved students who were studying to become a science teacher (16–18 year-olds). Making is also used to improve understanding in the social and economic disciplines, e.g. history and social sciences.

Besides testing and tinkering, building a community that engages in sharing and reflecting on experience is needed. Roël-Looijenga (2021) introduced the idea of joint reflection with eight year olds in a Montessori class and noticed that without such sharing of ideas, less iterations in the design and make process were made. A balance between stimulating tinkering and self-constructed knowledge and explanations around concepts seems to be needed. Mentors, peers, books, videos and other knowledgeable others should help learners in making sense of what happens in the embodied activities.

Similar Koski, Klapwijk and De Vries (2011) argue that the learning process should ideally move between three knowledge domains, the social context, the concrete object and abstract knowledge including concepts from both the engineering and natural sciences. The central position of the concrete, materialized product in this three-domain model is not arbitrary. The product may invite the learner to explore the social context in which the product is used as well as the concepts that are helpful in the exploration, design and making of the object. However, one could also start in the social domain (with the need and desires to make something) or in the domain of the concepts. Ideally, each domain enriches and inspires the learning in other domains and learners move iteratively between the domains.

Making is also a good vehicle to develop many of the so-called 21st century skills as well as agency. Klapwijk and Stables (2023) and Klapwijk et al. (2019) have summarized key skills in the context of formative assessment of design learning to make learners and their coaches more aware of what they are learning during the design and make processes. Seven skills are defined including divergent thinking, productive mistakes and bringing ideas to life (through different media), empathy, communication (and cooperation), deciding on directions and understanding the design process. These skills related to the 21st century are not developed in a void, but need a context and making is one of the vehicles for their development.

Through making, empathy is developed. Learners may either start with a social need they relate to. Making also prompts makers to think about how their families and other stakeholders may make use of certain technologies. The actual making stimulates agency, through making learners discover that they can be relevant to others and make positive changes possible, e.g. pupils developed a game to learn math in a new and fun way (Klapwijk, 2017) or contribute to re-using waste by making products from waste for a loved-one. It is important to note that most of the projects will not solve the world's problems, however, through these projects learners will discover the relevance of technology and science for society and develop positive attitudes towards making in general and careers in STEAM.

Last but not least technological literacy is developed through making in a broad sense, but also in the sense of craftmanship. Especially, makers spaces offer a variety of tools and materials in which expertise is developed. Through making and being part of a community of practice, expertise in using digital and non-digital fabrication technologies is developed and ideally transferred from one project to another. How to exactly use a technology, whether it is a hammer or a 3D printer, is a critical maker ability.

Another claim or hope is that through making, children will learn to learn. Papert, Blikstein and others expect that self-directed learning and agency developed during making will be transferred to other contexts (Blikstein, 2013). Making helps them to become self-directed learners who pursue their own process. As this is not always easy, they learn to endure and to make productive mistakes. Although there is in the form of case studies, ample evidence that this happens in maker spaces (Martin & Betser, 2020) and in schools (Riikonen, Seitamaa-Hakkarainen, & Hakkarainen, 2020), this is not always the case. The same two studies also show that not all students are in all circumstances able to manage and pursue their own projects successfully. Smith, Iversen, and Hjorth (2015) found that loosely framed projects with no criteria or guidance led to student frustration, while Schut (2023) discovered that feedback from real clients and peers may often lead to resistance and fixation.

Finally, it is hoped that making will help students to enter in deep-learning processes in which they feel the need for more knowledge, skills or expertise to pursue a certain make or design goal. Just-in-time educational models are advocated, learning should be driven by demand and instruction limited (Dijk, Meij, & Savelsbergh, 2020; Stager & Martinez, 2013). It is thus hoped, that through increased motivation, children and other maker space participants become self-directed learners and that the agency developed through (digital) making will be transferred to other contexts.

5   Maker Education and School Subjects

Although the roots of the Maker Education movement go back at least a hundred years ago, the popularity it has now emerged around the beginning of the 21st century. At that time, in most countries a lot of making took place in school, in a subject with varying names (Technology Education, Design & Technology Education, Industrial Technology Education, and many equivalent names in other languages). Technology Education also has roots that go back at least a century in craft education. But the school subject as we know it now in most countries emerged around the 1970s (some countries being earlier than others and still there are countries that only now give it a solid place in the school curriculum). That means that Technology Education was already in place for about three decades before Maker Education started gaining popularity. This quick rise of Maker Education surprised and also annoyed many technology teachers in schools who had been toiling for many years to get a stable position in the curriculum and now suddenly saw activities very similar to what they were doing become more popular than their school subject had ever been. An obvious reason for the popularity of the FabLabs and Makerspaces in general is that they were well equipped with high-tech devices like 3D-printers. School technology was often still focused on hand and machine production and the novelty of the automated making devices no doubt appealed strongly to both the general public and young people in particular. Other schools went to the other extreme and threw out their "shop" equipment and instead installed computer stations where pupils would simulate making processes rather than working with real material themselves. Many of such stations were developed by commercial suppliers and often it was clear that commercial interests had prevailed over educational relevance in the development of these ready-made stations. No wonder that a local Makerspace then had easy opportunities to become more popular than technology education classrooms, as youngsters felt that it was more rewarding to make something yourself than just creating something on a computer screen. Although relations with schools were propagated early in the Maker Movement, for instance by Mike Eisenberg, a computer scientist at the University of Boulder in Colorado, who set up a Crafts Technology Lab there. Also one of the best known Maker Education stimulators, Paulo Blikstein, in the Mid 2000s increasingly propagates links between Maker Education an schools. But many FabLabs and other Makerspaces remained at distance from schools in the realm of informal education. In the course of time, an increasing number of FabLabs and Makerspaces, however, were initiated in schools and the number of relations between FabLabs/Makerspaces and schools increased (mostly with an informal nature but often very effective). Schools began to see the potential of making activities for learning school subjects. For instance, pupils got a better understanding of the ingenuity of medieval "engineers" (that title is, of course, from much later times) by making some of their inventions and experiencing how much effort it requires to get them working. Understanding of polyhedrons in mathematics education deepens when pupils make a model of these regular shapes. In 2011 the first FabLearn conference was held at the Stanford University, USA, with a focus on maker education in schools or related to schools. A total of 38 such conferences have been held, which indicates a continued interest in the relations between schools and (primarily digital) maker education. The remaining differences in focus of Maker Education and school Technology Education can be mutually corrective. School Technology, which today is mostly broad in its maker activities (most classrooms still have hand tools and machines but now they also have digital making equipment) can remind the FabLabs and Makerspaces that there is value not only in digital making but also in having the basic experience of holding hand tools and feeling the material. On the other hand, FabLabs and Makerspaces can remind school teachers of the fact that the world has moved beyond hand and machine production and that pupils should see and experience something of the more contemporary production devices.

6   Maker Education and Environmental Sustainability

A serious concern related to the strongly increased popularity of making through the Maker Movement is the increased use of materials and the effect this has on the natural environment. According to Klemichen, Peters, and Stark (2022), considerations of environmental sustainability are not a primary concern for many maker enthusiasts. The easy access to making equipment and the easiness with which products can be made in Makerspaces have given rise to serious doubts about the effects of making activities on the natural environment. Maker enthusiasts often lack knowledge about the environmental effects of their making activities and do not see that as a real concern (Kohtala & Hyysalo, 2015). They find pleasure in making objects that are not to be used for any practical purpose but thrown away after the making activity as the fun was more in the making itself than in the resulting object. Although the possibilities of re-using materials constantly increases thanks to new research studies in (sustainable) engineering, the amount of materials use can increase so rapidly due to the increase in popularity of making activities that not only precious resources are lost but also waste is created that needs to be processed. Even when there is an awareness of the need to think about sustainability in doing the maker activities, that does not always lead to changes in behaviour (Klemichen, Peters, & Stark, 2022).

Fortunately environmental sustainability has become the focus of some dedicated projects, such as the ecoMaker project in Germany (Klemichen, Peters, & Stark, 2022). Maker Education certainly has the potential of raising an awareness of the need for sustainable living among citizens. Although materials use is only one of the many aspects of sustainable living, it is certainly not the least important one. When considerations related to environmental sustainability become a constant element in maker activities, this can be a powerful instrument for stimulating responsible use of material. Here, too, Maker Education and Technology Education (as part of formal education) can stimulate each other. In Technology Education, too, there is still a similar gap between awareness and practice. A continuous cooperation between

Maker Education and Technology Education can enable the sharing of good practices and thus improve the sustainable use of materials in both settings.

7 Set-up and Structure of This Book

The set-up and structure of this book are similar to a previous volume in the International Technology Education Studies book series, namely the volume "Analyzing best practices in technology education", edited by De Vries, Custer, Dakers, and Martin (2007). Both in that volume and in this one we have commissioned two types of chapters. The first type is case study chapters. These chapters are descriptions of a certain practice with a focus on the particular features of that practice and not so much a thematic comparison with other practices or with theory. That happens in the second type of chapters. In those chapters the authors have used the case studies to reflect on different themes associated with Maker Education in relation with Technology Education. Not all case studies have been used in all chapters, but the authors have selected the material in the case studies that they needed to support their theoretical considerations with empirical material. The fact that the previous volume in 2008 won the Silvius-Wolansky Award (ITEA) was a stimulus to use the same concept again for our current book. The case studies and thematic chapters are preceded by an introductory part of the book in which we introduce the domain this book deals with and some more general chapters that provide an overall understanding of the domain. At the end of the book we tie together the conclusions of the thematic chapters in order to draw some general conclusions about the nature and possible future of the relation between Maker Education and Technology Education.

More concretely, that leads to the following content of this book. After this opening chapter, two more introductory chapters follow. Chapter 2 is a study about China that shows how Maker Education emerged there. We have chosen China because in this country Maker Education developed at several levels in cooperation. There was a national policy to support developments, expertise at universities to stimulate the development of content and schools and teachers to realize its practice. This makes it likely that Maker Education will remain over time. The sustainability of Maker Education is also the concern of Chapter 3, in which a six-step process is described that has been proven in Denmark to lead to a sustainable practice of Maker Education.

Part 2 contains the case studies at local level. Chapter 4 contains a case study on makerspaces in Dutch libraries with focus on 8–12 year-old children's informal learning. Chapter 5 is from Mexico and shows how Maker Education for primary education can contribute to their awareness of the need for a circular economy. Chapter 6 from Kenya gives an impression of the challenges for Maker Education of an African context under covid-conditions. Chapter 7 focuses on teachers' roles in Maker Education for the case of Korea. Chapter 8 is from China, as was Chapter 2, but now the focus is on individual local initiatives. Chapter 9 is again from the Netherlands, but now at tertiary education level. All together the cases have a variety in continents and levels of education that creates a very nice overview of the different shapes Maker Education can take.

In Part 3, the case study chapters are used as material for reflection on certain themes. Chapter 10 discusses the aspect of pedagogy in Maker Education: what contribution can Maker Education make to learning and what does that require? In Chapter 11 the focus is on the materiality of making and what that means for the way learning takes place. Chapter 12 is on the aspect of social learning, which is characteristic of many Maker Education practices. Chapter 13 deals with the contribution of making activities to learning spatial skills. Chapter 14 discusses the differences and communalities between Maker Education as informal and as formal learning. Chapter 15 is about the sustainability of Maker Education, as shown in the various cases. This chapter compliments Chapter 3, which was written from a more theoretical stance.

The book ends with a synthetic chapter in which we as editors try to bring together the experiences from the various cases as analyzed in the thematic chapters to gain some insights into pros and cons of Maker Education and to imagine a possible future for Maker Education.

Notes

1   https://makezine.com
2   https://www.instructables.com
3   https://fablearn.org/fellows/
4   https://www.cbsnews.com/news/electronics-product-repair-manufacturers/

References

Anonymous. (1984, September 13). Boer daar ligt een kip in het water. *Sinclair Gebruiker, 1*, 12–15.
Barton, A. C., Tan, E., & Greenberg, D. (2017). The makerspace movement: Sites of possibilities for equitable opportunities to engage underrepresented youth in STEM. *Teachers College Record, 119*(6), 1–44.

Biber, E. (1831). *Henry Pestalozzi and his plan of education; being an account of his life and writings with Copious extracts from his work and extensive details illustrative of the practical parts of his method.* John Souter, School Library.

Blikstein, P. (2008). Travels in Troy with Freire: Technology as an agent of emancipation. In *Social justice education for teachers* (pp. 205–235). Brill.

Blikstein, P. (2018). Maker movement in education: History and prospects. *Handbook of Technology Education*, 419–437. https://doi.org/10.1007/978-3-319-44687-5_33

Buechley, L. (2006). A construction kit for electronic textiles. In *10th IEEE international symposium on wearable computers* (pp. 83–90).

Buechley, L., & Hill, B. M. (2010). *LilyPad in the wild: how hardware's long tail is supporting new engineering and design communities* (pp. 199–207). Proceedings of the 8th ACM conference on Designing Interactive Systems (DIS), Aarhus, Denmark.

Buechley, L., Peppler, K., Eisenberg, M., & Yasmin, K. (2013). *Textile messages: Dispatches from the world of e-textiles and education. New literacies and digital epistemologies* (Vol. 62). Peter Lang Publishing Group. https://www.peterlang.com/document/1109415

Danticat, E. (2013, August 27). All immigrants are artists. *The Atlantic.* http://www.theatlantic.com/entertainment/archive/2013/08/all-immigrantsare-artists/279087/

Dewey, J. (1938). *Experience and education.* Touchstone.

Dijk, G. v., Meij, A. v. d., & Savelsbergh, E. (2020). Maker education: Opportunities and threats for engineering and technology education. In *Pedagogy for technology education in secondary schools* (pp. 83–98). Springer.

Gershenfeld, N. A. (2005). *Fab: the coming revolution on your desktop–from personal computers to personal fabrication*: Basic Books (AZ).

Isaacson, W. (2007). *Einstein: His life and universe.* Simon & Schuster.

Kafai, Y., Fields, D., & Searle, K. (2014). Electronic textiles as disruptive designs: Supporting and challenging maker activities in schools. *Harvard Educational Review, 84*(4), 532–556.

Klemichen, A., Peters, I., & Stark, R. (2022). Sustainable in action: From intention to environmentally friendly practices in makerspaces based on the theory of reasoned action. *Frontiers in Sustainability, 2, 675333.* https://doi.org/10.3389/frsus.2021.675333

Klapwijk, R. (2017). Creativity in design. In C. Benson & S. Lawson (Eds.), *Teaching design and technology creatively* (pp. 51–72). Routledge.

Klapwijk, R., & Stables, K. (2023). Design learning: Pedagogic strategies that enable learners to develop their design capability. In D. Gill, M. Irving-Bell, M. McLain, & D. Wooff (Eds.), *Bloomsbury handbook of technology education* (Chapter 19, pp. 271–289). Bloomsbury Publishing.

Klapwijk, R., Holla, E. M., & Stables, K. (2019). *Make design learning visible.* Delft University of Technology.

Kohtala, C., & Hyysalo, S. (2015). Anticipated environmental sustainability of personal fabrication. *Journal of Cleaner Production, 99*, 333–344.

Kroes, P. (1995). Technology and science-based heuristics. *New Directions in the Philosophy of Technology,* 17–39.

Litts, B. K., Kafai, Y. B., Lui, D. A., Walker, J. T., & Widman, S. A. (2017). Stitching codeable circuits: High school students' learning about circuitry and coding with electronic textiles. *Journal of Science Education and Technology, 26*(5), 494–507. https://doi.org/10.1007/s10956-017-9694-0

Looijenga, A., Klapwijk, R., & de Vries, M. J. (2015). The effect of iteration on the design performance of primary school children. *International Journal of Technology and Design Education, 25,* 1–23.

Martin, L. (2015). The promise of the maker movement for education. *Journal of Pre-College Engineering Education Research (J-PEER), 5*(1), 30–39.

Martin, L., & Betser, S. (2020). Learning through making: The development of engineering discourse in an out-of-school maker club. *Journal of Engineering Education, 109*(2), 194–212.

Martinez, S. L., & Stager, G. (2013). *Invent to learn: Making, tinkering, and engineering in the classroom.* Constructing Modern Knowledge Press.

Mersand, S. (2021). The state of makerspace research: A review of the literature. *TechTrends, 65*(2), 174–186. https://doi.org/10.1007/s11528-020-00566-5

Osborne, R. (1983). Towards modifying children's ideas about electric current. *Research in Science & Technological Education, 1*(1), 73–82.

Papert, S. (1991). *Situating constructionism.* MIT Press.

Papert, S. (2005, reprinted from 1980). Teaching children thinking. *Contemporary Issues in Technology and Teacher Education, 5*(3/4), 353–365.

Papert, S., & Solomon, C. (1971). Twenty things to do with a computer. *Artificial Intelligence Memo #248,* 1–40.

Ramey, K. E., & Uttal, D. H. (2017). Making sense of space: Distributed spatial sensemaking in a middle school summer engineering camp. *Journal of the Learning Sciences, 26*(2), 277–319.

Riikonen, S., Seitamaa-Hakkarainen, P., & Hakkarainen, K. (2020). Bringing maker practices to school: Tracing discursive and materially mediated aspects of student teams' collaborative making processes. *International Journal of Computer-Supported Collaborative Learning, 15,* 319–349.

Roël-Looijenga, A. (2021). *Enhancing engagement for all pupils in design & technology education: Structured autonomy activates creativity* [PhD thesis]. Delft University of Technology.

Rooijendijk, C. (2010). *Alles moest nog worden uitgevonden; De geschiedenis van de computer in Nederland* [The history of the computer in the Netherlands]. Olympos.

Rose, M. (2005). *The mind at work: Valuing the intelligence of the American worker.* Penguin.

Rouse, R., & Rouse Gillespie, A. (2022). Taking the maker movement to school: A systematic review of preK-12 school-based makerspace research. *Educational Research Review, 35,* 100413.

Schad, M., & Jones, W. M. (2019). The maker movement and education: A systematic review of the literature. *Journal of Research on Technology in Education, 52*(1), 65–78.

Schut, A. (2023). *"But, it's just a really good idea!": Investigating the guidance of design feedback processes to mitigate pupils' fixation and stimulate their creative thinking.* Delft University of Technology.

Smith, R. C., Iversen, O. S., & Hjorth, M. (2015). Design thinking for digital fabrication in education. *International Journal of Child-Computer Interaction, 5,* 20–28. https://doi.org/10.1016/j.ijcci.2015.10.002

Stammes, H. (2021). *Matters of attention gaining insight in student learning in the complexity of design-based chemistry education* [PhD thesis]. Delft University of Technology.

Tofel-Grehl, C., Fields, D., Searle, K., Maahs-Fladung, C., Feldon, D., Gu, G., & Sun, C. (2017). Electrifying engagement in middle school science class: Improving student interest through E-textiles. *Journal of Science Education and Technology, 26*(4), 406–417. https://doi.org/10.1007/s10956-017-9688-y

Van Breukelen, D., Van Meel, A., & De Vries, M. (2017). Teaching strategies to promote concept learning by design challenges. *Research in Science & Technological Education, 35*(3), 368–390. https://doi.org/10.1080/02635143.2017.1336707

Vossoughi, S., Hooper, P. K., & Escudé, M. (2016). Making through the lens of culture and power: Toward transformative visions for educational equity. *Harvard Educational Review, 86*(2), 206–232. https://doi.org/10.17763/0017-8055.86.2.206

Vries, M. J. de (2007). Reflecting on reflective practitioners in technology education. In M. J. de Vries, R. Custer, J. Dakers, & G. Martin (Eds.), *Analyzing best practices in technology education* (pp. 1–10). Sense Publishers.

CHAPTER 2

The Development and Evolution of Maker Education in China

Jianjun Gu and Qiuyue Yang

Abstract

In the age of education informatization 2.0, Maker education is becoming one aspect of an increasingly universal education. As a new educational model, Maker education is expected to cultivate innovative and compound talents in the 21st century, as well as being considered to be an effective way to cultivate students' communication, cooperation, innovation ability, and critical thinking. In this chapter the emergence and evolution of Maker education in China is described as an example of its development at the national level.

Keywords

China – maker education – innovation – cultivation – Xingzhi Tao

1   The Origin of Maker Education in China

Chinese Maker education and its ideology have a long history. The embryonic form of Maker education was established in the early 20th century. Xingzhi Tao is the pioneer of modern Chinese education and of modern Chinese creative education. In 1926, Tao founded Xiaozhuang Experimental Rural Normal School (now Nanjing Xiaozhuang College) with the motto of "Integrating Teaching and Doing". In 1927, Tao gave a speech in Shanghai entitled "Creative education" and proposed that "doing" is the beginning of Chinese education, and "creation" is the completion of Chinese education. Tao's work has been fundamental to the development of theories and practices of creative education in China.

After the founding of the People's Republic of China in 1949, the educational system of our country went through several changes. After the reform and opening up starting in the late 1970s, the educational mode dominated by an "examination-oriented education" system was formed. From the 1980s to the 1990s, Maker education took root within this national education reform. Maker education was put forward with its historical practical logic and realistic social political and economic background. The Central Committee of the Communist Party of China (CPC) issued a decision on education reform, reiterating its emphasis on "improving the quality of the whole nation". In 1985, the National Education Commission has set up a national working group to correct the existing one-sided pursuit of higher education rates, as well as the first national conference on education was held after the reform and opening up. In the same year, The Central Committee of the Communist Party of China issued the decision on education reform, reiterating its emphasis on "improving the quality of the whole nation".

Since then, Maker education has gradually developed. In the 21st century, the driving force of Chinese economic development has shifted from factor-driven and investment-driven to innovation-driven, and innovation education and Maker education has become the source of economic development. In 1997, Tsinghua University has introduced innovation education. In December 1998, the Ministry of Education mentioned for the first time in *the Action Plan for Revitalizing Education towards the 21st Century* that "cultivating a group of talents with innovative ability". In October 1999, the China Education Daily stated on its front page that "Innovation is the key to quality education". Since then, China has carried out large-scale quality-oriented education, among which innovation education is regarded as the soul of quality-oriented education. More generally, Maker education is an innovation education that improves learners' innovative thinking and innovative literacy through "learning by doing" and "creative learning".

At the beginning of the 21st century, Maker education was mostly organized and carried out spontaneously by primary and secondary school teachers and non-governmental forces. Subsequently, a new round of Reform of National Curriculum Standards was launched to promote Maker education to an important position. On January 26, 2006, the Central Committee of the CPC and State Council issued the "Decision on the Implementation of the Outline of Science and Technology Planning to Enhance Independent Innovation Ability", which aimed to: "Deepen education reform, speed up the development of education, promote quality education and innovation education, for the construction of an innovative country to cultivate rational structure, and excellent quality of personnel at all levels". In basic education, from the perspective of national education policy, new requirements are put forward for developing innovative education and maker education and the training of innovative talents.

The origin of Maker education in China is life-long and meaningful. When it started, it was organized and carried out spontaneously by non-governmental forces. In this process of independent exploration, there was a lack of unified overall system management and top-level design. With the requirements of national education policies and the scientific research strength of universities entering the field of Maker education and gradually becoming an important supporting force to promote the transformation and upgrading of Maker education in China, it has advanced to a new level. This will be described in the next section.

2 The Development of Maker Education in China

In 2013 and 2014, the Ministry of Education initiated the reform of the curriculum plan of ordinary senior high schools and the revision of curriculum standards of various disciplines. Professor Jianjun Gu of Nanjing Normal University, one of the authors of this chapter, was appointed as the leader of the revision team of general Technical Curriculum Standards of ordinary senior high schools. After four years of efforts by dozens of experts, the *General Technology Curriculum Standards for Senior High Schools* (2017 *Edition*) was officially published in 2017.

There are three important modules of the compulsory curriculum content in these Standards: Technology and Creation series of creative development and technological invention module; the technology and creation series of product 3D design and manufacturing module; and the technology and creation series of science and technology humanities integration innovation module, all of which were proposed to strengthen students' technology education and Maker education.

Subsequently, educational administrative departments have issued special policy documents to promote the deepening of Maker education. In 2016, the Education Bureau of Shenzhen Municipality formulated *The Construction Guide of Maker Education Curriculum for Primary and Secondary Schools in Shenzhen* (*Trial*), which means that the construction of Maker education curriculum in primary and secondary schools in Shenzhen was still in the trial. This *Curriculum Trial* document was elaborating the curriculum of maker education from eight aspects, namely curriculum objectives, curriculum nature, curriculum elements, curriculum structure, curriculum setting, curriculum development, curriculum implementation, and learning evaluation and implementation guarantee. *The Guidelines for the Construction of Maker Education Practice Spaces for Primary and Secondary Schools in Shenzhen* (*Trial*) were also formulated to put forward detailed requirements for Maker education for practice laboratories from seven aspects, namely overall requirements, site selection and decoration, tools and consumables configuration, cloud service platform, curriculum construction, room organization and management, and service provider selection. This puts forward specific requirements for the construction of practice spaces or practice bases, such as makerspaces, in primary and secondary schools with conditions in Shenzhen. These two documents have regulated the development of Maker education in primary and secondary schools in Shenzhen at the institutional level, and have important reference significance for the implementation of Maker education in domestic primary and secondary schools in Shenzhen.

Moreover, many universities have come to provide important support for Maker education. In November 2015, representatives of technology and engineering education from nearly 30 countries, regions, and organizations gathered at the Chinese Academy of Engineering to hold the International Maker Education Alliance Conference (IMEAC). The IMEAC was initiated by the Engineering Training Center of Tsinghua University, the School of Education Science of Nanjing Normal University, and units, organizations, and well-known experts from 21 countries and regions. Professor Jianjun Gu serves as the executive chairman of the IMEAC. Starting from the value of the discipline of technology and engineering education, the conference gathered consensus and resources, discussed the plan of alliance, so as to improve the professionalism, and organize the international level of Maker education.

In December 2015, the International Maker Education Summit Forum was held at Nanjing Normal University, jointly organized by the UNESCO Chair for Industry-University Cooperation and the School of Education Science of Nanjing Normal University. The conference was attended by more than 140 experts and scholars from more than 10 countries, including the United States, Russia, and the United Kingdom, as well as from Hong Kong, Taiwan, and 28 mainland provinces. The conference focused on the theory, methods, and cultural construction of Maker education, the disciplinary basis of Maker education, the relationship between Maker education and technology education, engineering education, STEM education and other disciplines, and Maker education and technical and vocational education and training (TVET).

In November 2018, the K16 Fusion Innovation Education Alliance and the K12 Technology and Engineering Education Alliance were established in Nanjing Normal University. Professor Jianjun Gu is the chairman of the K16 Technology and Engineering Education Alliance. The goal of the alliance is to adapt to the needs of the era driven by global economic and technological innovation. It is committed to bringing children into the world of technology and engineering from a young age, and cultivating K12 students who have ideas, can design, can do, and are good at creating, so as to serve the innovation-driven development of the country. Professor Gu shared the latest research results of Maker education from the perspective of technology and engineering education, which promoted the practice, enriched the connotation of Maker education, and promoted the cultivation of international innovative talents at the conference.

In December 2020, the *Maker Education Base Alliance 2020 Alliance Conference and the K16 Technology and Engineering Education Summit Forum* were successfully held in Xiamen. *The Conference and Forum* was closely focused on the core theme of selection and cultivation of innovation and maker talents, and released demonstration units of online platform cooperation of the mass innovation community. The *Forum* held Tsinghua University, Harbin Institute of Technology, Huazhong University of Science and Technology, Zhejiang University, Xi 'an University of Technology, Xi 'an University of Science and Technology and other universities as the online platform of mass innovation community demonstration unit award ceremony.

The online platform of mass innovation community builds a simulated innovation practice environment with clear goals, cooperation much win and optimal engineering benefits, quantifies students' knowledge, ability and comprehensive literacy, and provides new ideas for universities to carry out innovation and Maker practice curriculums and activities. A number of Maker spaces of different sizes have emerged across the country, also becoming an important factor in promoting the development of Maker education. For example, in 2010, the maker space "XinCheJian" was established in Shanghai. Shenzhen Graduate School of Tsinghua University, Shenzhen Graduate School of Harbin Institute of Technology and Shenzhen University, and maker groups or associations have emerged. In 2014, Tsinghua University held a Maker education Forum sponsored by Intel. In the same year, the first China-US Young Maker Competition (CUYMC) was held by the Ministry of Education of China, organized by the Overseas Study Service Center of the Ministry of Education, Tsinghua University and ENN Group.

In addition, the emergence of Maker workshops in universities is also an important embodiment of the upgrading of Maker education in China. The college student Maker Workshop is a Maker workshop with college students as the main body, which may have different titles, such as College Student Entrepreneurship Center. The workshops on campus gathered fans with the same interest to create an innovation garden. As a result, entrepreneurship projects have become more demonstrable and interesting, and students' innovation and entrepreneurship ability are enhanced. For example, the "College Students Cultural Creativity Workshop" of the School of Humanities and Law, Oujiang College, Wenzhou University, with literary creation as the core, has become a media base for the school to turn literary creative works into products, and a medium for literature lovers to demonstrate their personal qualities and realize their own values. The operation mode of Maker workshops is improved from the traditional entrepreneurial mode of "design and production first, then marketing and sales" to the mode of "studio plus production workshop", and the links of "creativity, design, output and sales" are more innovative and rapid (Liu, 2016). In 2015, the Innovation Education Studio of Zhejiang University launched the first college student Maker training camp, which, as an early example of supporting campus maker entrepreneurship, led high-quality students to tap their potential and produce new ideas, encouraged free exchange of ideas and opinions, and established new ideas based on others' opinions.

Primary and secondary schools mostly explore Maker education by excellent teachers and demonstration schools. In 2013, Wenzhou Middle School established a Maker space for primary and secondary schools, and integrated the school's original STEAM curriculum, forming a relatively complete Maker curriculum group. It is one of the earliest Maker Spaces in primary and secondary schools in China (Zhu & Sun, 2015). In August 2013, with the support of Wenzhou Education Technology Center, a number of Maker education teachers in Wenzhou Middle School held the "STEAM Education Forum" in the form of completely private and informal, inviting domestic teachers, researchers, and entrepreneurs interested in the field of Maker education, establishing a dialogue platform between teachers and makers, and strengthening the cooperation between the school and social forces.

In the STEAM teaching practice, Beijing Jingshan Middle School proposed a simple Maker education model, integrated the original teaching resources of robotics courses, and opened Maker curriculums for students from primary school to senior high school. The Maker educational model was based on the procedures of teaching and textbooks, which many Maker teachers and scholars, Beijing New Workshop and other social organizations are invited to participate in the Maker curriculum design for primary and secondary schools (Liang, 2016). In the process of Maker education, Beijing Bayi Middle School takes "STEM+" education as its key development project. A large number of regular extracurricular activities of science and technology are carried out, science and technology festivals are held every year, dozens of elective courses of science and technology are set up, and technology subject learning is carried out in the way of project research. Since 2014, the Beijing Bayi Middle School has introduced 3D printer production, an Arduino Maker course, and projects on My Moon Rover, simulation satellite design, multi-legged robot creative design, and so on. The junior middle school set up a number of Maker projects, such as electronic musical instrument making, simulated aircraft making, underwater car making, and so on.

Nanjing 27 Middle School in Jiangsu province established the "Zhong Shan Maker Workshop" to guide students to master design skills and operation techniques. Based on the general technology curriculum of the school, the innovation and practice of teaching research and the construction of curriculum resources are actively carried out. Wuxi Tianyi Middle School of Jiangsu province guides students to analyze real problems existing in the process of reality so as to achieve the purpose of training students' innovative design thinking in hands-on practice. In 2017, the Youth Maker Science Challenge was held at Jianping Middle School in Shanghai, bringing together young students from Carnegie Mellon University, Fab Lab founders, education experts, and young makers from home and abroad to discuss Maker education. This was a special exchange opportunity between distinguished makers and younger makers, as well as a new attempt of Maker education concepts and practices at home and abroad.

With the implementation of comprehensive education, innovation education and the advancement of the new curriculum reform, more and more universities and primary and secondary schools have begun to set up Maker platform and Maker spaces to encourage students to get in touch with all kinds of technological innovation and Maker products as early as possible. It's beneficial to improve the whole national qualities, as well as achieving the innovation education and Maker education goals.

References

Liang, S. S. (2016). *Chinese maker education (Basic education edition)*. People's Posts and Telecommunications Press.

Liu, Q. (2016). Student makers and their workshops from the perspective of education. *Chinese Higher Education, 5,* 44–46.

Zhu, Z. T., & Luo, L. (2015). From maker movement to maker education: Cultivating mass innovation culture. *Research on Audio-visual Education, 7,* 5–13.

CHAPTER 3

A Participatory Design Approach to Sustaining Makerspace Initiatives

Katrine Holm Kanstrup, Ole Sejer Iversen, Maarten Van Mechelen, Christian Dindler and Marie-Louise Wagner

Abstract

This chapter proposes a framework consisting of six steps for sustaining makerspace initiatives by use of infrastructures developed through a participatory process.

Our framework derives from eleven cases in which we have supported the initial stage of a makerspace initiative for eleven Danish municipalities and a private foundation. The aim of this work was to create sustainable infrastructures around the initiatives and to provide the makerspace initiatives with a shared vision for development in accordance with the individual ambitions and circumstances of the municipality.

In this chapter we condense our experience into a six-step framework to inspire future makerspace initiatives globally. The six-step framework is based on current research in Participatory Design (PD) and draws on principles of stakeholder involvement, infrastructuring and vertical and horizontal alignment. Here we exemplify how this work may lead to more sustainable and robust makerspace initiatives.

Keywords

MakeEd – participatory design – sustainability

1 Introduction

As makerspaces are gaining acceptance globally as laboratories for digital creativity and learning, many existing makerspaces are struggling to extend their funding and to maintain their relevance after the first years' attention as a new and politically potent learning environment.

Makerspace initiatives are undoubtedly expensive to establish but perhaps even more costly to maintain, develop and run as vigorous and open hubs for digital creativity, innovation and learning. Whereas many guides and tutorials provide good starting points for purchasing equipment and hiring staff to a makerspace initiative, only few research-based initiatives address the importance of establishing infrastructure around the makerspace initiative that secures a sustainable and robust structure for developing the makerspace beyond the initial project phase and into a long-lasting resource for learning and creativity. In this chapter we provide a framework for developing local and robust infrastructures based on a PD process. By infrastructure we refer not only to technical structures but to the organisational, political and personal structures that are needed for long-term success of makerspaces. The framework is distilled from 11 cases in which we have developed local makerspace initiatives for a private foundation. All of the eleven makerspace initiatives were located in formal educational settings in relation to K9 teaching. Our work draws on PD principles emphasising how social and technical initiatives can be sustained. In the following sections we briefly introduce these principles before presenting the framework and demonstrating how the framework was put into practice with stakeholders from schools, municipalities, libraries and educational institutions during the past two years.

2   Participatory Design

In this section we provide a brief introduction to PD as an approach to makerspace development. PD is a design tradition that grew out of Scandinavia emphasising the direct and continuous involvement of future users and stakeholders in the process of design (Simonsen & Robertson, 2012). For PD, the reason for involving people directly in design is not only that their knowledge is valuable in terms of creating the best design results. It also reflects a democratic ideal of giving voice to those that will be affected by the results and making sure that they benefit from design. As such, PD embodies a commitment to ensuring that participants enjoy lasting gains from their participation and that the things that are developed through design are sustained after the project ends. Historically, PD has primarily been associated with the design and introduction of digital technology although it has also been applied in other areas such as organisational development and within education.

We suggest that PD is a fruitful approach to makerspace development because it integrates concerns for designing physical and digital spaces, educating and creating organizational commitment. Furthermore, PD explicitly addresses the challenge of how new initiatives will be sustained over time within an organisation. These concerns are of pivotal importance for successful makerspace development and hence PD is a potential good match. Moreover, PD has already been applied within the area of digital fabrication and the broader challenge of supporting digital design literacy in education (e.g., Smith & Iversen, 2018; Iversen et al., 2018).

To provide a conceptual scaffolding for the framework proposed in this chapter, we now dive into some of the central PD principles derived from Bødker et al. (2017) that we will use to articulate how and why PD works as an approach to makerspace initiatives.

Principle 1: Collaborative Hands-on Activities Involving Stakeholders

As noted, a central tenet in PD is the direct involvement of stakeholders in design activities. Not only do future users and stakeholders take part in making overarching design decisions and setting project goals; they take part in very concrete hands-on activities exploring future practices, design ideas or ways of organising work. Collaborative hands-on activities serve several purposes in PD.

Getting first-hand experience with what you are designing, whether it be technology or teaching environments, provides a strong platform for understanding the problem and the possible solutions. Abstract and perhaps intangible concepts become very real and tangible in hands-on activities as participants engage their bodies and minds. Also, hands-on activities are particularly useful as a way of facilitating shared understanding between stakeholders and as such they are important when working with diverse participants.

Principle 2: Working Frontstage and Backstage

Since PD engages directly with future users and stakeholders a significant part of the design work taking place in PD involves activities where designers and users collaborate. This may include developing new ideas or concepts through workshops, evaluating existing working procedures or learning from each other's expertise. These kinds of activities are referred to as the frontstage of PD. But this is obviously not all of the work going on in PD. Much work takes place backstage. This is where participants have informal dialogues, plan activities, reach out to stakeholders and manage the ongoing process. Frontstage and backstage are a metaphor for describing how and where PD work is arranged and also provides a way of understanding how a PD process progresses.

Principle 3: Infrastructuring

In order for initiatives to last when the project ends, PD is particularly concerned with creating the tangible and intangible structures that support this. Infrastructures in general refer to the facility needed to make something operational (a city, a household, a school, etc.). Infrastructures can be physical structures such as the facilities needed for makerspaces but, importantly, it can also be more intangible such as a professional networks or arrangements between teachers that will eventually be important for a makerspace to function. Infrastructuring refers to the work where these structures are created. It is well-documented in PD research, that these infrastructures are crucial in terms of ensuring that initiatives, such as makerspaces, are sustainable.

Principle 4: Working Horizontally and Vertically

For initiatives to gain momentum and eventually be sustainable it will most often be beneficial to consider how participation and engagement with different stakeholders has horizontal and vertical aspects. Working horizontally entails engaging with stakeholders in similar positions or with similar challenges. In terms of makerspaces, this might mean reaching out to other teachers to engage a wider audience in maker activities or to create professional technical forums around fabrication technologies. Working vertically entails looking at other levels of managerial or political power. For most initiatives striving to grow or for sustained existence it will most often be necessary to gain managerial support of several levels.

3   Participatory Strategies for Sustainable Makerspaces in Denmark

The participatory approach for sustaining makerspace initiatives derives from our current research within a Danish context from 2019 to 2021. A private Danish foundation has supported 11 municipalities with donations ranging from 0.7 to 1.2 Mill € to establish, operate and sustain local makerspace initiatives with the general aim of increasing children's interest in creating digital technologies and understanding how emerging technologies affects our everyday lives. Funding for makerspace initiative was provided from the private foundation for a period of three to five years based on three main criteria:

Ownership: To what extend the municipality took ownership at all organisational levels and beyond the funding period.

Spread: How many pupils, schools, and percentage of total teachers the municipality involved in the makerspace initiative.

Depth: To what extent the municipality invested their own time and resources in teacher training in STEM related matters in relation to digital fabrication.

Our research team was engaged by the foundation to conduct a start-up workshop for each of the eleven municipalities based on their individual makerspace set-ups, existing organisational structures and political objectives. The main objective with the start-up workshop was to ensure that the sustainability of the makerspace initiative was considered in the initial phase of the project designs. The eleven makerspace initiatives were fundamentally different from each other. This was partly due to the size of the municipalities ranging from 3.860 to 22.857 pupils and including from 7 to 52 primary and secondary public schools in their makerspace initiative. Moreover, the initiatives funded were very different in relation to strategies for makerspace location(s), outreach, scaling, competence development, prior knowledge of makerspaces, and partnering with local libraries and other existing networks.

Each of the workshops involved 12–30 participants from the municipality on various levels in the existing organisation ranging from the director of the school departments, project leads, 3–5 school principals, teacher trainers, teachers with expertise in digital technologies and to some extent other external partners from industry, museums or libraries. A total of 198 participants took part in the eleven workshops.

The 11 municipalities have individual setups in regards to the chain of command within education and school management. We have identified eight archetypal roles in the municipalities and around the task of sustaining makerspace initiatives. These categories are crucial to understand when identifying how sustainable makerspace initiatives are primed in collaboration between these different levels of authority.

Director of education: the highest level of authority in the municipality with regards to K-12 education who develops strategies and allocates budgets in close collaboration with elected politicians.

Project lead: assists the director of education and is responsible for the makerspace initiative, which includes acquiring funding and purchasing more expensive equipment at the municipal level.

Makerspace manager: runs and maintains the makerspace and purchases most of the equipment; provides training and guides teachers in how to use the makerspace and integrate 'making' in their teaching practice; can be someone at the municipal level, school level or both.

School principal: responsible for a particular school that participates in the makerspace initiative; not every school might

	aspire to an in-house makerspace but instead rely on the yet to be established municipal makerspace.
Teachers:	provide education to pupils but do not necessarily have an understanding of makerspaces and how to integrate making in their teaching practice.
Project partners:	has a strategic interest in co-developing makerspace initiatives together with the municipality and one or more schools (e.g., library, youth club).
Funding agency:	private or governmental institution that provides funding to develop and realise a makerspace initiative within the municipality, typically for the first 3 to 5 years.
University researcher:	responsible for the workshop program (i.e. the six steps) and some of its content.

Each of the workshops were ideally conducted during two or three-days – the first day one month before the next. The workshops took place in an existing well-established public makerspace engaging the local makerspace personnel in the workshop as inspiration for the participating municipalities. Due to the pandemic restrictions in 2020–2021 six of our makerspace workshops were transformed into virtual environments with all six municipalities together.

Based on the eleven unique cases of makerspace workshops, we identify six general steps that were present in all cases to support the sustainability of makerspace initiatives. The six steps were implemented differently in the 11 cases depending on local circumstances. In the following section, we will present the six steps with the aim of providing other projects with guidelines and inspiration for conducting their own participatory process for sustaining public makerspace initiatives. For each of the six steps we provide a general description of the activities, how they reflect PD principles and details in terms of how the individual step played out in our 11 cases.

4   The Six Steps towards Sustaining Makerspace Initiatives

In this section we provide a description of the six-step framework that led to more sustainable makerspace initiatives in the eleven Danish municipalities. We will go through the six steps highlighting the main objectives of the different steps, the participants and activities conducted to reach the suggested outcome. We have provided an overview of six steps in Table 3.1.

Step 1: Understanding the Complexity of a Makerspace Initiative

The overall objective of the first step is for project leads and school principals to develop a thorough understanding of the complexity of makerspaces, and related to this, of the role of the makerspace manager. A common misconception is that providing access to state-of-the-art digital fabrication and maker technologies will in itself lead to valuable educational practices with these technologies, which is rarely the case (Van Mechelen et al., 2021).

A vibrant makerspace requires not only technical but also strong organisational infrastructures to sustain the initiative. One such infrastructure revolves around professional and competence development enabling managers to run and maintain the makerspace and teachers to use the facilities for educational purposes. It further requires infrastructures for knowledge sharing within and between makerspaces and different organisational levels in the municipality and participating schools. As for the role of the makerspace manager, apart from technical skills and assuring safety, they need diversity and interpersonal skills, the ability to train and give feedback to teachers with diverse backgrounds and engage students in maker education. Project leads and principals need to be aware of this extensive function description when hiring a makerspace manager on the municipal and/or school level. In sum, a vibrant makerspace initiative needs substantial infrastructuring to establish strong communities of practice involving a wide range of local stakeholders, including a skilled makerspace manager.

The activities in our cases took about 5 hours and started with a short pitch by the project leads, explaining their vision and objectives for establishing a new makerspace in their respective municipality. This activity was followed by a short discussion and ensured that all participants understood the ongoing initiatives in their own and other municipalities. Afterwards, participants were invited for a guided tour in an existing makerspace where they could interact with teachers and pupils who were using the facility. Meanwhile, the makerspace manager explained how he enables and inspires teachers to set up meaningful activities with their pupils, and he talked about the technical and organisational requirements for running a makerspace more broadly. Finally, after the tour, participants developed plans for community-based training and knowledge sharing within and across schools that could be sustained in the long run.

Step 2: Hands-on Introduction to Makerspace Education

During the second step, teachers with different disciplinary backgrounds from the participating schools who did not participate in the first step are invited

TABLE 3.1   An overview of the six-step framework in relation to objectives, activities, actors and relevance

Step	Objectives	Activities	Actors
1	Understanding the function description of a makerspace manager at the municipal and/or school level; Understanding the need for long-term competence development for managers operating the makerspace and teachers using it with their pupils; Understanding the need for knowledge-sharing within and across schools and municipalities	Short pitch by project leads, explaining their vision and objectives for establishing a new makerspace in their municipality; Guided tour in an existing makerspace; manager explains technical and organisational infrastructure and daily practice of running a makerspace; Opportunity for participants to talk to pupils present in the makerspace about their experiences	Main participants: municipal project leads; school principals; aspiring makerspace managers Lead organiser: university researchers and makerspace manager
2	Hands-on experience with digital fabrication and making; Understanding the learning potential of maker education beyond operational skills; Developing teachers' ability and confidence to integrate digital fabrication and making in their teaching practice; Shared understanding about the challenges teachers may face and the type of competence training this requires	Introduction to design brief followed by group work in a makerspace under guidance of a more capable peer; Discussion on the role of the teacher in maker education and how to deal with recurring challenges	Main participants: teachers with various disciplinary backgrounds Lead organiser: municipal project leads
3	Situate maker education within the broader political landscape and digitization of society; Develop a shared understanding of makerspaces not only as places for collaboration, creativity and design, but also for critical reflection on how digital technology transforms society (macro-level); Providing research-based arguments to achieve buy-in from policy makers and other stakeholders	Presentation of international research on maker education and its societal relevance by a knowledgeable researcher followed by discussion; Participants write down main takeaways and ideas for the next step	Main participants: director of education, school principals, teachers, municipal project leads Lead organiser: university researchers

(cont.)

TABLE 3.1 An overview of the six-step framework in relation to objectives, activities, actors and relevance (cont.)

Step	Objectives	Activities	Actors
4	Developing a vision and strategy for each makerspace within the larger organisational infrastructure (micro-level); Support participants' ability to communicate the initiative clearly to colleagues and other stakeholders; Creating enthusiasm and sense of ownership around the initiative	Participants reflect individually on ideal learning environment for a makerspace; Participants break out in small groups to develop a makerspace canvas including a shared vision for and the resources needed to realise that vision; Each group prepares a presentation of their makerspace canvas	Main participants: school principals, teachers, municipal project leads Lead organiser: university researchers and makerspace manager
5	Commitment from management on the municipal and school level to sustain the initiative beyond the initial funding; Securing financial stability	Each group presents their makerspace canvas to the other groups and the director of education; Director of education links the initiatives to the strategic vision of the municipality; Researchers elaborate on how to bridge the strategic vision of the municipality and the school; Representative of the funding agency explains criteria for evaluating makerspace initiatives; Participants write down main takeaways and ideas for later use	Main participants: director of education, school principals, teachers, funding agency Lead organiser: project leads
6	Understanding of the different types of technologies that can be purchased; Awareness about safety risks, maintenance requirements and other criteria that can be used to make a selection of technologies	Guided tour in another makerspace; the manager explains the different technologies in the makerspace, their purpose and use, etc.; University researcher presents a framework that maps digital fabrication and making technologies onto learning objectives; Participants decide on what technologies to purchase for their makerspace initiative	Main participants: school principals, aspiring makerspace managers, municipal project leads Lead organiser: university researchers

for a workshop to get hands-on experience with design and digital fabrication technologies by addressing real-world challenges in small groups. This activity is facilitated by a more capable peer such as a makerspace manager who introduces the design brief and helps participants with navigating the design process and using the equipment. The activity culminates in one or more tangible artifacts and, through continuous reflection, in arguments for why these artifacts address the challenge introduced in the design brief.

The main objective of this step is for teachers to become familiar with the types of activities that take place in makerspaces and develop a shared understanding of the learning potential of maker education. Since these teachers will be the ones introducing pupils to design and digital fabrication, a related objective is for teachers to develop the ability and confidence to integrate maker education in their teaching practice. Teachers tend to think that the goal of maker education is for pupils to learn how to operate digital technologies and produce tangible artifacts, but the design process and collaborative learning that takes place along the way are far more important. The value of maker education lies, arguably, in the potential for learning and knowledge production, which far exceeds the particularities of a single design brief.

For other participants such as project leads and school principals, this step provides insight into the challenges experienced by teachers, and the type of competence training they might benefit from most. More so, it helps participants to understand that collaboration and 'horizontal work' are vital to realise makerspaces' educational potential.

The activities in our cases took about 1.5 to 3 hours. The makerspace manager, a local teacher, introduced assignments she had previously done with her pupils (e.g., using 3D modelling to design a sign for the school library). She explained how she integrated learning goals and framed the design assignment in a way that avoids pupils from choosing the easiest way to a solution and often results in poor argumentation. The participants then started working on the assignment in small groups with the help of the makerspace manager. After each group had presented their design concept and argumentation, she facilitated a discussion on the role of the teacher in maker education and how to deal with challenges such as pupils being more tech savvy than you are, faltering collaboration, and student groups that value quick and 'shiny' results over process.

Step 3: Establishing the Grand Narrative of a Makerspace Initiative

In the third step, all participants from the municipalities (incl. the director of education), schools and external project partners are invited for a state-of-the-art overview of international research on maker education. This overview is provided by an acknowledged researcher in the field and followed by a discussion. The main objective is to situate maker education within the broader political landscape and digitization of society and, for participants, to develop a shared understanding of makerspaces not only as places for collaboration, creativity and design, but also for critical reflection on how digital technology is currently transforming society. This rapid transformation requires different types of education and learning, equipping pupils with a thorough understanding of digital technology and its ethical and societal impacts. Makerspaces could fill this gap and help pupils on their journey towards becoming active and critical citizens who keep the advancing digitization in check.

Introducing participants to this macro-perspective is important as it increases the likelihood that those involved in establishing a new makerspace, ranging from the director of education to teachers, embark on the same journey. The state-of-the-art overview furthermore provides participants with input for creating a vision for their local makerspace initiative (see Step 4), and equips them with research-based arguments to achieve buy-in from policy makers, parental school committees, other local schools that are currently not involved in the initiative, and so forth. In short, Step 3 focuses on research-based alignment between all participants involved in the makerspace initiative and reflects the PD principle of working vertically to ensure support and shared understanding among stakeholders at different levels of authority.

In the cases with Danish municipalities, this step took about 1.5 hours. The talk was provided by a distinguished professor who had been collaborating with the ministry of education to establish a curriculum on technology comprehension, the objectives of which are closely aligned with those of maker education. During the talk and discussion, participants were encouraged to write down ideas on sticky notes, which they used in the next step to further develop their local makerspace initiative.

Step 4: Developing the Makerspace Initiative within the Existing Municipality Landscape

The fourth step involves all participants from the municipalities, schools and external partners, except for the director of education. Whereas the previous step presented participants with a research-based perspective on maker education and its societal relevance, this step is all about the micro level and further developing the makerspace initiative. Participants first reflect individually on their 'dream' for an ideal makerspace learning environment and then break out in small groups to map existing resources and develop a 'makerspace canvas', that is, an overall strategy for their initiative within the context of their local municipality and school. This is achieved through a series of exercises in which participants take a human-centered perspective to discuss and describe (1) the envisioned users of their makerspace, (2) the channels through which these users can be reached, (3) their motives for visiting, using and returning to the makerspace, (4) the activities and practices they might engage in, and (5) the human and material resources this might require, both existing and new ones. Each group visualises the outcome of these exercises on a big canvas, which they present to the other groups and the director of education in the next step.

The main objective of this step is for participants to recognise that there is no standardised method or approach to realise their vision, and to situate the makerspace within the existing organisational infrastructure. Participants furthermore learn to communicate the initiative in a convincing manner, thereby focusing on both high-level values and operational requirements. This step reflects the PD principle of infrastructuring and, again, uses hands-on activities to foster participant engagement.

In our cases, this step took 3 hours and was facilitated by a professional with extensive experience in change management within organisations. To inspire participants at the start of the session, a vision statement was read out loud by a makerspace manager who had been successfully running a makerspace in a school. The vision statement was co-created by teachers and pupils and did not only serve as an objective to strive towards, but also as a means to create ownership of and enthusiasm about the makerspace initiative. After this introduction, the participants broke out in their municipal groups and started working on their makerspace canvas with the help of the professional facilitator.

Step 5: Confirmation and Articulation of Management Support for the Makerspace Initiative

In the fifth step, each municipal group presents their makerspace canvas, which they developed in the previous step, to the other participants and director of education of the participating municipalities. The director, in turn, explains how the initiatives fit the strategic vision of the municipality, expressing their interest and support on a political level.

The envisioned outcome of this step is shared commitment from all participants, and the directors of education and school principals in particular, to further develop the makerspace initiative beyond the project duration, and ultimately, to secure financial stability. Compared to the third step that focuses on vertical alignment between participants regarding the societal impact of maker education based on international research, the fifth step is geared towards the local policy level and obtaining structural support. It reflects the

PD principle of working both backstage and frontstage to ensure that initiatives can be sustained over time. In our cases this step took about 1 hour.

Step 6: Choosing and Purchasing Technologies for the Makerspace

In the sixth and last step participants across schools and municipalities receive practical insights about buying, using and maintaining digital fabrication and making technologies. All too often, makerspace initiatives start by purchasing expensive equipment without first establishing a shared vision and strategies for sustaining the initiative in the long run, including educational objectives and community-driven competence development. Therefore, in this step, participants visit another makerspace (see also Step 1), but this time by focusing on the available technology. The makerspace manager takes the participants on a guided tour, and explains which equipment has been purchased over the years, how it has been used, which safety and maintenance regulations need to be considered, and any other challenges and opportunities related to these technologies.

After the makerspace tour, a researcher explains how to best choose technologies in support of educational objectives, thereby explaining core concepts (e.g., open-source, age-appropriate interfaces, interoperability) and elaborating on the pros and cons of commonly used makerspace technologies (e.g., Arduino, Little Bits, Makey Makey). This overview is followed by a few practical exercises for which participants use the outcomes of the previous steps to select equipment for their makerspace. In short, the sixth step is about the backstage work required to equip makerspaces with adequate technology.

In our cases, this step took about 3 hours. After the participants visited a makerspace, a university researcher presented a framework for selecting makerspace technologies and the participants broke up in small groups to apply the framework to their local initiative.

5 Concluding Remarks

In this chapter we have provided a six-step framework for sustaining makerspace initiatives through a PD process. The framework is generated by distilling knowledge and experiences from eleven cases in Denmark which provides a solid ground for introducing a participatory approach to sustaining makerspace initiative. Based on the experiences from the workshops in 2020 the funding agency decided that six new municipalities should follow the steps in 2021, and again based on experiences another six municipalities in 2022.

Several points are important to notice in relation to constructing a generalized process framework based solely on Danish makerspace initiatives. First, school systems are very different from country to country and so are the levels of authority within school systems. Second, funding agencies have different approaches and different requirements when supporting makerspace initiatives. Third, the willingness and culture of seamless collaboration between different levels of authority might differ significantly from culture to culture. Finally, the six-step framework requires substantial resources in relation to planning time, stakeholder participation, expert engagement, access to existing makerspace initiatives etc. These resources are not necessarily present when makerspace initiatives are initiated. These limitations to the proposed framework demand a high degree of contextualization and adaptation of the framework when applied in different circumstances and with different constraints.

As such, the framework is not a fixed recipe to ensure a sustainable makerspace initiative but a source of inspiration when planning the initial stages of a makerspace initiative based on collaboration and participation among teachers, management and makerspace experts.

References

Bødker, S., Dindler, C., & Iversen, O. S. (2017). Tying knots: Participatory infrastructuring at work. *Computer Supported Cooperative Work (CSCW), 26*(1–2), 245–273.

Iversen, O. S., Smith, R. C., & Dindler, C. (2018). From computational thinking to computational empowerment: A 21st century PD agenda. In *Proceedings of the 15th participator design conference: Full papers-volume 1* (pp. 1–11).

Simonsen, J., & Robertson, T. (Eds.). (2012). *Routledge international handbook of participatory design.* Routledge.

Smith, R. C., & Iversen, O. S. (2018). Participatory design for sustainable social change. *Design Studies, 59,* 9–36.

Van Mechelen, M., Wagner, M. L., Baykal, G. E., Smith, R. C., & Iversen, O. S. (2021, June). Digital design literacy in K-9 education: Experiences from Pioneer teachers. In *Proceedings of the 20th annual ACM interaction design and children conference* (pp. 32–42). Association for Computing Machinery

PART 2

Case Studies on Maker Education

∵

CHAPTER 4

Informal Learning in a Public Library Makerspace for Youth in the Netherlands

Monique Pijls, Tom van Eijck and Bert Bredeweg

Abstract

Informal learning spaces create opportunities for children and youth to develop their talents and to experience new social roles. In recent years, several public libraries in the Netherlands have established makerspaces to empower youth by facilitating the development of their digital skills in conjunction with their creativity. The Amsterdam Public Library created a network of makerspaces (Maakplaats021) and provided training for the makerspace-coaches. These coaches – former librarians or other professionals – have a central role in the makerspace and fulfill several functions. This contribution describes informal learning of children in these makerspaces and distills critical features that enforce learning through the lens of children aged 8–12 and their makerspace-coaches.

Keywords

public library makerspace – informal learning – empowerment – community involvement

1 Introduction

Over the past decades, many museums and libraries have created makerspaces where children can develop their creative, social and technological skills (Bevan et al., 2020; Escudé et al., 2020; Lin & Schunn, 2016). With trained staff facilitating and scaffolding these young makers' learning processes, these makerspaces have become regular learning environments in the 'educational playing field' (Gahagan & Galvert, 2020; Nagle, 2020; Slatter & Howard, 2013; Willett, 2018). The Amsterdam Public Library created a network of ten makerspaces (Maakplaats021) where children can attend school- and after-school programs. These makerspaces were established in various urban neighborhoods to reach

© KONINKLIJKE BRILL NV, LEIDEN, 2023 | DOI:10.1163/9789004681910_004

children from families with a lower socio-economic status. These children generally have little access to technology and creative resources at home, while schools in these communities often lack time and staff to focus on creativity and digital literacy.

In the first four years of the project Maakplaats021, the development of makerspaces was monitored through a formal research project examining what children and makerspace-coaches did and what they experienced during the school and afterschool programs in the library makerspace (Pijls, Van Eijck, & Kragten, 2020; Pijls, van Eijck, Kragten, & Bredeweg, 2022). In this contribution we present a new qualitative analysis of a portion of the data collected during this formal study (27 interviews with children and 12 interviews with makerspace-coaches), focusing on the characteristics of informal learning in the afterschool programs. We have selected typical passages of the interviews and use *thick description* to illustrate and explain learning in afterschool-programs in the makerspace and extract critical features of this learning environment. We also elaborate on the question what it takes from makerspace-coaches to support learning of the children. After a short general description of the project, we provide eight 'vignettes', i.e. snapshots that each highlight a particular aspect of the informal learning context. Five of these focus on the development of the children within the makerspaces and three on the professional development of the makerspace-coaches.

2   The Project Maakplaats021

Maakplaats021 was initiated by a consortium consisting of the Amsterdam Public Library and three partner organizations (Waag, the organization that started the first Fablab in Amsterdam in 2011; Pakhuis de Zwijger, an organization that focuses on community development; and the Amsterdam University of Applied Sciences, which performed the monitoring research). The project was funded by the municipality of Amsterdam. At ten library locations throughout the city, a makerspace was built, sequentially over a period of four years (2017–2020). Each makerspace contained the same basic equipment, consisting of two or three 3D-printers, a laser-cutter, a vinyl-cutter, fifteen laptops, glue guns, two sewing machines and pencils, paint, paper, etc. The library-makerspace offered after-school programs for tinkering, community development and computer programming (coding) for children between the ages of 8–12. The name Maakplaats021 (Dutch for Makerspace021) is derived from the concept of 21st century skills (OECD, 2021), which include digital literacy, collaboration, communication, citizenship, critical thinking and self-regulation.

All after-school Maakplaats021 activities took place on weekday-afternoons. Children could sign-up for free and the administration of the participants was carried out by the makerspace-coach. Each program admitted twelve to fifteen children, who were guided by two to three makerspace-coaches. A program consisted of ten weekly classes, often concluded with a closing presentation for parents in the last week. During school holidays, special activities were scheduled. The programs comprised digital fabrication and tinkering, designing, community-art, programming/coding, each often based on a theme.

When a new makerspace opened its doors, experienced maker-educators from other locations 'ran' the programs in the first months, coaching the library-makerspace-coaches in their new role. A training program for staff was developed, while additional staff training comprised of a yearly two-day-course, monthly meetings ('maker morning') and weekly 'developing time' as well as additional courses in pedagogy, maker education, digital fabrication, and design. Initially, maker educators of the partner-organizations developed the new programs, but gradually some of the makerspace-coaches created their own programs.

Makerspace-coaches were recruited from the library staff. Librarians with a passion for creativity and technology were schooled in digital fabrication. In addition, external staff, with experience in art, craft and technology was attracted. Ultimately, four of the twelve makerspace-coaches were current or former librarians. Whereas makerspace-coaches were scheduled to rotate the various locations, each makerspace had one coach who was in charge of that location only. This was particularly important for the maintenance of the equipment, tools and materials. Supplies were ordered centrally and distributed over the ten makerspaces by a 'makerspace-producer', hired by the public library.

In addition to cooperation within the project by the three partner organizations and library, the consortium also collaborated with various cultural foundations, museums and entrepreneurs in the city that offer art education and technology education. Student teachers assisted in the makerspaces, under supervision of the makerspace-coaches. The makerspaces also offered programs for school classes, again guided by the makerspace-coaches. All in all, the public library makerspaces have evolved into dynamic locations were children aged 8–12 come and visit school and afterschool programs, guided by maker-spaces coaches, whose professional development is arranged by the organization. In total, the Maakplaats021 registered 23,826 children visits in the after-school programs over its establishment period (2017–2020), with an approximate binary gender distribution of 50/50.

The following eight vignettes describe typical examples of learning in the public library makerspaces.

3   **Developing Skills by Creating Creatures**

On Tuesday afternoon, a group of nine children sit around their table, concentrated on their project. The atmosphere is calm and focused. Some of the children have been visiting the makerspace for three years already, while others are relatively new. Children mention that they came to know about the makerspace by friends, or their mother signed them up, as 'she saw the makerspace when she visited the library and she thought I would like it'. A subscription list for the next season-course with handwritten names is lying on the table. There are twelve places, and the list is almost full. There will likely be a waiting list, like there was before.

The children are proud of what they make and have made. A girl says:

> I made so many things. Once I made a bag with hamsters on it. It was really a beautiful bag. I used it very often. I also made a gym bag, and we once made a forest of fairy tales. I was very proud of that, too.

Within these projects, the children learned to work with a laser-cutter and a sewing machine, Tinkercad software for the 3D-printer, Inkscape and a sticker cutter. The experienced children became very skilled over time.

> He is the youngest child of the group. He can work with all that software and with the sewing machine very well. His mother likes that too.

One of the successful programs was 'Creating creatures', which involved designing your own animal, cutting the fabric with a laser-cutter, sewing it – first inside-out! – and finally designing small ornaments, such as eyes, with the 3D-printer. Figure 4.1 shows the cut fabric of a Pikachu.

The makerspace-coaches have designed programs with structured assignments. They say:

> Children need this structure. We also teach them a lot of social skills, to help each other, to wash their hands and so on. The children love it; they want to prepare the drinks for the break. One week ago, we were sitting with the children, chatting a bit and I asked them 'Who feels happy now?' Many raised their hands. The atmosphere was so peaceful.

This vignette illustrates the makerspace as a fruitful training site for digital skills. Further typical characteristics of this informal learning environment are:
– The makerspace is accessible.
– Some children spend a lot of time in the makerspace, 100–250 hours.

FIGURE 4.1   Creating creatures: fabric cut with laser-cutter in the shape of Pikachu

- The children are motivated.
- Children develop technical skills and creativity.
- The makerspace is a space where children feel safe.
- The activities are structured but focused on individual development.

4   I Learned So Many Things in the First Week

A child is visiting a makerspace that was recently built. On this particular afternoon he is the only visitor. He mentions very enthusiastically the many things he learned over the past few weeks.

> I love making things. My mother heard from somebody else about this place',
> he says. 'Here I work with my hands, and that is the difference between
> school and this place. And I use computers and a 3D printer, all very cool. At
> this moment I am working on a sticker with my name. Over the past three
> weeks we worked with all the equipment, and we learned how it worked:
> laser-cutter, vinyl-cutter. We used paper and pencil and Inkscape. Last week
> I worked together with another child, and we helped each other.

This vignette shows that although this child recently started in the makerspace, it already experienced that it learned a lot. The new technologies are fascinating and are distinctive from his experiences at school. Although children work on individual projects, helping each other comes naturally.

Another typical phenomenon of new makerspaces is that there are few visitors. In contrast to makerspaces that already existed for several years and often have a waiting list (see vignette #1), this place still must attract new visitors. This often goes by word of mouth or by people passing by, since these library makerspaces are often located near other shops and services.

5   Making a Robot to Help Grandma

It is Wednesday afternoon in the public library in the shopping center, and the makerspace is upstairs; a rectangular space with six large tables with stools. Today's activity is 'Codeteam', a ten-weeks program about coding and programming. Eight children are divided into groups of two or three. On their table a sheet of paper, with a map drawn on it. They are working with little cars and Micro:bit, which they program to make the cars follow the path.

> 'I can speak robot-ish: T. taught me', says one of the children.
> 'Can you teach me that language too?' the other says.

Then they explain about the 'confetti-canon' they made last week: a robot that could move and throw confetti. Hence brightening up other people. A girl says:

> I want to learn to work with things like robots and programming. I think it is important that a robot can move, can go somewhere. Catching things is also important: things like food or drinks, or the mouse of a computer. When elderly people are not able to walk or to grab things, the robot can do things for them. My great grandma, for instance, is alive but in the hospital. Sometimes she goes home. She lives nearby. I sometimes visit her with my mother and little brother. It is nice to see her. Then I can tell her what I did in the makerspace. That is nice to tell.

At the end of the afternoon, her mother, with her little brother drops in to pick her up. The mother tells how happy she is that her daughter can visit the makerspace. Her daughter says:

> I don't know yet what I want to become when I grow up. Now, I like working with people, and with computers and programming, and I also like dancing and swimming.

This vignette shows that this girl enjoys programming and is very motivated to learn more. Her residence indicates that she is from a low-income family. She thinks about technology and programming as something to help other people, so as a social tool. It also shows that she is confident in learning and considers programming as equal to dancing or swimming. Furthermore, this child wants to share her pleasure in learning with her family. What she experiences in the makerspace affects her family directly.

6   Collaboration with the Local Outdoor Market

Thursday afternoon, the makerspace has a large window adjacent to the week-day market. On this afternoon, the atmosphere is restless. 'The children are a bit upset this afternoon, because of a violent incident that happened yesterday in the street', the makerspace-coach says. 'One of the kids knows one of the people involved and you can see that it bothers him'. Two children are sitting in the corner, playing with a 3D-pen, making a little 'dino'. 'We leave them quiet today; they usually collaborate well'.

Here, Makerspace021 directly collaborates with an established community program led by a local cultural foundation (The Beach). The makerspace-coach says:

> I learn a lot from the maker educators from The Beach, who stimulate the children's autonomy and make them reflect on ideas, instead of taking an initial idea as a definite plan. Every week we look back: 'What did you do last week and where are you now?' Children made a neighborhood walk and photograph what they like and dislike. We also collaborate with market vendors, by recycling their packing material. This black plastic is used to pack fruit, now it became a fancy handbag.

Here, some of the clothes and accessories that the children made in the makerspace were sold on the local market as well. The open window of this makerspace symbolizes how it is connected to the urban neighborhood. Events in the community affect the children while the makerspace is a safe space where they can recover and connect with other children. They learn to reflect and to create. The cooperation with the local market vendors is a win-win situation for all: waste is cleaned up and the makerspace has free and interesting materials to work with. Children experience that they can contribute to the community by making and remaking.

7 Developing Confidence

A makerspace-coach talks about the way she coaches children in their personal development in the makerspace.

> A child that was very shy when she came for the first time, started to blossom after a few times, her mother said. She gained confidence and started to express herself. This is a safe space for her. I think it is very important that children feel safe. Once they do, the rest will follow. Children learn to cooperate with others, also people that are new to them. Parents are very happy with this development.

The coach explains how she creates an open atmosphere.

> They have so much fun here. That is important, I think. If they have questions, they can come to us. If they have complaints, they should tell us too. You must always remain open to criticism, really.

Children learn to overcome personal barriers and beliefs.

> Often, children can do more than they think. In the end they say: I first thought I couldn't make it. Like last week, there was one child; he wanted to sit apart, to focus. Two weeks later, he joined the group and he wanted to show something. It appeared that he continued to create at home; he made a story in Scratch, an animation. We always work with freeware and a login, so he continued making at home and was proud of that.

Initially, many of the children that come to the makerspace are not used to learning through open tasks and the freedom to come up with ideas and multiple solutions instead of one correct answer.

> I notice that children are insecure or lack self-confidence. They often ask me: 'Is this correct, did I do this well, do you like it? Then I ask them: 'What do YOU think of it? If you don't like it, you can make it better'. They are afraid to make mistakes, but programming is mostly about debugging, I tell them. And making is about repairing or remaking. Every child can do this and make it in its own way. Each at their own pace.

The makerspace-setting can be inviting for personal conversation, both during after-school programs and school visits.

> This also works for school visits. Last week, at the end of the lesson, a child came to me: 'Can I give you a hug?' While they are involved in a project, they tell you about their lives. Sometimes only a little, sometimes even a little too much.

This vignette shows the opportunities for personal development in the makerspace. Programming and making require new approaches and new skills and these help children to gain confidence.

8   'Thinking in 3D Is... Mind-Blowing'

One of the librarians who was involved in the setup of the very first makerspace had to master a lot of new skills. At that time, all makerspace-coaches had to learn from scratch to work with the software and the machines. This makerspace-coach makes clear what it meant to then to learn a new skill.

> Thinking in 3D is what everybody must learn, the children too. It doesn't matter what age you have, when you do that for the first time, your brain must get used to it. It takes a few weeks, and then you know how to think. That is what we teach them here. To broaden your mind.

She explains that many of the new skills she coaches she had to learn by doing herself.

> When I still worked in the library, I got time to work on my own in the makerspace. From now and then I asked my colleague for help. But you had to discover everything for yourself. I learned everything while I was here [in the makerspace] from morning to night. I had to dive in and discover how it works. We practiced and practiced and practiced.

This vignette shows that for future makerspace-coaches without a background in technology or programming, the new skills can be fascinating but require many hours of practice.

9   The First Time I Had to Present for a Group

Some of the makerspace-coaches do have a background in designing and technology, but not in education. They must learn how to manage a group, like this makerspace-coach tells.

> During the summer program, there were moments that I thought: there is too much noise, now I have to set stricter rules. I find that difficult. The first time I had to present for a group, I felt so shy. Because I also think 'just make fun'. It all went well. But there is a rule that children are not allowed to run in the makerspace. I want to learn how to address children if they do not behave.

The struggles and concerns of this makerspace-coach are comparable to those of beginning teachers. Since the groups of children are smaller and the setting less restrained than at school, the situation is less urgent, but makerspace-coaches must develop these leadership skills too. This makerspace-coach experiences that she could learn from a teacher-training student, who did an internship in the makerspace.

> Last month, a student teacher came to help us weekly. She is interested in the makerspace and must learn to work with the equipment. But she helped me too, pedagogically she is more skilled than me.

10   Hands Off That Keyboard

One of the new makerspace-coaches is a photographer. When asked about his main learning objectives, he talks about the pedagogy of inquiry-based learning.

> In the first place, of course, I had to learn to handle the equipment. And we had to learn to coach the children and to keep order within a group of children and to know the right moment to intervene. I had to learn to hold back. It is so easy to take over and push the button yourself on a computer. Instead, we have now learned to use words and stimulate the children to learn, to provide more distant instruction so that children can find out for themselves. Corona has helped to normalize keeping distance too... [laugh].

The coach mentions that in the end he learns through practice and from and with colleagues.

> I learned a lot from colleagues, you are left to dive in at the deep water after two days of technical training. How to cope with children is something that you learn through practice.

11   Critical Features of Informal Makerspaces

1. The makerspace provides opportunities for children to learn and to get acquainted with creativity and technology. Altogether, children can spend a lot of time in the makerspace. By visiting the makerspace weekly, they develop technological skills and creativity. Even a few visits to the makerspace can impress and motivate children and give them the feeling that they learned a lot.
2. After-school programs in the makerspace attract intrinsically motivated children and the activities stimulate their motivation.
3. The personal guidance in the makerspace enables children to overcome anxiety and to experience those times of frustration are allowed in the process of making. Children gain confidence over time.
4. The makerspace is embedded in the community. The physical embedding of the makerspace in a public library and near other public spaces or shops attracts children from local communities. It also allows parents to easily contact the program.
5. Makerspace-coaches need continuous professional development. They wear many hats in the makerspace (expert in technology and creativity, coach, developer of new learning materials, organizer). Especially the pedagogical role requires proper training and coaching.
6. Cooperation with local organizations and institutions and universities stimulates the development of makerspace-coaches. Maker educators from cultural organizations bring in expertise, while teacher students from universities can assist in makerspaces too.

12   Conclusions and Discussion

After-school programs in a public library makerspace fulfill an important role in the development of talents and to motivate children. There are requirements to fulfill in order to realize this rich learning environment. It takes time to reach children in the community and set up the makerspace. After-school makerspaces put high demands on staff, which needs to reserve time and require training and support. A makerspace-coach is a jack-of-all-trades who coordinates several roles (Pijls, van Eijck, Kragten, & Bredeweg, 2022). For the realization of training and support, collaboration with (local) organizations and universities is very important. The after-school context is an interesting learning space for teacher-students too.

It is challenging to keep children connected to the makerspace when they grow older. This seems especially important for stimulating children who are interested in technology and programming. Another challenge is to keep this service free of cost for children. One way to ensure continued participation may be by establishing a peer-tutor system, where older youth with experience in the makerspace can tutor the younger children (Sheridan, Clark & Williams, 2013).

Acknowledgements

We wish to thank the makerspace-coaches and the children for their willingness to share their experiences in an interview. We are grateful to Hester Jiskoot for thoroughly reading and commenting an earlier version of this manuscript.

This research was funded by the Municipality of Amsterdam as part of the project Maakplaats021, by the Amsterdam Central Library (OBA), Waag, Pakhuis de Zwijger, and the Amsterdam University of Applied Sciences.

References

Bevan, B., Ryoo, J. J., Vanderwerff, A., Wilkinson, K., & Petrich, M. (2020). "I see students differently": Following the lead of maker educators in defining what counts as learning. *Frontiers in Education, 5*, 121.

Escudé, M., Rivero, E., & Montano, J. (2020). Designing for belonging and becoming in an afterschool tinkering program. *Afterschool Matters, 31*, 42–50.

Gahagan, P. M., & Calvert, P. J. (2020). Evaluating a public library makerspace. *Public Library Quarterly, 39*(4), 320–345.

Lin, P. Y., & Schunn, C. D. (2016). The dimensions and impact of informal science learning experiences on middle schoolers' attitudes and abilities in science. *International Journal of Science Education, 38*(17), 2551–2572.

Nagle, S. B. (2021). Maker services in academic libraries: A review of case studies. *New Review of Academic Librarianship, 27*(2), 184–200.

Organisation for Economic Co-operation and Development (OECD). (2021). *Building the future of education*. Retrieved July 31, 2022, from https://www.oecd.org/education/future-of-education-brochure.pdf

Pijls, M. H. J., van Eijck, T. J. W., & Kragten, M. (2020). *Leren in Maakplaats021: Praktijkonderzoek naar het leren van kinderen en maakplaatscoaches in de maakplaatsen op verschillende locaties van de Openbare Bibliotheek in de periode 2017–2020*. Hogeschool van Amsterdam, Kenniscentrum onderwijs en opvoeding.

Pijls, M. H. J., van Eijck, T. J. W., Kragten, M., & Bredeweg, B. (2022). Activities and experiences of children and makerspacecoaches in a public library makerspace. *Journal for STEM Education Research, xx*, 1–24.

Sheridan, K. M., Clark, K., & Williams, A. (2013). Designing games, designing roles: A study of youth agency in an urban informal education program. *Urban Education, 48*(5), 734–758.

Slatter, D., & Howard, Z. (2013). A place to make, hack, and learn: makerspaces in Australian public libraries. *The Australian Library Journal, 62*(4), 272–284. https://doi.org/10.1080/00049670.2013.853335

Willett, R. (2018). Learning through making in public libraries: Theories, practices, and tensions. *Learning, Media and Technology, 43*(3), 250–262. https://doi.org/10.1080/17439884.2017.1369107

Using "EcoMakerKits" to Stimulate Maker Mindset and Circular Thinking in Mexico

*Álvaro Núñez-Solís, Suneel Madahar, Nathan Eskue and
Miroslava Silva-Ordaz*

Abstract

This chapter provides a recount of Maker Education using e-waste to stimulate the Maker Mindset and Circular Thinking in a Mexican context and the need to engage primary school children in this area.

It explores how the usage of "Eco Maker Kits" enables or hinders the learning concept of Circular Thinking and Maker Mindset by active learning introducing basic electronic hands-on experience and reusing materials that would normally end up in the landfill.

The results show that using a lesson plan with learning activities turns out to be useful to stimulate curiosity for Circular Thinking. The "EcoMakerKits" also helped to expand the Maker Mindset of the participants by assembling artifacts and electronic circuits. This provides an opportunity for young children to build upon their technical skills and motivate them to tackle global issue, such as electronic waste, highlighting the importance of reusing, repairing and repurposing.

Keywords

circular thinking – maker mindset – constructivism – hands-on learning – elementary

• • •

I hear and I forget. I see and I remember. I do and I understand.
CONFUCIUS, 6th century BC

∵

© KONINKLIJKE BRILL NV, LEIDEN, 2023 | DOI:10.1163/9789004681910_005

1   Circular Thinking and E-Waste as Global Challenge

As an educator you might wonder how to foster sustainability awareness among your students. This chapter focuses on one of the many areas of sustainability: waste. Specifically, "How do we stimulate the Maker Mindset and Circular Thinking using e-waste"?

Making creates knowledge, builds environments, and transforms lives (Ingold, 2013). The resources for making are not always renewable resources. In this chapter we will explore how Circular Thinking requires a Maker mindset and Makers benefit from Circular Thinking in a Mexican context.

The Circular Economy thinking is based on the principles of design, repair, and reuse to keep products and materials in use, thus demanding less resources and energy (Korhone, Honkasalo, & Seppälä, 2018). "Now we have entered the Age of Anthropocene, the geological epoch signifying that human activity has become the dominant driver of change for the Earth's climate and ecosystems. Discarded garbage, plastics and e-waste have risen to unheard-of heights" (Wackman & Knight, 2020, p. 57).

E-waste following a linear economical model, that hasn't been designed to be recycled, is known as planned obsolescence (Bolow, 1986; Guiltinan, 2009; Waldman, 1993). The constant growth of obsolete electronic products generates a problem worldwide due to the lack of processes to reincorporate raw materials to a Circular Economy model, thus causing the overexploitation of virgin natural resources (Böni, 2005). Today, in the complex Covid 19 pandemic situation, there has been a rise in the purchase and the waste of electronic equipment since people have been forced to acquire or renew their electronic devices to meet the needs of work, school, family, and friends.

Meeting the contemporary social needs involves environmental and human health impacts (Kiddee, Naidu, & Wong, 2013); which could be addressed in a more sustainable way through Circular Thinking.

2   Maker Mindset Connecting with Circular Thinking

We are all makers; Dougherty (2016, p. 143) defined making as "the process of realizing an idea and making it tangible". Therefore, with the global challenge we are facing with e-waste and realizing that this linear economic system is no longer sustainable, the maker society is already present in the creative process of solving the problem. Makers are doing this by coming up with tangible solutions and alternatives to this linear economy and integrating more Circular Thinking into the development of new, more sustainable products. Later in this chapter we will share how a Mexican company has successfully addressed this problem and is using it as part of their business model.

But as educators, how do we prepare the new generations to learn about the principles of design, repair and reuse that characterize the Circular Thinking? How can we link circular thinking to Maker education by democratizing technology into a more sustainable living environment? Paul Blikstein (2018) suggests that the best way to foster curiosity and guide students to explore and construct their own knowledge is by letting them become makers.

The Maker Education mindset is based on skills, attitudes and knowledge that fosters active learning, curiosity, engagement, playfulness, and resourcefulness (Dougherty, 2016, p. 144). These attributes help the maker to transform their ideas into tangible artifacts using the tools and technology available. So, what if the technology available is based on Circular Thinking principles?

Andrews (2015) suggests that Circular Economy should also be embedded when designing the curriculum, so that it also becomes integral to the educational practice. It would enable sustainability issues to be addressed implicitly. For example, students would learn to design for longevity (creating products that can be repaired, upgraded and remanufactured, and have a high perceived value) and to design for reduced environmental impact and increased efficiency (via dematerialization, designs using waste/discarded products/parts, closed materials loops and service design; Andrews, 2015, p. 313).

In this chapter we explore how sustainability and especially the Circular Thinking approach can be added to STEAM. This term has been used regularly in Maker education. Martinez & Stager (2019) define it as a way to explore, tinker, imagine and create solutions to problems while developing skills in science, technology, engineering, art, design, and/or mathematics (STEAM). By adding Sustainability with the Circular Thinking approach, the term used in this chapter is STEAMS.

STEAMS is a project-based approach to create artifacts made out of reused, repurposed or repaired objects. It gives young children the opportunity to wonder and explore technological skills like electric circuits, multimedia, tinkering and engineering among others. Furthermore, 21st century skills like computational thinking, creativity, communication, collaboration and critical thinking are fostered while taking action to reuse, repair and repurpose objects. The aim of STEAMS is to make the new generations curious about the Circular Thinking and encourage educators and children to foster creative ways to solve problems using reused, repaired or repurposed materials.

This chapter recounts the connection between the principles of Circular Thinking and the Maker Mindset in a Mexican educational context.

2.1 *Designing Mechanism to Take Action against E-Waste*

In 2006, in Queretaro, Mexico, Alvaro Nuñez, the CEO of "*Recicla Electrónicos México S.A de C.V*". started the adventure of putting together a company to recycle e-waste, they call themselves "Eco Makers". Ever since, his company has been working with different partners and putting together a framework to address the local and national problem of electronic obsolete products. This framework provides a management system to reuse and recycle obsolete products. The framework has six sections represented in Figure 5.1.

The mechanism of the framework is human based design. By using Maker Mindset elements such as tinkering, engineering and problem solving, the Eco Maker team has come up with different strategies that make it accessible to the community by collecting their e-waste and creating a culture to recycle it and turn it into profitable products.

The company has developed an easy way to collect the e-waste from the community by using an app. They have developed an app in English and Spanish

FIGURE 5.1   Management system to reuse and recycle obsolete products

where people can request to collect their electronic waste[1] and the Eco Makers send a delivery company to collect it.

To share knowledge the company has created different channels. For example, the "Circular Economy podcast",[2] their blog[3] and Maker workshops.

2.1.1   Reusing E-Waste to Design "EcoMakerKits"

The Eco Makers put special effort on the educational part of their framework. They developed an "Innovation Lab" based on the maker principles of engagement and resourcefulness. Its members are a team of engineers and mechatronic students working collaboratively to reuse different parts of the e-waste and turn it into upcycled new products to support Circular Economy education. After several design cycles they have created many innovative prototypes, and some of them make it into the Maker Store as innovative products. For example, in Figure 5.2 you can see how at the front a mechatronic student is developing a 3D printer using the e-waste of an old printer. The idea is that some of the parts of the old printer will be used for other 3D printers.

The Eco-Maker store reincorporates e-waste to new cycles and products and make these accessible to the society. For example, they have refurbished laptops and desktops. They also have put together "EcoMakerKits", each kit contains e-waste parts to build products like a Bluetooth loudspeaker and an electric Fan. These EcoMakerKits" provide users with the opportunity to develop technical skills while using electronic waste, highlighting the importance of reusing, repairing and repurposing.[4] In Figure 5.3 you can see some

FIGURE 5.2   Innovation lab

FIGURE 5.3   Eco-maker store

of these products like a desktop computer, a Bluetooth loudspeaker, a Fan, an electricity convertor, and an LED lamp.

The philosophy of the company shares the Maker Education principle of "invention literacy". Silver (2016) advocates to foster "invention literacy" as part of the contemporary education. He suggests that people should learn, understand and name how things are made. He implies that there is a "hidden literacy" in the man-made world, and when putting apart objects, this gives the opportunity explore and name the parts of what it is made of and hopefully give insights and inspiration to build new things.

There are many products being developed by the Eco Maker team, but with the inventor's mindset, the technical and understanding skills using e-waste, we will focus on the Bluetooth loudspeaker and the Fan, where we have documented information from educators and students using them.

2.2   *Hands-on Learning with the "EcoMakerKits"*

The Eco Maker team has come up with two ways to share their "EcoMakerKits" to the educational community. One is focusing on educators through donations campaigns, and the other is focused on students and extended community through trainings and access to the products in the web shop.

2.2.1   Educational Campaigns to Share "EcoMakerKits"

In Mexico every May 15th is the Teachers National Day. In 2021, the Eco-Makers team came up with the idea of making a "Fan Maker Kit" based on what they had on storage (Figure 5.4). They donated the Fan Maker Kits to teachers interested in STEAMS education. The campaign reached 147 schools, with 219 kits

FIGURE 5.4   Teacher with Fan Maker Kit

donated to 86 municipalities in 24 out of the 32 states in Mexico. Some of the reactions of the teachers were: "Thank you Eco-Makers, I will use them in my robotics class", "I am looking forward to using it when we come back to face-to-face learning", and "I will use it as a complement to my STEAM class". In Figure 5.4 you can see Eduardo Chamodi, who is one of the teachers that applied for the STEAMS education campaign.

This example shows how part of the Maker Education principles goes beyond the profit purpose and embraces the sharing knowledge values. Through the "EcoMakerKits", Maker Education and Circular Thinking principles accessible to an extended community as well as linking it to the Global Goal from the United Nations of "Quality Education".

2.2.2   Hands-on Learning Using the "EcoMakerKits"

The educational perspective of Circular Thinking focuses on extending the life of a product and valuing the materials coming from nature. This concept is not easy to grasp for primary students. Therefore, the Eco Maker team developed a pilot workshop to stimulate curiosity for Circular Thinking, especially assembling artifacts with electronic circuits by making a Bluetooth loudspeaker and an electric Fan.

The pilot of the workshop took place in July 2021 in Querétaro, México, at a "Summer Course" that lasted four hours. The participants were fourchildren between 10 and 13 years old, the 13 years old participants having just finished primary school. The facilitator was a retired engineer that volunteered to facilitate the workshop and gave special input on the technical part of the activities.

The researcher, the last author of this book chapter, developed the instructional design and documented the pilot.[5]

The learning activities were based on the constructivist approach from Roger Bybee (Walia, 2012) called the "5E Model": Engage, explore, explain, elaborate, and evaluate. The learning goal was to practice the following 21st century skills: Creativity, collaboration, communication, and critical thinking.

The learning objectives were:
- Introduce the Circular Economy concept
- Explore digital tools to create a melody inspired on Circular Economy
- Follow a sequence of steps to build a Bluetooth loudspeaker and an electric Fan using e-waste
- Test the Bluetooth loudspeaker and the electric Fan
- Reflect on their learning

The first activity was to engage the students with the topic by asking them about what they already know about Circular Economy and documenting their answers using a self-assessment worksheet. The participants self-assessed the following learning goals based on their previous knowledge:
- I can explain what the Circular Economy is.
- I am able to create a melody with digital media.
- I am able to plan a sequence of steps to build a Bluetooth loudspeaker.
- I am able to play the melody on the Bluetooth loudspeaker.

They had to choose between three different answers:
- I can do it with support.
- I can do it by myself.
- I can do it and explain it to others.

The second activity was to explore the concept of Circular Economy. The participants watched a video[6] made for children by the Eco-Maker team. Afterwards the facilitator helped them discuss the global challenge that every year, tons of obsolete electronic products are discarded in the world, causing environmental pollution and damage to the health of living beings on the planet. After the discussion they had to come up with keywords that represent the Circular Economy, then present it to the group and finally write a sentence with their own definition of Circular Economy.

Music and melodies are an important part of humanity (Martinez & Stager, 2019) and a great way to explain how humans interpret their world. Therefore, the third activity was to explain how to create an original melody that would represent the concept of Circular Economy using an open-source website.[7]

The fourth activity was to elaborate on the conceptual understanding of Circular Thinking by a hands-on activity. They had to put together the Bluetooth loudspeaker (represented in Figure 5.5) and an electric Fan (represented in Figure 5.6). The facilitator explained how these products were made of electronic components recovered from damaged or obsolete electronic products, preventing more kilos of electronic waste from being erroneously deposited in landfills. After putting the kit together, they had to play their "Circular Economy melody" using the speaker, and they had to turn on the electric Fan.

Both the speaker and the electric Fan "EcoMakerKits" come in a box with all the parts to build it, including the case, engines, and wires to connect it.

The participants had to put them together using a set of instructions and video tutorials. The electric Fan had a hard copy with instructions represented in Figure 5.7, as well as a video tutorial.[8] The Bluetooth loudspeaker had a digital version of the instructions[9] and a video tutorial.[10]

FIGURE 5.5   Bluetooth loudspeaker

FIGURE 5.6   Electric fan

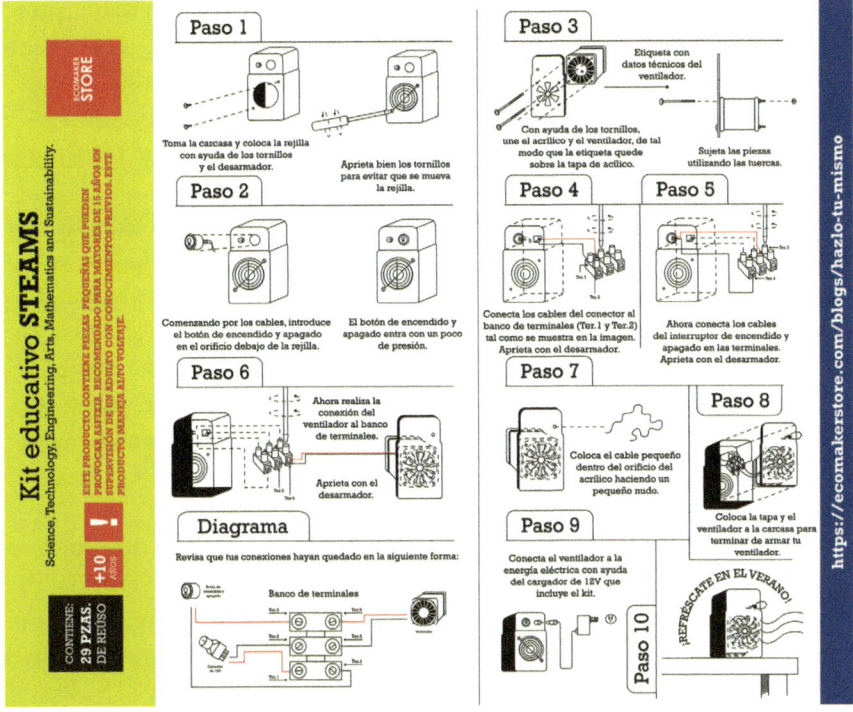

FIGURE 5.7   Set of instructions for electric fan

Finally, the fifth activity was to evaluate and self-assess their understanding and knowledge based on the rubrics from the first self-assessment activity and to reflect on their learning by answering the questions:

– What did you learn?
– What made you curious?
– What worked well?
– What did not work?
– What else would you like to learn?

In the next section we describe the results of the pilot workshop as an example of STEAMS hands-on learning activities.

3   Findings and Insights Using the "EcoMakerKits"

The two "EcoMakerKits" help to showcase how hands-on learning can impact the vision and understanding of Circular Thinking and Maker Mindset. As a result, we share some findings and insights based on two questions:

– What enables or hinders the understanding of Circular Thinking using "EcoMakerKits"?
– What enables or hinders the Maker Mindset using "EcoMakerKits"?

3.1   *The Enablers and Disablers of Understanding of Circular Thinking Using "EcoMakerKits"*

The teacher's campaign to share the "EcoMakerKits" was a great initiative for educators to have access to STEAMS resources, but it didn't include a lesson plan to explain what Circular Economy is. Therefore, a pilot was organized to showcase how educators and students could use these resources and to document their understanding of "Circular Economy" while using these resources.

In the next paragraphs the finding and insights of the five different activities of the workshop can be found. The participants were two boys and two girls, the facilitator, and the researcher. The two boys decided to work together, and the two girls worked as a team as well.

The first, second and fifth activities were done individually, they focused on grasping the conceptual understanding of what "Circular Economy" is. The participants practiced their critical thinking and communication skills. The third activity focused on their creative and tinkering skills to create an original melody that would represent the concept of "Circular Economy".

The original melody of the girls represents the disassembly process of e-waste and turning it into reusable electronics.[11] The boys decided to write the word "economy" using Morse Code.[12]

During the first activity and the self-assessment, the participants acknowledge that they needed support to explain what "Circular Economy" is but after the video and the discussion they were able to give their own definitions. It is interesting to see that three out of four definitions focused on electronics, except for "Participant 1". We believe that the influence of the video made by the Eco Maker team and the discussion around e-waste impacted on this narrowed vision of what "Circular Economy" is. During the group discussion the facilitator did mention that Circular Economy goes beyond electronics. It can also take place with fabrics, metal, and other types of materials. Thus, even though there is a broader definition to it, the participants came up with their own definition based on the experience from the first and second activities.

The positive effect is that the participants were able to develop technical skills, a limitation, considering that the learning goal is about "Circular Economy" using resources based on e-waste, but it seems that they needed support to grasp the "Circular Thinking" skills.

3.2   *The Enablers and Disablers of the Maker Mindset Using "EcoMakerKits"*

The students that participated in the workshop were able to benefit from the lesson plan that guide them through the technical skills and Maker Mindset, like resourcefulness, playfulness and especially focused on the technical skills to assemble the artefact and to connect the electric circuit practicing engineering, tinkering and critical thinking skills.

They put together the Bluetooth loudspeaker and an electric fan in pairs. The girls chose to build an electric fan represented in Figure 5.8 with the facilitator's assistance. The boys chose to build the loudspeaker represented in Figure 5.9.

They followed the video tutorial and the steps to build it. The resources provided by the Eco Maker team were very useful to guide them step by step to put it together.

FIGURE 5.8   Assembling the electric fan with the facilitator's assistance

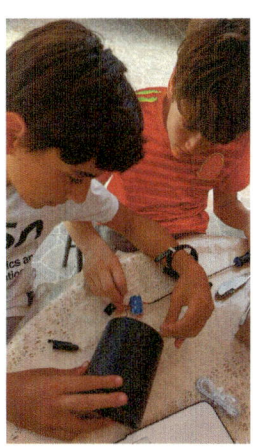

FIGURE 5.9
Boys assembling the bluetooth loudspeaker

One major observation during the workshop was that it was a positive impact to invite a retired engineer as he has plenty of experience, patience, and time to share his knowledge with young generations. Especially, when it came to assembling the Bluetooth loudspeaker and the electric Fan. He was able to give some suggestions to use the tools and how to carefully follow the instructions to make sure that the electric circuits were put together in the correct order.

The participants found it challenging to put together the electronic circuits and had to go back to the video and the instructions many times to do it correctly. Their curiosity went beyond the novelty of the product and went deeper into scientific curiosity (Jirout et al., 2012). The participants were able to express it in the reflection activity. For example, in the last reflection activity they shared that they were curious to know how the electric Fan works, where energy comes from, realized how small the Bluetooth hardware is, and how wires work. These insights that might encourage them to find out more about technical skills related to assembling and electronic circuits.

The educators that participated in the teachers' campaign with "EcoMakerKits" have also access to the video tutorials and manuals made by the Eco Maker team. Hopefully these resources make it easier for them to integrate the technical skills into their educational environment and share the Maker Mindset with their students. Unfortunately, this has not been documented yet.

The workshop helped to document how in using "EcoMakerKits" the participants can actively learn how it is not acceptable that the society continues to send products to the trash when there is a high probability that many of their parts and/or components still work or can be repaired.

The limitation of this workshop is that is the educational part focuses on e-waste, leaving aside other industries such as fashion and plastic packaging that are part of the linear model of take-make-waste.

Another limitation is that the "EcoMakerKits" are part of a well-defined business model that provides the infrastructure to make it sustainable to provide to the society this type of maker education. As a result, there is limited access to this type of educational resources.

4   Conclusions

We can conclude that in the workshop the "EcoMakerKits" resulted in growing curiosity of "Circular Thinking" and technical skills to ensemble artifacts made out of e-waste, especially with the older participants.

In the workshop, the participants received practical experience in a country with a lack of resources for materials in education. They learned to follow a manual, develop basic electronic understanding, and gained the experience of re-using materials to assemble something useful.

It was possible for the participants to develop a certain understanding of Maker Mindset and the technical skills to build their "EcoMakerKits". It would be advisable to have a facilitator with technical knowledge to explain how electrical circuits work, how to essemble them, and to help solve technical questions from the participants.

The instructional design focused on the Bluetooth loudspeaker "EcoMaker-Kit". It gave specific learning goals and steps that were used in the workshop to give more emphasis on concepts like "Circular Economy" and "Electronic Circuits" to build the loudspeaker and a website to make the melodies to be played using the Bluetooth loudspeaker. The participants might also benefit from a lesson plan that could give a functional context to use the electric Fan.

For further research, it would be interesting to consider adding to the Eco Makers educational campaigns the educational resources that go beyond teaching technical skills as a strategy to approach the "Maker Mindset", but also help to grasp the concept of "Circular Thinking". This could help other educators locally and globally to have inspiration on how to approach these concepts using hands-on learning activities.

It would also be interesting to dig deeper into the business model of the Eco Maker company who supplies these kits, especially to see if this business model can be adopted by others in order to increase the amount of e-waste recycling and increasing the supply for educational kits like this. Further research could take the lessons learned from the company and package it as a template for others, perhaps other areas within or even outside Mexico could get up and running quickly, managing a sustainable business model with an important environmental/educational purpose.

The current environmental crisis calls us to carry out actions that mitigate the effects of Climate Change. It is through the Circular Thinking and the type of educational resources used in this chapter, that we may also demonstrate the importance to incorporate e-waste in education.

Educators could consider using components with a useful life for the creation of new maker educational resources as alternatives to reduce the environmental impact; As well as helping to accomplish the following Sustainable Development Goals: Quality Education, Responsible Consumption and Production, and Climate Action (Morton, Pencheon, & Squires, 2017).

We also find a positive impact on the education of young generations to foster the curiosity and to expand their Maker Mindset. This can be done through STEAMS activities like the two presented in this chapter with the "EcoMakerKits". These activities provided hands-on learning that helped the participants to raise awareness of Circular Thinking, grasp the concept of e-waste, and develop electronic circuits technical skills. The participants were also able to make a melody that helped them to represent these concepts in a personal way, providing them with more agency to own their knowledge.

It might be interesting for other educators to have next to their "Maker Space" a "Breaker Space" designated to dismantle e-waste and help to make the connection on how things work and are made, and how they can be reused or repaired to extend their usable life.

Hopefully the children participating in this type of maker education are inspired to become professionals that can develop new products with the knowledge and methodology of the Circular Thinking and Maker Mindset.

Acknowledgements

The authors would like to thank the participants, the facilitator, and the Eco Maker team for their support.

Notes

1   www.juntaentregayrecicla.com.mx
2   https://open.spotify.com/show/3t90009ft4VCODBfiO5F70?si=2VRQy_
    zaR4WxZV7lvg0pmQ&nd=1
3   https://ecomakerstore.com/blogs/ecomakerstore/crean-bocina-bluetooth-con-materiales-
    reciclados?_pos=1&_sid=853e4ffcf&_ss=r
4   https://ecomakerstore.com/
5   A slide deck in Spanish was used to support the workshop and is available following this link:
    bit.ly/planeacioneconomiacircular
6   https://youtu.be/Eete-R14_a8
7   https://musiclab.chromeexperiments.com/Experiments
8   https://youtu.be/t2gcOk1UPas
9   https://issuu.com/ecomaker_store/docs/instructivo-ecomakerbox-bocina-bluetooth
10 https://youtu.be/6tj5_WfFNg0
11 bit.ly/team1girls
12 bit.ly/team2boys

References

Andrews, D. (2015). The circular economy, design thinking and education for sustainability. *Local Economy*, *30*(3), 305–315.

Blikstein, P. (2018). Maker movement in education: History and prospects.
In M. J. de Vries (Ed.), *Handbook of technology education* (pp. 419–435). Springer.
https://doi.org/10.1007/978-3-319-44687-5_33

Böni, H. (2005). Global perspectives on e-waste. *Environmental Impact Assessment Review, 25*(5), 436–458.

Bulow, J. (1986). An economic theory of planned obsolescence. *The Quarterly Journal of Economics, 101*(4), 729–749.

Cruz-Sotelo, S., Ojeda-Benítez, S., Jáuregui Sesma, J., Velázquez-Victorica, K., Santillán-Soto, N., García-Cueto, O., Alcántara Concepción, V., et al. (2017). E-waste supply chain in Mexico: Challenges and opportunities for sustainable management. *Sustainability, 9*(4), 503. http://dx.doi.org/10.3390/su9040503

Dougherty, D. (2016). *Free to make: How the maker movement is changing our schools, our jobs, and our minds.* North Atlantic Books.

Engel, S. (2011). Children's need to know: Curiosity in schools. *Harvard Educational Review, 81*(4), 625–645.

Ergin, I. (2012). Constructivist approach based 5E model and usability instructional physics. *Latin-American Journal of Physics Education, 6*(1), 14–20.

Guiltinan, J. (2009). Creative destruction and destructive creations: Environmental ethics and planned obsolescence. *Journal of Business Ethics, 89*(1), 19–28.

Ingold, T. (2013). *Making: Anthropology, archaeology, art and architecture.* Routledge.

Jirout, J., & Klahr, D. (2012). Children's scientific curiosity: In search of an operational definition of an elusive concept. *Developmental Review, 32*(2), 125–160.

Kiddee, P., Naidu, R., & Wong, M. H. (2013). Electronic waste management approaches: An overview. *Waste Management, 33*(5), 1237–1250.

Korhonen, J., Honkasalo, A., & Seppälä, J. (2018). Circular economy: The concept and its limitations. *Ecological Economics, 143*, 37–46.

Merckel, G. (2021). Breve texto sobre Educación Maker en el contexto de la economía circular. Retrieved September 11, 2021, from https://medium.com/@gusmendez/breve-texto-sobre-educaci%C3%B3n-maker-en-el-contexto-de-la-econom%C3%ADa-circular-586fe6dbc2eb

Morton, S., Pencheon, D., & Squires, N. (2017). Sustainable Development Goals (SDGs), and their implementation: A national global framework for health, development and equity needs a systems approach at every level. *British Medical Bulletin, 124*(1), 81–90.

Silver, J. (2016). *Invention literacy.* Retrieved October 16, 2022, from https://medium.com/startupgrind/invention-literacy-5915a411e29d

Wackman, J., & Knight, E. (2020). *Repair revolution: How fixers are transforming our throwaway culture.* New World Library.

Waldman, M. (1993). A new perspective on planned obsolescence. *The Quarterly Journal of Economics, 108*(1), 273–283.

Walia, P. (2012). Effect of 5E instructional model on mathematical creativity of students. *Journal of Golden Research Thoughts, 1*(10), 1–4.

CHAPTER 6

Playful Learning by Design in Kenya
Remote Development of Design Education Workshops for Rural Kenya

Marten B. Westerhof, Mathieu Gielen, Annemiek G. C. van Boeijen and James Otieno Jowi

Abstract

Design projects can function as a carrier for learning a subset of 21st century skills – but how does that play out in a rural community in Kenya that is unfamiliar with this approach to design education, and in a culture and context that the developers of such design education are not familiar with? This chapter recounts the development of a workshop programme that aims to teach design-related skills to primary school aged children in the non-formal context of a community centre in rural Kenya. As a collaboration between a Dutch academic design school and a local Kenyan non-profit organisation, the project required rethinking design education for a different cultural and economic context. This impacted the educational approach, including learning goals and design goals, didactics, educator support, and communication channels. Travel restrictions due to the Covid-19 pandemic enforced a remote development process, which created space for increased agency of the participating children and facilitator. The resulting workshop instruction guide scaffolds the local facilitators' design (education) knowledge and supports playful group learning processes.

Keywords

co-design – playful learning – design education – culture – maker activities

1   Kenyan Children Designing Toys: The Initial Assumptions and Aims

Times of hardship can spark initiatives with unforeseen value. In 2020, the Covid-19 pandemic brought formal primary education in rural Kenya largely to a standstill. In West Kenya, in Kisumu County, there is a local community centre run by Sustainable Rural Initiatives (SRI). The director of SRI sought opportunities to provide the local children with alternative informal learning experiences. He contacted old acquaintances from the Dutch design school Industrial Design Engineering (IDE) at Delft University of Technology. At IDE, a research and development project had previously been conducted on co-design as an educational format for children in primary education in The Netherlands (Gielen et al., 2020; Klapwijk et al., 2021). Hence our thoughts went towards creating a programme that would implement design education for children in the specific cultural and economic context of rural families in SRI's community.

The project was loosely defined around various assets at SRI. The community centre housed workshop facilities for crafts such as woodworking and tailoring that could be used. A facilitator was available to support children's learning process. At IDE, knowledge was available of design methodologies (Van Boeijen et al., 2020), including culturally sensitive design (Van Boeijen & Zijlstra, 2020). The previous project at IDE had identified factors that enhance design as a learning process (Klapwijk & van den Burg, 2019) for training a subset of 21st century skills (Voogt & Pareja Roblin, 2012), such as creative problem-solving and communication. Finally, IDE could provide a Master student eager to develop a design education format. Designing and building toys was deemed an appropriate focus for the workshops, based on the following assumptions: toys relate to children and motivate them to engage in the design process; designing toys would enable the children to replace their current imported toys with ones that reflect their own cultural identity and individual play preferences; it could replace plastic with more sustainable locally sourced materials; and it might even provide a basis for setting up production and sales of toys – an opportunity to train their entrepreneurial skills. Combining the perceived assets and focus on toys, an assignment was drafted to develop an educational design programme for the children attending workshops at SRI's community centre. Over the course of five months and within the evolving constraints of the Covid pandemic, this project was carried out by a graduating Master student in Industrial Design Engineering (1st author), operating as education developer. During this period, a series of workshops with supporting instructions and videos were developed, sent to the local SRI employee, discussed before and after each session for as far as communication channels were available, and improved in an iterative design research process. In some cases, the results of the workshops were shared with the education developer, who could send feedback to the children through video messages. After several iterations, the final workshop instruction sheets and supporting videos were integrated in a toolkit that aims to aid in hosting a series of educational design workshops for children at SRI, and for the workshop facilitator to independently host follow-up workshops. This chapter recounts the insights evolving from the project and the playful design toolkit in which it resulted (Westerhof, 2021).

2   Drivers for the Workshop Development Process

Designing is dealing with uncertainty. The result is never clear at the start and the solution space may alter, depending on intermediate insights and contingencies. Five main drivers that influenced the solution space of this specific project are identified and discussed below.

2.1   *Remote Collaboration during a Pandemic*

Usually, designers attach great significance to experiencing a context they are not familiar with themselves (Van Boeijen, 2015). As an outsider (Banks, 1998), it is key to participate closely with local people to avoid biases and to understand what is relevant for the design and what not. Subtle details are difficult to understand from, for example, literature alone (Hao, 2019; van Boeijen & Stappers, 2011). However, due to the COVID-19 pandemic the education developer was not able to travel and study the context locally or facilitate early versions of the workshop himself. Therefore, new ways of research and development were implemented via remote collaboration with SRI's employees and the involved children.

To cope with remotely developing the education programme, the education developer's efforts focused on facilitating 'learning by doing' by preparing digital instruction materials. With the help of these materials, the local facilitator took on the role as organiser and facilitator. Conversations after each workshop and the photos and videos of the activities that the workshop host recorded allowed the education developer to acquire an understanding of the local context and to improve the workshop materials.

Few funds were available at SRI, which put heavy constraints on how the communication could be sustained. Video or audio calls between the education developer and the workshop host and participating children were too costly and unreliable to maintain during the workshops. To limit these costs, it was essential that the toolkit would make the facilitator function independently during the workshops. Thus, the workshop toolkit came to focus on instructions for the facilitator rather than the children. It was the facilitator who needed to understand and apply the characteristics of the workshop that triggered children to learn design skills.

2.2   *Co-developing Culturally Embedded Workshops*

For the workshops to be effective, a culture-sensitive design approach (Van Boeijen & Zijlstra, 2020) is key. The way in which the workshops are structured and fleshed out is important to the suitability of their use in the context, but also to what they teach and in what way. A variety of aspects was considered, including the topics for the design challenges, design terms (language and jargon), and the language and music that are used in the supporting videos in the toolkit.

During the development of the toolkit, the children's opinions of the activities were mainly interpreted by the facilitator and then relayed to the education developer. Because of the constant dialogue between these two during the project, the facilitator, and indirectly the children, could suggest changes or specific additions or omissions from the workshops, and thus had a strong say in the development of the toolkit. Because the facilitator performed the bulk of the activities after the education developer had prepared the materials, he could not only tailor the instructions for hosting the activities to better fit the occurring situation, but also translate, interpret, and adapt specific aspects of the workshops to better fit the context. For the education developer, this meant that the toolkit needed to be developed with a strong focus on supporting an effective transfer of the necessary knowledge to the facilitator.

2.3   *Children's Participation Motives*

The absence of the education developer during the workshops not only put more responsibility on the facilitator, but it also affected children's motivations to participate. As the community centre does not provide formal education, children are free to come and go as they wish. Their initial curiosity towards what the design educator could teach them dwindled once it became clear that these workshops followed a strict task-based structure that felt like formal schooling. Not being present during the sessions, the education developer could not improvise on the spot to mitigate the negative aspects of the set-up. He had to rethink the programme from the perspective of children, as recounted by the facilitator, and decide how to keep them engaged. The workshops had to be inviting, have exciting relatable topics for the children, be fun to partake in, and give the children a sense of accomplishment. And for a large part, the facilitator had to accomplish this with the support of the workshop toolkit.

There already is a variety of educational programmes that aim to teach children design skills. The first activities organised at SRI were based on the 'Your Turn' design education programme (Klapwijk et al., 2021). This programme focuses on letting the children experience working on real design challenges in multiple design sessions in structured classroom settings. The workshops at SRI were initially also planned as a series of sessions, each dedicated to a phase in the design process. It turned out to be difficult to make this set-up work in SRI's context. The children experienced the organised activities as school-like and quickly lost interest in taking part in them, which meant they would also not experience the joy of seeing their design come to life. To enthuse the children for joining the activities, it helped to give them tangible design goals that were feasible to reach in a single workshop. It also helped if assignments were relatable and interesting to a diverse group of boys and girls.

2.4 *Scarcity of Resources*

The scarcity of resources available for the project had a strong influence on the workshop activities. Initial proposed formats, based upon Dutch examples, made use of a variety of materials, e.g., printed paper templates for brainstorming activities, colour pencils for sketching, raw materials to build models through woodworking and tailoring, and a mobile phone or computer (including internet costs) for recording videos. All of these materials proved difficult to make available, possibly because the children's activities were not deemed economically relevant. To make a viable programme that would survive in the economic conditions after the project had ended, it was essential that SRI could independently organise these workshops with the toolkit alone without external funding after the collaboration ended. Thus, it was decided to only make use of materials that are widely available for free in SRI's surroundings, such as twigs and clay. The children collected the materials before creating artefacts as integral part of the workshops to limit the costs. The use of local, freely available materials makes the workshop less dependent on external contributors, more resilient to adverse circumstances, and hopefully also easier to disseminate to other locations.

2.5 *A Shift from Toys to Playful Design Experiences*

The original intent of the Kenyan stakeholder for this project was for the designer to co-design and craft toys with the children, that could potentially also be sold locally by the children to train their entrepreneurial skills. Creating their own toys would have allowed children to develop crafting skills and get access to toys that were potentially more affordable and durable than the current supply of imported plastic goods. Furthermore, these toys would reflect the local cultural context, as the children having access to 'appropriate toys', as an extension to 'appropriate technology', was deemed important. Although play itself is a universal phenomenon, what children play with is informed by the context and surroundings. Through play, children explore and acquaint themselves with the rules and symbols of their communities (Else, 2009, pp. 44–45). Appropriate toys were thus seen as a valuable medium to support their social development.

However, early in the development process of the workshops, the emphasis shifted away from the end-product (available, affordable, sustainable toys) to the playful learning experience of design and creation. The low durability of the local materials that were available during the workshops greatly reduced the feasibility of creating durable toys. Thus, the building activity itself became more dominant. Initially, the shift in focus away from creating usable toys was perceived as a great setback and loss of value. However, crafting is a universal form of play and toys are a popular crafting category. So, could the activities in the workshops become a form of play and still have the desired educational effect?

A review by Zosh et al. (2017) concludes that, although free play is an important part of child development, adults can also help to facilitate learning by structuring children's play. When adults guide children's play, they can help them to develop skills by providing them with joyful, engaging, iterative and socially interactive play experiences. By extension, in this case the workshops could help children develop design skills in a fun and engaging way through structuring children's crafting and building during the workshop as a design process, an exploration of form and function. In a conventional design cycle (Van Boeijen et al., 2020, pp. 45, 47, 57), the prototyping stage follows on ideation. Here, the building activity itself became the core of the ideation process. Making, assessing, and altering the artefact became a fluent process which encapsulated divergent, convergent, presentation, and feedback activities, as a form of iterative 3D-sketching. The artefact was no longer a prototype or model referring to a possible future product; the artefact was the nascent toy – or rather, the clay and twigs were the toys, and designing was the play. The distant collaboration made it hard to assess the actual playfulness during activities. However, some indications were found through video reports and discussions with the facilitator.

Children could freely explore the materials and their expressive potential. Construction play, the process of 'creating meaning', was the dominant play type. Artefacts showed a variety in design, level of detail, and backstories. This suggests that the children experienced freedom to express personal fascinations, which is an indication of an open-ended playful process. The joyful pride of the children for their final artefacts signals the importance of working towards an end goal, but there was ample room for enjoying the process: this is an important aspect of playfulness as well.

The above-mentioned drivers for the solution space of the project (remote collaboration, culture-sensitive co-development, children's participation motives, scarcity of resources and focus on a playful design process), helped shape the final design of a toolkit that allows local facilitators to independently carry out educational design workshops. It offers a blueprint that structures the activities and supports the facilitator in applying productive didactic techniques but becomes more open-ended with every follow-up workshop.

3   The Design: A Workshop Format and Toolkit

A workshop format and several workshops based on this format were developed through which the children can learn design skills, based on design skill didactics (Klapwijk & van den Burg, 2019). Several tools were developed to support the facilitator to host these workshops independently, and thereafter create more workshops based on the same format: instruction materials and challenge suggestions collected in a manual, as well as supporting videos. The series of workshop descriptions and tools together thus form an open-ended toolkit.

3.1   *Workshop Format*

The workshops are divided in three distinct phases: Exploring, Building, and Presenting. See Figure 6.1 for an illustration of the three phases. The structure of the workshop is based on contemporary design methodologies (Van Boeijen et al., 2020). Typical elements of these design processes are adapted to fit an afternoon-long workshop, e.g., the iterative element present in many design processes is given a subordinate position in the final format. This helped to put more emphasis on the joy of building (in contrast to deliberate and time-consuming iterations) and to streamline the process for both the children and the workshop host.

In the first phase, a topic is introduced and explored by asking several questions to provoke discussion between the children, as illustrated in Figure 6.2. With each question and subsequent discussion, the children further elaborate on their design goal

In the second phase, the children gather the materials they want to use, and then build their solution with those materials. See Figure 6.3 for an example from one of the workshops. Throughout the process of building, the children further ideate, test, and iterate on their initial ideas to develop their ideal solution.

In the third and final phase, the children present their designs to each other, and discover and celebrate the great diversity of possible solutions to come out

Phase 1 - Exploring
Exploring the topic
and defining your goal

Phase 2 - Building
Building and testing
your idea

Phase 3 - Presenting
Presenting and
celebrating the designs

FIGURE 6.1   The workshops are divided in three distinct phases: Exploring, building, and
presenting

FIGURE 6.2   The facilitator introduces the children to the topic of a workshop through a video

FIGURE 6.3   A child in the process of building an artefact as his answer to his design goal

FIGURE 6.4   Children presenting their designs in the third phase of the first workshop

of the design goal they defined in phase 1. An example from the third phase of one of the workshops is given in Figure 6.4. This three-part process provides a minimal logical structure to the children's design process, guiding them through the design process, while maintaining an enjoyable pace and a natural flow throughout the workshop.

3.2   Predefined Workshops

A sequence of several workshops was developed. The first two of these workshops are predefined through videos that introduce the topic and pose questions that help the children define their design. In the first workshop the children design a toy car. In the first phase of the workshop, a video is played to introduce the topic of car design to the children, after which it poses questions to define their design goal. The questions relate to the aspects of the design, such as what it will be used for, by whom, when, where, and how. The video prompts the facilitator to pause the video after each question to allow the children to discuss it. At the end, the video gives the children examples of how they could prototype specific parts of their design e.g., how they can use clay and twigs to make wheels affixed to an axle to allow their toy car to be rolled around. Figure 6.5 gives an overview of the first workshop video through a selection of stills.

In this video the children are first shown how clay models are used in car design processes. Then, several questions are posed in the video to help the children specify the aspects of the car they will design through discussions. The video concludes with a question to trigger them to think about what they

FIGURE 6.5   A selection of stills from the first workshop video

want to design. In the second phase of the first workshops, the children are asked to collect clay and some wood from around SRI's grounds, after which they can start to build their toy car. The children inspire each other, but also have distinct ideas about what the function of their toy car is. As they figure out how to build the functions of their car into their design, the children experience the fun of creating something. Finally, in the third phase, the children show off their designs to each other and celebrate all the different outcomes of the workshop.

The topic in this first workshop is narrowly defined. As the children develop their design skills with each subsequent workshop, they are given a bigger 'solution space' for the challenge they are faced with while receiving less strict support in how to address the design challenge, as illustrated in Figure 6.6. The video structuring the second workshop in the sequence poses fewer constraints, and consequently the second workshop itself is more open as well. In this workshop the children are asked to design 'a building' that aims to serve a specific purpose in their own community. The video poses several questions to make them think about what kind of building would be of value to their village, and lets the children discuss that amongst themselves. In contrast to the previous video, this one does not give examples of what materials the children

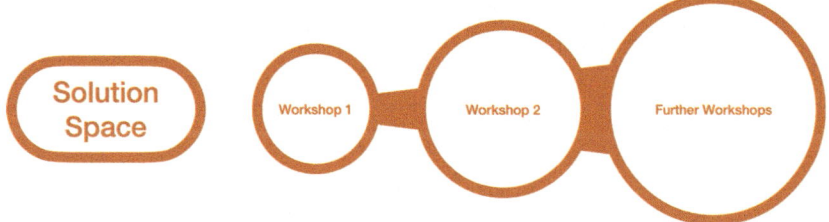

FIGURE 6.6   The solution space gradually increases with each workshop through the way in which topics are introduced and the design goals are formulated

could use and how they could answer the other questions in the video. The larger solution space in this workshop as compared to the first challenges the children's design and problem-solving skills more extensively. The focus thus also further shifts from building a specific toy, to an artefact that is more like a scale model for a solution in the real world.

The facilitator may refer to the manual for a structured instruction on how to independently organise the third and further workshops. The instructions contain several suggestions for topics with a large solution space to be used in workshops, such as e.g., challenging the children to design something to help someone cross a river or to make a boat that can stay afloat. After having organised these workshops, it is up to the facilitator to come up with more workshops with the appropriate solution space to challenge the children.

3.3   *Toolkit and Tools*

The toolkit consists of a manual and several videos that help the facilitator to host the workshops, which are illustrated in Figure 6.7. By using these tools to organise the workshops, the facilitator becomes acquainted with the workshop format and proposed didactics and gradually becomes independent in designing more workshops himself.

The manual contains an introduction to the toolkit, explanation of the workshop format, elaboration on the suggested progression of difficulty in the workshops, and step-by-step instructions for organising the first two workshops in the outlined sequence. Additionally, it contains a format to help the facilitator come up with topics and challenges for further workshops. It also

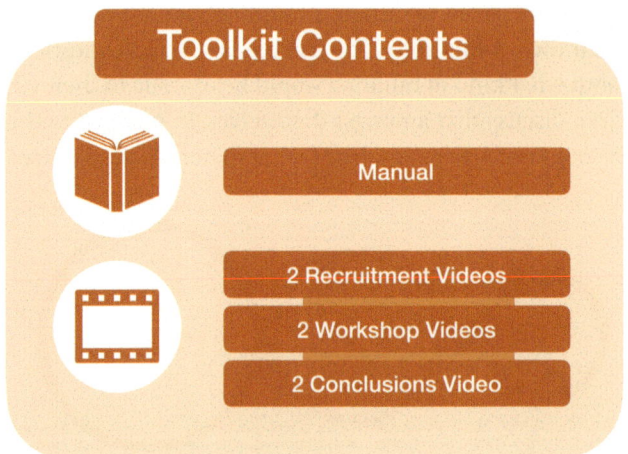

FIGURE 6.7   Overview of the contents of the developed toolkit

contains several suggestions for workshops based on that format e.g., letting the children design something to help someone cross a river. This format aims to help the host to become self-reliant in carrying out subsequent – more open – assignments.

The toolkit also contains several instructional materials, which are illustrated in Figure 6.8. The videos in the toolkit support the workshop host in preparing, facilitating, and concluding the workshops. From the third workshop onward the workshop host has the responsibility to introduce the topic and questions to the children without the support of a video. The manual provides the facilitator with suggestions through several 'challenge sheets'. Each challenge sheet presents the story of a main character who faces a problem in reaching their goal. The children are then invited to help solve the problem through their design.

In addition to the videos that aid the workshop host in organising the first two workshops in the sequence, the toolkit contains two recruitment videos and a conclusions video. The two recruitment videos briefly introduce the workshops and theme in an uplifting way, to help the host enthuse local children for joining the activities. These videos are played to the children at the community centre.

The final video in the toolkit, the conclusions video, helps the workshop host communicate to the children which skills they are developing. Klapwijk (2017) describes seven key design skills that are considered the most relevant for primary school pupils: 'thinking in all directions' (divergent thinking), 'developing empathy', 'making productive mistakes' (early and frequent iteration), 'making ideas tangible' (convergent thinking), 'sharing ideas' (communication), 'defining your direction', and 'making use of the process' (meta-cognitive skills). All these skills come into play during the design workshops, and they are illustrated in the conclusions video by the narrator, who links them to the phase of the workshop in which the children applied them and celebrates the children's work. The facilitator can point at evidence of applying these skills in the children's designs and design processes to increase the learning outcome.

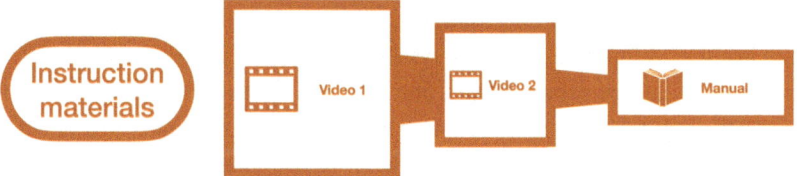

FIGURE 6.8   The developed instruction materials: With each workshop, the supporting materials become less prominent and elaborate, transferring the responsibilities for hosting the workshop to the facilitator

4   Conclusion

This chapter explained the remote development of a workshop to introduce children living in small villages in rural Kenya to design in a playful way. The original goal of the project was to help children build their own toys. These self-made toys would reflect their environment and cultural background better than imported toys. The project took on a longer-term focus in which building toys or other objects served a higher-level goal; children who are skilled at design. In this new focus, learning to design is ascribed a quality similar to what toys represent, that is 'playing'.

The following paragraphs present reflections on each of the five drivers of the workshop development process that were introduced in Section 2.

4.1   *The Remote Collaboration during a Pandemic*

During the development of the workshop format and toolkit a disadvantage unexpectedly turned into an advantage. The travel restrictions due to the Covid-pandemic enforced a remote collaboration and made the education developer highly dependent on the facilitator, in which the latter became more involved and influential on the end result, leading to a reciprocal relationship. Inadvertently, the specific remote collaboration approach taken in this project helped to further embed the workshops in the context effectively. Although it increased the responsibilities of the facilitator, who had the task of inviting children, hosting the workshops, and documenting the children's process during these workshops, it also helped to shift the agency in the design process from the education developer to the facilitator.

4.2   *Co-developing Culturally Embedded Workshops*

The result – a series of compact workshops accompanied with a toolkit – is based on an established notion of what design is and how designing, the design process, basically functions. This process is not universal but rooted in a specific design school culture. In this case, this was a design culture that can be typified as systematic, research-based, and problem-solving-focused. Although the education developer and his supervisors have done their best to approach the project in a culture-sensitive way, one should still stay critical towards the extent to which the result is attuned with the local situation, that is, in line with the local context, people's values, and practices. By default, a design, which is here the series of workshops and a toolkit, cannot be value-free. Many decisions are made in its creation, and they are partly based on designers' cultural backgrounds, understanding of the situation, and their beliefs about what is a good answer to the problem posed. Especially in vulnerable situations, such as the one here with children and with economic dependence, we need to be modest and give space for a discussion on possible long-term effects. For example, one could question whether the systematic design process, with three separated phases, is an appropriate export product that is useful to teach the children or whether the learning should address a more fundamental set of knowledge and skills: the understanding and ability to confront life's diverse challenges with a creative mindset of solution-focused flexibility. There are also more intuitive and artistic ways to approach design. Would they be more appropriate? We do not know. Another consideration is the kind of design assignments. In what way do they address the interests of children, for example regarding gender roles, but also regarding what they know about it. In the first workshop, the children were introduced to 'building a car'. Several archetypes for specific functions (truck, bus, pick-up, etc.) were shown to get the children started. In the following workshops the assignments were more open; from 'designing a building for the community' to 'something to cross the river', giving children the space to come up with their own interpretations, avoiding communicating norms about what a car, a house, or a bridge should look like. To what extent do we need to encourage children to follow the existing world with its current dominant values and practice? Or do we want them to think differently, imagining a world we could not even think of.

Furthermore, the division of roles has not been explicitly discussed. For example, the relationship between the facilitator and the children and the involvement of parents and other people responsible for the children's upbringing were not addressed. Moreover, the form of the instruction videos, the representation, is a point of attention. Practical aspects, such as orientation of illustrations in the manual that need to be read from left to right were attuned to local conventions. And we assume that the drawn figures in the video that represent the targeted children were rather abstract. Together with the chosen music, voice-over, and language, they were understood for their practical purpose, but what about the symbolic meaning of these manifestations?

4.3   *Children's Participation Motives*

Rewards in, for example, the form of seeing oneself and what one has made in a video proved important. Furthermore, informality and playfulness were needed to motivate the children to come to the workshop. Compared to prior primary school design approaches such as 'Your Turn' (Klapwijk et al., 2021), many of the formal design phases have been omitted or simplified, e.g., the well-known procedure of creating many ideas and then selecting or combining the best ones for further elaboration. This repeated divergent/convergent thinking process is regarded as an essential procedure to arrive at higher-quality design outcomes

(Van Boeijen et al., 2020, p. 51), yet it also leads to frustration in novice designers who cling to initial ideas (Schut et al., 2020). Instead of forcing each individual participant to produce many ideas, the SRI design workshop format and toolkit use the power of the group as it reviews and celebrates the diversity of outcomes of each workshop, thus conveying at least part of the learning experience that there are multiple solutions with various qualities for each problem. It may be less adherent to formal design-methodological training but superior in its support of children's intrinsic motivations to engage in the workshop.

4.4 Scarcity of Resources

As in every 'Base of the Pyramid' project in rural – often vulnerable – areas a holistic approach is key, which considers the principles Affordability, Accessibility, Availability (of resources), Reliability, Sustainability, and Acceptability (Van Boeijen et al., 2020, p. 27). Except for the internet costs needed to download the videos, the materials were chosen in line with these six principles.

4.5 A Shift from Toys to Playful Design Experiences

We might wonder if the children actually made toys in the end; a house, a car, a bridge to play with? Ultimately, we focused on the making itself and not on what the children could and want to do with the result at a later date. It would be worth investigating this further.

It is too early to answer the question if this design is scalable, which means that other rural community centres in Kenya or elsewhere, with similar circumstances, could successfully use the workshop format with the toolkit. It would be helpful to first see how the design is used at the SRI centre independently, without the background support of our education developer. More testing of the workshop format and toolkit at SRI's community centre and in other similar places is necessary to assess their robustness and long-term value.

References

Banks, J. A. (1998). The lives and values of researchers: Implications for educating citizens in a multicultural society. *Educational Researcher, 27*(7), 4–17. https://doi.org/10.2307/1176055

Else, P. (2009). *The value of play*. Bloomsbury Publishing.

Gielen, M. A., Klapwijk, R. M., Schut, A., & van Mechelen, M. (2020). *Vaardig in ontwerpen op de basisschool: Onderzoek naar het ontwikkelen van 21e-eeuwse vaardigheden via ontwerpprojecten met een externe partner* (Insitutional Repository). Delft University of Technology; TU Delft Research Repository. http://resolver.tudelft.nl/uuid:76339c1f-3e0e-4e8d-ab8d-c3faf8b1a8c4

Hao, C. (2019). *Cultura: Achieving intercultural empathy through contextual user research in design* [Doctoral thesis, Delft University of Technology]. TU Delft Education Repository. https://doi.org/10.4233/uuid:88322666-9cf1-4120-bbd6-4a93438bca74

Klapwijk, R. M. (2017). Creativity in design. In C. Benson & S. Lawson (Eds.), *Teaching design and technology creatively* (pp. 51–72). Routledge.

Klapwijk, R. M., Gielen, M. A., Schut, A., van Mechelen, M. P. P., & Stables, K. (2021). *Your turn for the teacher: Guidebook to develop real-life design lessons for use with 8–14 years old pupils* (Institutional Repository). Delft University of Technology; TU Delft Research Repository. http://resolver.tudelft.nl/uuid:aecf73d9-c54a-430b-a572-0e1fd92028b0

Klapwijk, R. M., & van den Burg, N. (2019). Formative assessment in primary design education—Involving pupils in clarifying the learning goal of divergent thinking. In S. Pulé & M. J. de Vries (Eds.), *Developing a knowledge economy through technology and engineering education* (pp. 277–287). University of Malta.

Schut, A., Klapwijk, R. M., Gielen, M. A., van Doorn, F., & de Vries, M. (2020). Uncovering early indicators of fixation during the concept development stage of children's design processes. *International Journal of Technology and Design Education, 30*(5), 951–972.

Van Boeijen, A. (2015). *Crossing cultural chasms: Towards a culture-conscious approach to design* [Doctoral thesis, Delft University of Technology]. TU Delft Education Repository. https://doi.org/10.4233/uuid:fc87dfd1-b7eb-4c84-b6c7-6835c5e837f8

Van Boeijen, A., Daalhuizen, J., & Zijlstra, J. (2020). *Delft design guide: Perspectives, models, approaches, methods.* BIS Publishers.

Van Boeijen, A., & Stappers, P. (2011). Serving the underserved: What can designers learn from rural appraisal techniques? In N. Roozenburg, L. Chen, & P. Stappers (Eds.), *Proceedings of the IASDR 2011* (pp. 1–9). TU Delft/IASDR.

Van Boeijen, A., & Zijlstra, I. (2020). *Culture sensitive design: A guide to culture in practice.* BIS Publishers.

Voogt, J., & Pareja Roblin, N. (2012). A comparative analysis of international frameworks for 21st century competences: Implications for national curriculum policies. *Journal of Curriculum Studies, 44*(3), 299–321.

Westerhof, M. B. (2021). *Playful learning through designing toys: Developing a design education toolkit for a non-profit organisation in rural Kenya* [Master's thesis, Delft University of Technology]. TU Delft Education Repository. https://repository.tudelft.nl/islandora/object/uuid%3A8ae09e82-28bb-4000-b7da-0613b1e3d0a2

Zosh, J. N., Hopkins, E. J., Jensen, H., Liu, C., Neale, D., Hirsh-Pasek, K., Solis, S. L., & Whitebread, D. (2017). *Learning through play: A review of the evidence* [White Paper]. The LEGO Foundation.

CHAPTER 7

Connecting Maker Education to Secondary School Technology Education in Korea

A Case of the Technology Teachers' Learning Community in Republic of Korea

Hyuksoo Kwon

Abstract

This chapter introduces trends and cases of maker education in South Korean technology education. In particular, this study investigates a technology teachers' professional learning community for maker education. Four themes were drawn from a qualitative analysis of the four technology teachers' interviews and relevant literature reviews: sharing and communication, we are makers, technology teachers as practitioners for maker education, and diffusion and movement. MAKERS, a technology teachers' professional learning community is focused on sharing and communication. In addition, MAKERS became makers and experienced making and collaboration presenting a balanced interest and practical ability in both hardware and software parts. Lastly, MAKERS is very active in practicing and spreading maker education and technology education.

Keywords

maker education – technology teachers – Professional Learning Community – Republic of Korea

1 Introduction

Our society is developing through innovative technologies and transitions. These changes have brought about a shift in the educational paradigm. Therefore, the global educational community has been interested in new ways to solve complex problems creatively and cooperatively, moving away from passive education in which only transmitted knowledge is acquired (Taylor, 2016). The core idea of this educational innovation is learner-centered learning participation. To this end, many researchers and practitioners have studied and practiced approaches to the maker education. From a practical point of view, maker education prompts students to learn and experience their needs, goals, and activities and then share the results (Blikstein, 2013; Bullock & Sator, 2015; Martin, 2015; Martinez & Stager, 2013).

Specifically, maker education in schools refers to self-directed activities in the context of problem solving according to student needs and interests, and includes various values subsequently used in future education (Gerstein, 2017; Kim, 2018). Interest in maker education is increasing globally, and the Korean government implements maker education in various forms under the leadership of national and local organizations. In addition. the Korean government introduced the philosophy of maker education into the school curriculum, and teachers have shown great interest in a problem-based approach centered on hands-on activities (Kim, 2020).

This chapter introduces trends and cases of maker education in Korean technology education. In particular, this study includes key issues on maker education by a technology teachers' community through the case of maker education.

2 Maker Education and School Technology Education in South Korea

South Korea is one of the countries that establishes and implements educational policies based on a national standardized curriculum. Moreover, technology education is one of the national curriculum subjects that must be completed in elementary and middle school in the national curriculum. However, Korean technology education has a problem with its identity because it has been merged with home-economics education. In addition, there has been a struggle with public's low perception or misunderstanding of technology and technology education.

The Korean government's interest in maker education in an effort in the context of educational innovation, and the Ministry of Education and regional offices of education have also made great efforts to embrace the key philosophy of school maker education and worked toward an efficient diffusion of the approach (Lee & Kwon, 2020). In promoting convergence education and software education, which were already being promoted in Korea, the philosophy of maker education provided a foundation for good practice. The Seoul Metropolitan Office of Education (2017) introduced maker education based on creativity, cooperation, and sharing. The Busan Metropolitan Office of Education (2017) introduced a Busan-type maker education that combines science, technology, arts, and culture with the vision of fun, sharing, and growth. Each provincial office of education has also established various types of school maker spaces and has been planning and operating student-centered making activities.

As these educational efforts continue, the need for teachers who are capable of taking charge and leading school maker education has been emphasized. One study explored which teachers have most practiced maker education, and found it was technology teachers (Jeon & Song, 2019). Furthermore, in the context of Korean maker education, the most frequent content areas include Arduino, software, and 3D printing (Jeon & Song, 2019).

The core concepts for technology education currently presented in South Korean curriculum are shown in Table 7.1. The core concepts refer to the fundamental idea being employed in the current Korean national curriculum (Go, 2021). All core concepts are strongly related to the maker education. In addition, technology education curriculum includes learning content such as 3D printer, software education, invention, etc. (Ministry of Education, 2015)

In addition, technology classes use strategies such as problem solving and engineering design a lot in terms of teaching and learning and emphasize collaboration and communication. Technology teachers have actively participated in various national-led projects and demonstrated exemplary application of the philosophy of maker education in school classes and projects.

3   Design

This chapter used the method of case study to show examples of maker education in Korean technology education. The purpose of this study is to describe how the Korean technology teachers' community has been practicing maker education in the school setting.

The subject of this study is a professional learning community (MAKERS, a pseudo name) running a technology teachers' association in Seoul, the capital of South Korea. This group started as a learning community of voluntary technology teachers and is now playing a leading role in the field of maker education. This group participated in projects related to the maker education for various government office and Seoul Metropolitan Office of Education. The main activity is a teachers' community meeting, which is developing from the past workshops and seminars to a recent Maker-A-Thon meeting and a movement to spread the making culture.

To achieve the research objectives, this study reviewed MAKERS websites, professional development sessions they conducted, the making activities they developed, and their research reports. In addition, an interview was conducted

TABLE 7.1   Technology education in Korean National Curriculum

Core concepts	Learning content for elementary school	Learning content for middle school
Creation	Biotechnology system Plants and animals	Manufacturing system Manufacturing problem solving Construction system Construction problem solving Emerging technologies and biotechnology
Efficiency	Transportation technology in life Safety management for transportation mean	Transportation technology Transportation problem solving New/renewable Energy
Communication	Understanding software Procedural problem solving Programming elements and structure	Communication system Communication problem solving Media and mobile communication
Adaptation	World of jobs and careers Self-understanding and career exploration	Technological development Technology and social transition
Innovation	Inventions and problem solving Personal information and intellectual property protection Function and structure of robotics	Technological problem solving Invention ideas and implementation Application and standards of technology
Sustainability	Eco-friendly future agriculture Agricultural experience in life	Appropriate technology Sustainable development

with two technology teachers (Daehan & Minkook) experienced in maker education training and workshops as well two leading teachers (Hyukshin & Changjo) for MAKERS. All participants in the interview gave consent, as shown in Table 7.2.

Participants voluntarily participated in the interview indicating that it was a good opportunity to contribute to the spread of technology education and maker education. For data analysis, a theme analysis was employed for

TABLE 7.2   Participants

Pseudo name	Position	Years of teaching
Daehan	Technology teacher, a member of MAKERS	6
Minkook	Technology teacher, a member of MAKERS	6
Hyuksin	Technology teacher, a leading teacher for MAKERS	15
Changjo	Technology teacher, a leading teacher for MAKERS	16

qualitative data, and efforts were made to triangulate the findings from various data analyses additionally to reach a conclusion.

4   Maker Education and Technology Teachers' Effort

The results of the collected data can be expressed four themes. In South Korea, the efforts of technology teachers of maker education can be explained by focusing on the following themes: sharing and communication, we are makers, technology teachers as practitioners for maker education, and diffusion and movement.

4.1   *Sharing and Communication*

The MAKERS started as a meeting to improve the competency and professionalism of technology teachers. They mainly participated in regular meetings, lectures and seminars, and training in various ways. Through these activities, technology teachers had time to talk about difficulties in the field of technology education classrooms that could not be learned at teacher education institutions and finding solutions together. This philosophy of sharing and communicating was the starting point for technology teachers to easily accept and practice the culture of the maker education.

What is very impressive is that the attitude of technology teachers who are willing to share their work has spread rapidly through website management, training, and regular meetings.

> I was really inadequate, so I went to the MAKERS and got a lot of help. The content that I did not learn during my undergraduate days, and the problems of the school field have been resolved. Because of the willingness

and interest in giving out what they have, I have personally received tremendous help, and I wanted to be of some help. (Daehan)

My full-scale experience with maker education started with my interest in Arduino. Let's practice sharing by teaching Arduino tool with technology teachers in the MAKERS! Isn't this what maker education points out? (Hyukshin)

We believe in maintaining the teacher community with this mindset. 'I like what you did. Share it! Sharing will create an ecosystem, and then I can influence other people, and from that person I can be influenced, build relationships and form networks.' (Changjo)

In a recent workshop by MAKERS, technology teachers practiced sharing and communication through group projects activities (see Figure 7.1). In the interview, the technology teachers showed spontaneity and actively shared and communicated. In this respect, technology teachers could more easily accept the culture of maker education. In summary, MAKERS is a teacher community that started based on the philosophy of communication and sharing and has been able to practice the spirit of maker education well by practicing voluntary sharing and communication with each other.

4.2   *We Are Makers*

After the educational policy for maker education was launched, many technology teachers announced that they were makers in their community meetings

FIGURE 7.1   Sharing and communication in a workshop by MAKERS

and that they had been conducting various workshops and voluntary professional development sessions on maker education.

> The title of the professional development sessions for technology teachers for the past five years was "We are maker." Every time I attended the sessions, I felt that it is the word that best describes a technology teacher. What I experienced during that professional development was that of a maker. (Minkook)

Technology teachers have included a Maker-A-Thon or project-based activities in most training sessions (see Figure 7.2).

The technology teachers themselves became makers and experience making and collaboration. In addition, technology teachers have a balanced interest and practical ability in both hardware and software parts, so they are suitable as makers.

> MAKERS once ran a Maker-A-Thon with a company. As the technology teachers participated and experienced it together, I thought that the experience of diverse making and collaboration activities was valuable for maker education. I was convinced at Maker-A-Thon that I can never do it alone! Collaboration is important. (Daehan)

> If you look closely at the activities of maker education, there is a hardware component as well as the software. Those who are interested in both areas at school are technology teachers. When such teachers gather, a learning community is formed, and we are becoming makers. (Changjo)

FIGURE 7.2   Maker-A-Thon project by MAKERS

4.3   *Technology Teachers as Practitioners of Maker Education*

Technology teachers who have directly experienced making activities often noted that there are many similarities in teach methods between technology education and maker education. Teachers of MAKERS emphasized that technology classes have the same flow of maker education because many technology teachers start with a problem in their class and structure the class as a problem-solving process.

> Technology teachers are very accustomed to the experience of recognizing and solving problems from real life. I think that most technology teachers are accustomed to divergent thinking and excel at problem-solving strategies. The reason is that the class emphasizes the flow of problem solving. The core of maker education is a focus on building on what has already been done to take it to the next level, rather than repeating. Technology teachers are strong in this area and show an active attitude toward collaboration. (Hyukshin)

Based on the making experience in the technology classes, MAKERS created the maker class model (see Figure 7.3). This model is derived from the accumulated class practice of technology teachers, and it can be said that the great ideas of maker education originate in the technological problem-solving process.

To finalize the model, MAKERS concentrated on the design thinking and Problem Based Learning (PBL) for maker education. This model can be implemented in both online and offline modes using open portfolio project. In

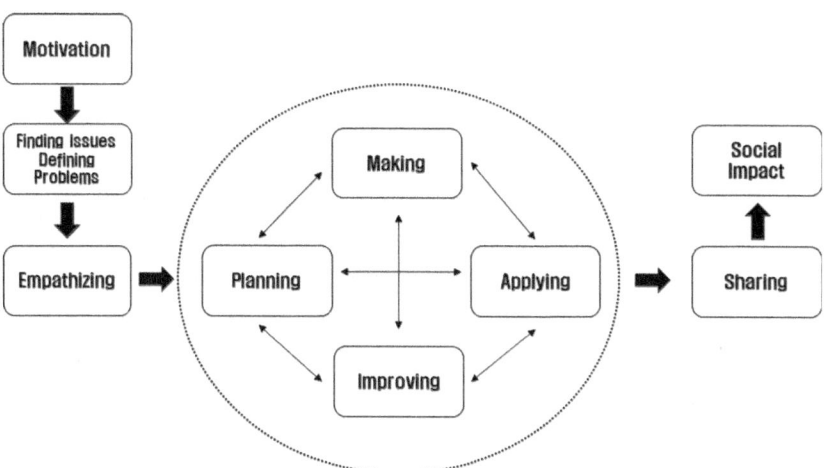

FIGURE 7.3   Teaching and learning model for maker education developed by MAKERS

addition, writing, sharing, and feedback process should be continuously implemented under this model.

4.4   *Diffusion and Movement*

Technology teachers have struggled with low public awareness of their field. The attitude that the MAKERS had at the initiation of the meeting of technology teachers was "Let's show the true value of technology education". Whenever technology teachers meet for the MAKERS, they practice a cultural movement that discusses and practices strategies that can inform technology education. Therefore, MAKERS are very active in practicing and spreading maker education and collaborating with other teachers in the school and implementing professional development sessions.

> There are many misconceptions about technology and technology education, including in schools. I was worried and upset about that. However, when technology teachers get together to share their concerns and discuss their own solutions, it miraculously leads to better practice. (Daehan)

> I think that the MAKERS's pride is in its' practical ability. Technology teachers from other regions also collaborate with us to practice maker education together. I once conducted a maker education professional development with professional learning community for maker education in Jeju-island. Maker education seems to be a good opportunity to properly promote the value of technology education in schools. (Minkook)

5   Conclusion and Discussion

Maker education has received a lot of attention in the context of educational innovation that emphasizes the flow of student-led learning in South Korea. The main group that practices school maker education in Korea is technology teachers. What is important here is that they are technology teachers who can together with on spirit rather than one excellent technology teacher. South Korean technology education has problems such as low awareness, merged subject name with home-economics, and insufficient infrastructure (Lee, Ham, & Kwon, 2020). However, the subject of this case study, MAKERS, is fighting these difficulties and is trying to solve current problems in technology education.

Through the examples of makers, this study identified how technology teachers connect maker education to technology education classes. The following conclusions were drawn from a qualitative analysis of the four technology teachers' interviews and relevant literature reviews. MAKERS started as a voluntary professional learning community that gathered to identify and solve problems on current issues in technology education classes. Technology teachers who experience the same difficulties and problems can practice and organize through sharing and communication. When the maker education policy was first introduced to the educational field, the MAKERS demonstrated his practical and organization abilities and conducted various professional development sessions and events to let the technology teachers see themselves as makers. In addition, technology teachers have played a role in promoting the value of technology education to others as a major leader in school maker education.

Based on the case study of the MAKERS and literature review, Korean technology teachers have contributed to Korean maker education. The justification and strategy for Korean technology education to further promote and convince school maker education can be summarized as follows.

First, technology education and school maker education have considerable commonalities in terms of their contents. Maker education is related to creative activities such as arts, robots, and programming, and is similar to the main learning contents covered in technology education of Korean national curriculum.

Second, technology education and school maker education have many things in common in terms of their process. The teaching strategies of school maker education, which explores problems and the process of solving problems using various materials, tools, and equipment, has many similarities to technological problem solving.

Third, there are various examples of upgrading and using existing technology laboratory in the school maker spaces project initiated by Korean government. This should be an opportunity for the technology laboratory, which was a relatively alienated space from the school, to receive relatively attention and be reborn as the most innovative space in the school. In addition, the current Korean school maker education is too limited to 3D modeling, Arduino, and coding education. If the dynamic teaching capabilities are facilitated by collaboration with the teachers' community, more diverse cases can be developed and implemented.

Acknowledgements

I would like to express my special thanks to Korean Technology and Engineering Teachers' Association and the sharing data and Maker model created by 'Seogimo' (Seoul Technology Teachers' Learning Community).

References

Blikstein, P. (2013). Digital fabrication and 'making' in education. The democratization of invention. In J. Walter-Hermann & C. Buching (Eds.), *Fablabs: of machines, makers and inventors* (pp. 203–222). Transcript Verlag, Bieledfeld.

Bullock, S., & Sator, A. (2015). Maker pedagogy and science teacher education. *Journal of the Canadian Association for Curriculum Studies, 13*(1), 61–87.

Busan Metropolitan Office of Education. (2017). *5 years plan of the creativity and convergence education for Busan maker education.* Busan.

Gerstein, J. (2016). Becoming a maker educator. *Techniques: Connecting Education & Careers, 91*(7), 14–19.

Go, I. (2021). Analysis on trends of technology education shown in national curriculum at the elementary level in Republic of Korea. *International Journal of Technology Education, 31*(2), 223–254.

Jeon, Y., & Song, U. (2019). Analysis of studies about maker education based on systematic review. *Journal of Korean Association of Information Education, 23*(6), 529–542.

Kim, S. (2020). Development of Artificial Intelligence (AI)-based maker education program using physical computing. *The Korean Journal of Technology Education, 20*(3), 76–95.

Kim, Y. (2018). Exploring the applicability of maker education theory to practical arts education at elementary school. *The Journal of Practical Arts Education Research, 24*(2), 39–57.

Lee, D. (2019). A meta-analysis of the effects in maker education. *The Journal of Educational Information and Media, 25*(3), 577–600.

Lee, D., & Kwon, H. (2022). Keyword analysis of the mass media's news articles on maker education in South Korea. *International Journal of Technology and Design Education, 32*(1), 333–353.

Lee, H., Ham, H., & Kwon, H. (2020). Research trends of integrative technology education in South Korea: A literature review of journal papers. *International Journal of Technology and Design Education. 32*(2), 791–804.

Martin, L. (2015). The promise of the maker movement for education. *Journal of Pre-college Engineering Education Research (J-PEER), 5*(1), 30–39.

Martinez, S. L., & Stager, G. S. (2013). *Invent to learn: making, tinkering, and engineering in the classroom.* Construction Modern Knowledge Press.

Ministry of Education. (2015). *The 2015 revision practical arts (technology & home-economics) curriculum.* Author.

Seoul Metropolitan Office of Education. (2017). *Seoul maker education mid-long term development plan.* Seoul Metropolitan Office of Education.

Taylor, B. (2016). Evaluating the benefit of the maker movement in K-12 STEM education. *Electronic International Journal of Education, Arts, and Science (EIJEAS)*, 2–22.

CHAPTER 8

Case Studies of Maker Education in China

Jianjun Gu and Qiuyue Yang

Abstract

With the promotion of national innovation and entrepreneurship education policy, makers have stepped out of old workshops, basements, coffee rooms, old factories, simple classrooms and laboratories, and stepped into the vision of government, industry, society, and schools. For this chapter, two typical cases have been selected to analyze the educational practice of Maker education in China. These cases could provide a reference for world education reform and the promotion of lifelong learning for all people.

Keywords

China – maker education – project teaching – tertiary and secondary education – entrepreneurship

1   Tsinghua University iCenter: A New Educational Model That Integrates the Spirit of Creativity into Teaching Practice

Tsinghua University iCenter is an interdisciplinary platform for innovation and entrepreneurship education built by the Tsinghua University Basic Industrial Training Center. It is one of the most important bases for engineering practice and innovation education in China.

The "I" concept refers to "Industry", "Interdisciplinary", "Innovation", and "International", as well as being "Student-oriented". The Tsinghua iCenter has always inherited the craftsmanship spirit of "actions speak louder than words", and innovated the trinity education concept of "value shaping, ability cultivation, and knowledge transfer", which is integrated with the culture of creators (Li et al., 2017). The Tsinghua iCenter, based on the university and open to the whole society, forms a scalable dual innovation education system and business incubation model to promote innovation and entrepreneurship education nationwide.

The iCenter formation included the following stages:

- In 2009, the Mechanical and Electrical Engineering Innovation Laboratory was established as a prototype of the iCenter, integrating innovation and entrepreneurship education into engineering practice.
- In 2010, the Tsinghua University Student Innovation Club was established, which launched the Design Technology Innovation Workshop and the Tsinghua Toyhouse Studio.
- In 2013, the first Student Creative Space Association and Creative Cross-Fertilization Space in domestic universities were established, proposing to focus on innovative practices and education models represented by creators.
- In 2014, the construction concept of the iCenter was proposed.
- In 2015, during Youth Day, Tsinghua University received a letter from Premier Keqiang Li.
- In 2016, the whole building was moved into the Zhaoji Li Technology Building, and the construction of the creator ecosystem was carried out from multiple dimensions, including hardware and software facilities, an operation mechanism, and dual-creation activities.

1.1 *Teaching and Learning Activities for Creative Tertiary Education*

The Tsinghua iCenter has explored and formed a new teaching model based on "student-oriented, creator-driven, project-guided teamwork and cross-fertilization". With the construction of "Manufacturing + Internet + Creative Space" as the core, the university integrates advanced manufacturing technology units and forward-looking system construction into the dual-creation education process, expands innovation and entrepreneurship services, and has built a new reorganizable, dynamic, digital and open innovation and entrepreneurship activity base.

In terms of the construction concept, it is committed to "making students' dreams come true", fully unleashing their creative potential and creating a good atmosphere of creativity, innovation, and entrepreneurship on campus; in terms of systems, it has built an open service platform and teaching system for creative activities, providing support in terms of incubation sites, technical training, product development, processing and production, management consultation, and so forth. In terms of the mechanism, an open construction mechanism has been formed to activate the campus into a more creative learning space through the active participation of relevant faculties, teachers, students, domestic and international enterprises, and the global creator community.

The iCenter at Tsinghua University has formed a training center curriculum based on the Engineering Training Series, the Innovation and Entrepreneurship Series, and the Engineering Culture Series. Creativity education

is implemented based on the Innovation and Entrepreneurship series. This series comprises several competitions and courses:
- the Comprehensive Ability of Engineering Training Competition,
- the Mechanical Innovation Design Competition,
- the Electronic System Design Competition,
- the Virtual Instrument Competition,
- the Construction Manufacturing Competition,
- the Energy-Saving Vehicle Competition,
- the Hardware Design Competition,
- the Digital System Innovation Design Competition,
- Entrepreneurship Awareness and Practice,
- Advanced Manufacturing Processes and Innovative Production, Entrepreneurship Guidance—Meeting with Entrepreneurial Famous Artists Face to Face and,
- Creative Design and Manufacturing.

1.2   *Science Based Innovation Workshops for Primary and Secondary Students at the Tsinghua University*

For example, the Tsinghua iCenter program established the "Science Base Innovation Workshop" in cooperation with the Basic Industry Training Center, an important support unit for the popular science base of Tsinghua University. The basic Industry Training Center provides popular science experts for the popular science base of Tsinghua University, provides projects for science week, projects for popular science tours, and has established innovation workshops as the place for popular science activities. The Training Centre for Basic Industries has built innovative workshops to provide a venue for popular science activities.

The Science Based Innovation Workshop focuses on science popularization projects and has built an "explosion-proof demining robot", a "3D printer", a "smart home", a "Smart Arm", and other projects to support science popularization. Through the construction of a photovoltaic power generation system, the Innovation Workshop has a green theme innovation environment. It also relies on the mechanical workshop and electronic craft workshop of the Basic Industry Training Center to provide a real engineering environment for popular science activities.

The basic industry training center is the first batch of experimental practice bases in colleges and universities focusing on primary and secondary school students and is established by the Beijing Municipal Education Commission. The establishment of an experimental practice base for primary and secondary school students in colleges and universities by relying on the advantages of teaching, scientific research, laboratories, and other conditions as well as teachers, promotes the reform of the new curriculum in primary and secondary schools and cultivates innovative talents. Meanwhile, it also serves society and basic education for colleges and universities, and provides a working platform for sustainable development.

As such, the Innovation Workshop of the Science Popularization Base of the Basic Industry Training Center provides teaching support and hands-on practice space and equipment for experimental practice activities of primary and middle school students with mature teaching projects. At present, the teaching activities include metal processing technology, electronic technology, explosion-proof demining robot design, 3D printer design and production, intelligent home design and production, and so on.

1.3   *Creative Space Societies*

Inspired by the Tsinghua iCenter project, Tsinghua University students started the Tsinghua Makerspace community. Founded in 2013, Tsinghua Makerspace is an on-campus science and innovation club focused on the development of creators and the incubation of projects. The club is made up of 18-to-24-year-old Tsinghua university students. The Tsinghua Makerspace not only provides a platform for college students to conduct Makerspace activities and training but also actively develops courses and instructional tools for primary and middle school students. Tsinghua Makerspace also provides consulting services for the construction of Makerspaces for primary and middle schools. The daily activities of Tsinghua Makerspace include skills training, brainstorming, guest sharing, and a creator marathon. The team has designed tools for brainstorming to gather the wisdom of the team and to produce the best ideas; guest sharing is to invite guests to share their ideas from time to time to broaden students' horizons; and the Makerathon is a semester-long competition to get students' projects off the ground and to win prizes.

Tsinghua Makerspace has incubated many projects (Figure 8.1), for example, the Little Yellow Bean Interactive Bird Kit (Figure 8.2). This is a DIY assembly kit suitable for children's creative education. Children need to put together the internal electronic modules with the shell by themselves and draw the appearance with crayons.

2   A Case Study of Creative Teaching in Tianyi Senior Middle School, Jiangsu Province: "The Design and Creation of a Small LED Green Energy-Saving Table Lamp"

Experts generally believe that technology is the innovation and transformation of nature or the surrounding environment in order to meet the higher needs

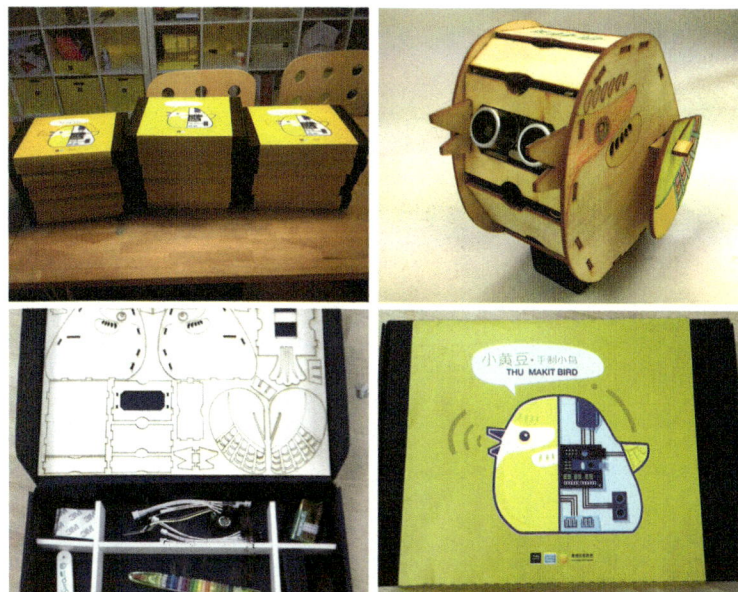

FIGURE 8.1   Students' creative projects

FIGURE 8.2   Students' work

of human beings. The case described in this section is from a Chinese middle school and is based on real-life problems.

The case "Design and creation of a small green LED lamp" is based on real-life problems in the classroom (see Figure 8.3). The students aged sixteen to eighteen are guided through the design and operation of the lamp so that they can develop their technical and behavioral skills in innovation and creation. Here are the details of the case study.

2.1   *Identifying and Clarifying Problems*
The teacher introduces the topic through the example of students needing a desk lamp for doing homework, and guides them to design a small lamp. Design requirements are presented in Table 8.1.

FIGURE 8.3   Students' work

TABLE 8.1   Design requirements

Dimension	Design requirements
Functional requirements	With the function of reading lighting, in line with the vision protection lighting requirements of senior high school students
Technical requirements	Reading illumination requirements > 500Lx; Livnglife lighting requires illumination about 150Lx
Material requirements	Metal, plastic, wood, and other panels, tubes, wire, preferably using scrap trim or semi-finished materials
Appearance requirements	Practical, beautiful, easy to use, reasonable switch position
Durability	Strong and stable structure, lamp base, lampshade, and lamp frame firmly connected, low power consumption, 1 old battery No.5 can also be used
Safety performance	The use of a low-voltage DC power supply, green environmental protection
Cost requirements	Less than 15 yuan
Completion period	Spans more than 5 weeks, with 10 classroom hours or less

2.2 *Development of Design Solutions*
2.2.1 Design Principles
The design objects of this design program are practical products for life created by the students themselves. In addition to grasping the principles of innovation, practicality, economy, and sustainability, the materials are required to be inexpensive and easily accessible. In addition, it should be able to develop students' awareness of green and collaborative learning; design and manipulative learning activities should be able to be carried out throughout the learning process of technical design, be based within a dedicated classroom, and be completed by all the first year high school students.

2.2.2 Structural Design
The overall structure of the LED Green Energy-Saving Small Table Lamp piece consists of seven parts: the battery component, the LED lamp assembly, the booster and voltage regulator circuit assembly, the switch, the base, the support frame and the lampshade assembly. The first four parts belong to the electronic circuit subsystem, while the last three parts belong to the mechanical component subsystem. The innovation of the whole device is that it can make effective use of the large number of discarded "three-layer new" or above dry batteries in our daily life; secondly, it can guide students to pay attention to their surroundings and develop their awareness and ability to turn waste into treasure. The conceptual design is shown in Figures 8.4 and 8.5.

2.2.3 Functional Objective Design
The overall design objective is that the LED light is convenient, practical, aesthetically pleasing, meets the reading lighting requirements of a study or dormitory, and is achieved through the specific functional objectives of the two subsystems consisting of seven component devices.

The electronic circuit subsystem should have boost and voltage regulator control functions: firstly, it can boost the input voltage below 3.3V to 3.3V (the

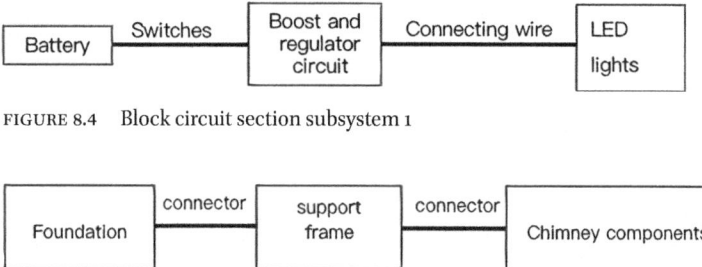

FIGURE 8.4 Block circuit section subsystem 1

FIGURE 8.5 Block circuit section subsystem 2

rated operating voltage required by the LED lamp assembly); secondly, it can reduce the input voltage above 3.3V to 3.3V; thirdly, when the input voltage fluctuates within a reasonable range, the output voltage can be kept stable.

The mechanical structure subsystem should have the function of supporting the whole work: firstly, the design of the base part can ensure the stability of the product; secondly, the design of the bracket part can ensure that the height and tilt of the light source can be flexibly adjusted; thirdly, the design of the lampshade part, which is both beautiful and generous, can play the role of guiding the direction of light dispersion.

2.3   Development of Design Solutions

The special room for production activities was equipped with the following tools and materials:

- a large common tool section: such as pincer workbench, grinding wheel polishing machine, drilling machine, wire saw, pistol drill, illuminator and other common equipment;
- a small tool section, requiring at least one group set: such as sharp-nosed pliers, diagonal pliers, scissors, a straight screwdriver, cross screwdriver, large file, hobby knife, tweezers, etc. (2 students/1 set); small file, internal heating type electric contact iron (2 students/1 set); and multi-meter (4 students/1 set);
- arrangements should be made to purchase equipment on behalf of students according to their individual needs.

The following materials had to be prepared by the middle school teachers before their students carry out maker activities to ensure the smooth progress of the activities. The steps are as follows:

- Raw material collection: 3 weeks in advance.
- Energy-efficient step-up voltage regulator circuit creation: the table lamp circuit is composed of a step-up printed board (including IC), three high-brightness white light-emitting LED tubes, one battery box, one switch, two 50cm wires, two capacitors, one inductor, one diode. It has strong versatility and a compact structure. The function is to convert a DC voltage of 0.8V-9.0V into a constant 3.3V output, ensuring that the obsolete batteries collected by the students can also be reused.
- The supplementary collection of raw materials: After the optimization of the design of the LED energy-saving lamp, students can make a second collection of raw materials to make up for any lack of materials (see Table 8.2). At this point, given the difficulty of collecting materials, the teacher can also provide some of the more heavily used "standard" components for students

TABLE 8.2   List of materials

Classes	Yes/No
Full line redone for $6	
LED lights 3 × 1.0	
Welding wire 0.25	
Hotmelt adhesive 0.5	
Push button switches 0.5	
Brackets 1.0	
Universal Board 0.5	
Circuit boards 3 RMB	
Subtotal amount	

to purchase as needed (e.g., a full set of circuit boards, solar panels, printed circuit boards, LED lights, battery boxes, 1 meter of wire, soldering wire, hot melt glue, push-button switches, brackets, universal circuit boards, etc.).
– LED desk lamp overall creation: first of all, the use of common hand tools (hacksaw, file, hobby knife, vise, scissors, tweezers, etc.), common machine tools (drill press, wire saw, sander, belt sander, laser cutter, etc.), and common adhesives (502 glue, universal glue, resin glue, etc.) should be taught and trained before large-scale creative activities can be launched.

2.4   *Testing, Evaluation, Optimization, Preparation of Specifications*
2.4.1   Testing Process and Methodology
Out of 90 participating students, a total of 89 individual completed tests on the created lamps. In terms of gender, 60.6% were female. After completing the LED Green Energy-Saving Lamp, students had to do at least four tests and fill in Table 8.3. The four tests include:
– Testing stability. Can the lamp be placed smoothly on the table without external forces? Can the lamp still be placed smoothly on the table when

TABLE 8.3   Evaluation of trial results

Stability	Robustness	Lighting brightness	Comfort	Overall assessment
25%	25%	25%	25%	100%

subjected to common external forces, such as hand impact or wind from an electric fan?

– Testing for sturdiness. Shake, vibrate, move by hand, and twist the joints to see if there is any significant structural deformation of the lamp.

– Testing the brightness of the lighting. Under normal use, select three evenly spaced test spots on the desk and test them with an electronic illuminance meter to see if the average of the three measurements meets the general illuminance requirements for reading lighting (>500 lux).

– Testing the comfort of use. Look at the overall aesthetics, the ease of use of the switch, the ease of hand holding, and the presence of angles that can easily hurt your hands.

2.4.2 Program Optimization

– Repair problems with unlit desk lamps. There are generally reasons such as incorrect component installation, incorrect wiring connections, reverse battery installation, poor solder joint contact, shorted solder joints, open connection lines, test points on the printed circuit board that are not connected, broken copper film on the printed circuit board, etc. The solutions to such problems include: Uniform explanation and demonstration for some common problems. For individual problems let the students in the group help each other to learn. The teacher sets up a repair table with some troubleshooting objects for struggling students to observe, and accepts repair requests from struggling students whenever and wherever possible.

– Problems with improving the robustness of the joints: increasing the contact area of the joints, rational selection of the gluing method, etc.

– Performance test of the improved and optimized device: student work that does not pass the overall assessment must be optimized and improved, and the results of the retest will be assessed after completion. For successful one-off student work, an evaluation event may be arranged.

– Evaluation of the results of the post-optimization technology trials. For one-off successes or works completed after optimization and improvement, each student is required to write a product instruction for their own LED energy-saving small table lamp, all of which will be completed before being sent to the teacher for final grade assessment.

3   Conclusion and Discussion

Maker education is a lifelong, whole-person development-oriented educational orientation that fosters individual DIY, a sharing spirit, and creativity, and promotes the cultivation of innovative talents in the era of crowdsourcing through maker spaces, courses, and activities. We showcased the implementation of maker education at the higher education level, represented by the iCenter at Tsinghua University, and at the basic education level, represented by Tianyi Senior Middle School and by the Innovation Workshop of the Science Popularization Base of the Basic Industry Training Center.

Maker education in primary and secondary education is the trend of social development. As Maker education aims for the development of the whole person, in the basic education stage, maker education mainly focuses on the development of a minimum level of maker literacy. Zhu and Luo (2015) pointed out that creator literacy is the ability to creatively use various technical and non-technical means to identify problems, deconstruct them, find solutions through teamwork, and form creative artifacts through continuous experimentation, which is related to learners' abilities in interpersonal communication, teamwork, creative problem solving, critical thinking, and professional skills, and also determines the learners' ability to adapt to society and work and achieve self-fulfillment in the future.

Tianyi Senior Middle School in Jiangsu Province has been actively carrying out maker teaching activities. The school focused on cultivating the maker literacy of all students, just as the typical case introduced in the first part – "The design and creation of LED green energy-saving small table lamp". First of all, the case teaching is based on the real problems in daily life, to find and clarify the problem; the second step is to formulate the design plan; the third step is model making; the third step is to test, evaluate and optimize the teaching process to guide students to learn the design and operation of desk lamp works. Thus enhance students innovation, creation of technical behavior ability and maker literacy.

Creative education is a form of learning that returns to the original human learning experience of learning while playing, incorporating the concepts of motivation, learning situations, active learning, collaborative communication, timely feedback, and respect for failure. Unlike traditional technology production classes, craft classes, and social practice classes in school education, the classes are arranged with simple half-finished assembly experiments that the children simply follow step by step. Through creative activities, learners' self-awareness, self-efficacy, and sense of teamwork can be continuously enhanced, enabling the development of a full range of skills including interpersonal communication, teamwork, creative problem solving, critical thinking, and professional skills. The development of creative literacy-oriented maker education in schools requires systematic promotion, including building distinctive maker spaces, training a group of maker education instructors, offering interdisciplinary maker courses, organizing maker activities, and conducting student maker work fairs.

Maker education in higher education is an education with the basic value of cultivating students' spirit of innovation, entrepreneurial consciousness, and entrepreneurial ability. In the context of the strategy of "mass entrepreneurship and innovation", innovation and entrepreneurship have become a national strategy, and colleges and universities in China have become an important position for innovation and entrepreneurship. The General Office of the State Council of the People's Republic (2015) of China has issued the Implementing Opinions on Deepening the Reform of Innovation and Entrepreneurship Education in Higher Education, pointing out that further guiding universities to carry out innovation and entrepreneurship education can be done at four levels.

Firstly, to stimulate students' awareness of innovation and entrepreneurship, and to cultivate the mindset of creators, through general education, we cultivate the entrepreneurial spirit of all students who think hard, question well, and dare to challenge authority, cultivate a culture of innovation, stimulate students' entrepreneurial motivation, entrepreneurial interest, and entrepreneurial ideas, and enhance students' market awareness, business awareness, and risk awareness.

Secondly, we develop innovation and entrepreneurship courses, create a space for university creators, integrate and share the academic and scientific research resources of the whole university, build an open and scattered "crowdsourcing space" to serve "creators" based on the existing foundation of the university and combined with various training programs for top innovative talents. "The university will also establish a system of cultural education, peer sharing, and public services to meet the needs of the "creators".

Thirdly, integrate innovation and entrepreneurship education into the whole process of training professional talents, highlighting "new theories, new technologies, new tools, and new methods", integrating innovation and entrepreneurship ideas into professional education, and focusing on the socialization and radicalization of professional knowledge.

Fourthly, the school provides highly efficient entrepreneurial services to ensure that students can share, start, operate, and secure their entrepreneurial projects.

Tsinghua University iCenter is committed to integrating the maker spirit into teaching practice, so as to set up a new interdisciplinary education model and platform. Inspired by the iCenter activities, Students at Tsinghua University launched Tsinghua Makerspace Club activities. The club has incubated many programs suitable for children's maker education, such as DIY assembly kits.

Through these children need to use their own hands and give full play to their imagination for the product's appearance. In this program, the children's practical ability, imagination, cooperation and communication and other aspects of innovation quality and ability have been fully practiced and improved.

References

General Office of the State Council. (2015, May 13). *Opinions on deepening the reform of innovation and entrepreneurship education in colleges and universities.* http://www.gov.cn/zhengce/content/201505/13/content_9740.htm

Li, S., Li, L., Sun, H., & Yang, B. (2017). The construction of the innovation and entrepreneurship training system in universities with "trinity and integration of three creations. *Tsinghua University Education Research, 38*(2), 111–116.

Zhu, Z. T., & Luo, L. (2015). From maker movement to maker education: Cultivating mass innovation culture. *Research on Audio-visual Education, 7,* 5–13.

CHAPTER 9

Maker Education in the Applied Physics Bachelor Programme at Delft University of Technology

Freek Pols and Rolf Hut

Abstract

Two mandatory courses that use maker education as learning activity are included in the applied physics bachelor programme at Delft University of Technology. In this chapter we provide the rationale for its inclusion, the associated learning goals, and the need for a makerspace with readily available makertools. We highlight the design of the makerspace and describe how it affected education. Finally, we illustrate how this all accumulates in a final project.

Keywords

Delft – The Netherlands – maker education – makerspace – engineering – applied physics

1   Building Future Engineers and Scientists

At Delft University of Technology, we 'build' engineers. Moreover, at the program of Applied Physics, students are trained to become the next generation scientist as well. Whether students pursue a career as a scientist or as an engineer, design skills are indispensable for physicists. When working at the frontier of our knowledge, e.g. building a quantum computer, or when solving problems as a consultant, e.g. climate control with 0.01°C tolerance, students have to have a grasp of what is technically possible, what limits the instruments, what the effect is of their design choices on their measurements and so on. Although they might not be required to build instruments themselves in their future jobs, in considering suitable solutions, discussing the merits and trade-offs of various options with technicians and other experts, they have to understand what is (roughly) possible, how their choices affect and propagate

© KONINKLIJKE BRILL NV, LEIDEN, 2023 | DOI:10.1163/9789004681910_009

throughout the entire design and result in obtaining the data with a required accuracy and precision within a reasonable amount of time.

Where many theoretical courses aim at the development of the physics conceptual knowledge, lab courses aim at the development of inquiry knowledge, the first- and second-year courses Design Engineering for Physics Students (DEPS) aim at teaching students skills to combine and apply their content knowledge in designing solutions to given problems (Hut, Pols, & Verschuur, 2020). The problems given and addressed in the course are related to their future careers: isolating instruments from environmental vibrations, calibrating instruments, reducing experimental uncertainties and so on.

2   Learning Goals, Structure, Workshops & Final Project for DEPS

To develop the required design skills, to have students gain experience in designing, to learn that there are different design approaches and to apply these, the following learning goals are set out for the first-year course:

After successfully engaging in DEPS1, a student is able to:

- design, realize and test a physical apparatus or a physical measuring or manufacturing process
- understand and use different design methods, applying a particular method depending on the problem/assignment
- understand elementary manufacturing techniques
- apply the acquired knowledge on sensors and data processing
- cooperate and work effectively in groups
- report and present a design
- use simulation software

In the second-year, the focus is on designing and building an instrument that measures a physical quantity. The following learning goals are set out:

After successfully engaging in DEPS2, a student is able to:

- design and devise an instrument that measures and digitally stores or displays a physical quantity
- understand pros and cons of equipment available in makerspaces and purposefully use these
- make 2D (vector) and 3D models
- work effectively in small groups
- apply physics content knowledge in design problems
- use design software
- understand and construct patents
- evaluate the sustainability of the product and process.

DEPS1 starts with a series of six design assignments taking a whole day each. The design assignments start with a brief (max 2 hours) introduction and instruction lecture, followed by a 6 hour period where the students have to design and build a functioning device. The assignments range from designing building and using a calibration setup for a sensor of their own choice, to designing, building and testing a setup that can isolate a measurement setup from outside vibrations. The learning goals of the coarse are addressed over the course of the six assignments. The maker education aspect of the assignments is two-fold:

- the students have to make (build) the solution they are proposing and are assessed based on.
- the students have the freedom to build their own solution within the constraints of the assignment: there is no single one right solution (though there are many wrong ones).

The gained insights have to be applied in a final project in which students build a physics demonstration which can be used by their former physics teacher in DEPS 1, and an instrument that measures a physical quantity in DEPS 2. Although the task is precisely formulated, many opportunities exist where students have to make choices. During the final project, they encounter various problems that need to be solved. Their knowledge gained in theoretical courses has to be combined with the knowledge gained in the design assignments in this course to overcome these and produce a working prototype.

In the remainder of this chapter we will focus on DEPS1 for clarity and conciseness. The experiences with DEPS2 are broadly similar to those with DEPS1.

3   The Need for and Realization of a Makerspace

Although we consider the brain the most important tool in designing, effectively building a prototype can hardly be done without other proper tools and equipment. In the first two years of teaching DEPS we have seen that a lot of time is 'wasted' on simple, jury rigged (Dutch: houtje-touwtje) solutions improperly using daily tools such as scissors knives and miles of duct tape. Rather than iterative prototyping and testing, time constraints and students' lack of motoric skills frequently resulted in handing in the first build prototype as the final product, see Figure 9.1. Moreover, in an educational setting where roughly 150 students work on the realization of their prototypes, one can easily see that there are inherent safety issues. There was thus an urgent demand for dedicated rooms that function as a makerspace with tools and equipment readily available to our students.

FIGURE 9.1
An example of a 'houtje-touwtje'
approach

Three adjacent rooms were found suitable for this purpose. The first author was allowed to design and equip the room within a given budget. In the design of these rooms, the main teacher of DEPS, the second author of this chapter, was frequently consulted. It was decided that one room was to be dedicated to the quick production of prototypes using the latest tools such as 3D printers and a laser cutter, this room is called the Maker room. One room was to be dedicated to more conventional and heavy machinery such as CNC and drills, jokingly called the Machine room. One room was to be dedicated to the assembly of the prototypes with handcraft available to students' disposal, named the Assembly room. One can get a glimpse of the rooms here (Pols, 2020).

The Maker room is equipped with a single 60W laser cutter, able to cut through 1 cm thick plexiglass or plywood. We considered this to suit most projects, where students have to use other machines when working with metals. To limit students' choice, and, honestly, reduce the workload for the technicians, students can choose all thicknesses of plywood or plexiglass as long as it is 3 mm. Four 3D printers are available to the students. Furthermore, the room is equipped with two tables with three workstations for soldering allowing six students to solder simultaneously.

The Machine room is equipped with a milling machine, lathe, a tap machine and a sand grinder. To increase the safety in the workspace, this room is equipped with lockers where students can store jackets, bags and so on. Other machinery, a circular saw, metal cutter, i.e., machinery that is considered unsafe to untrained students are available in a nearby workshops of technicians.

Most striking in the Assembly room is the work-island: three large tables in the middle of the room where students can solder, glue, tinker, assemble and so on. In the closets, students can find general tools and equipment such as duct-tape, screwdrivers, wrenches, and pliers, in other words, all tools required to assemble a prototype. One closet is equipped with electronic test equipment such as a digital multimeter, function generator, oscilloscope, voltage source. Furthermore, one dresser is fully equipped with a standard inventory of sensors and microcontrollers.

4   Change in Workshops with the Coming of a Makerspace

The introduction of the Makerspace both offered chances to streamline the design assignments and required additional learning activities to be implemented in DEPS1.

To kick-off event of the course, the first day where the students are introduced to the concept and context of the course, a tour of the makerspace was added. In this way students would be familiar with the fact that this place was available for them to use when needed during the course. During this tour, students were also pointed at the necessary safety regulations and the need to pass an (online) test on safety before they are allowed to work in the Makerspace.

To really hammer home that the Makerspace was available to the students, that the tools in there could be used for assignments in the course and finally to introduce them with the piece of machinery they are most likely to not have worked with previously, one of the design assignments was slightly changed. During one assignments (where students have to design and test an echo acoustic algorithm) students work with acoustic distance sensors placed in custom made standards. Previously the staff would provide both the sensors and the standards for the students to use during the assignment. With the Makerspace and the laser cutter now being available, two weeks before the assignment, students have to hand in a laser-cut-able design for their own standard that can hold the sensor at a given height. They are given a maximum of 30 × 30 cm of wood to work with (of the aforementioned 3 mm thickness). All 150 designs are cut out by staff and given to the students prior to the assignment[1] so they can work with their own standards. In this way the students learned how to make a 2D design for the laser cutter (a learning goal) and directly experienced that they can use things that they have designed themselves in follow-up assignments.

5   The Design of a Final Project

Already before the workshops are finished, students are introduced to the final project. They are asked to think of demonstration experiments that they would like to design and build. We use the plural form as students have to consider at least three different options and explore the pros and cons for each demonstration experiment. A first feasibility check is carried out by the teacher of the course. Once consented, the students further develop their ideas. They are asked to pick one of their ideas and present it to a physics teacher – all former physics teachers of the students are invited to participate – who then helps the students in evaluating the feasibility, identifying potential issues and concretizing the ideas. Often a Socratic approach – implying the teacher have students evaluate their own ideas using critical questions – is used. After receiving comments and recommendations, students ought to make a calculation related to their project. The calculation should demonstrate that the project is feasible and the phenomenon is observable. Furthermore, a calculation helps the students in identifying the variables that can be 'tweaked' so to optimize the effect, the so-called 'design parameters'. This is also a concept that is introduced and used in one of the design assignments.

The students again present their work and the teacher is allowed to ask critical questions regarding the calculations. Using this input, students are allowed to make changes and start working on their project. A budget of €50 allows them to identify and buy the materials needed. Their ordered products are delivered in the makerspace where they can assemble the prototype.

It is our intention that an iterative process is applied, where students quickly build a prototype version, test it, make adjustments and produce a better prototype version. To make sure students work in this iterative manner, they have a mandatory meeting with a teaching assistant (TA) once a week. In this meeting they report on progress made, tasks completed and how insights from the past week influence future actions. The TAs are trained to push the students towards an iterative planning instead of a single production run (which is the natural tendency of the students if not actively steered).

In helping students with the process and aspects of working together, they are given a lecture on modes of communication (the content – process – relationship model) and subsequently have to draft a code of conduct together. This code of conduct is referred to (and reflected upon) when troubles in the functioning of the team arise.

In the final assignment, all learning cumulate and students ought to show that they have mastered course' learning goals. The final assignment gives, intentionally, a lot of freedom to the students: the freedom to choose their own topic, to design their own design process and to plan their own actions during the assignments. This presents students with an extensive sense of agency and ownership. *They* are working towards building a product *they* choose themselves. As is known, agency contributes to the enhancement of intrinsic motivation (Deci & Ryan, 2012). Indeed, the intrinsic motivation to get this thing working is very high. To facilitate this freedom whilst assuring the learning goals are being attained, the team of supervisors (including teachers and TAs) must be constantly aware of these learning goals. During the start-up and middle phase of the final assignment supervision and help when students get stuck focus on the process, often with a Socratic method of helping by asking question: "where did it go wrong?" "what did you test to see how you can fix it?" "what does this new information mean for the project?" etc. During the final part of the assignment the focus of supervision shifts towards the content ensuring that student who have demonstrated that they attained the learning goals do not fail in building a working demonstration.

6 Change in the Final Assignment with the Coming of the Makerspace

Working in the Makerspace has allowed students to work with 'proper' tools for their final assignment. This has greatly reduced the level of 'Houtje Touwtje' fabrication mentioned before. Furthermore, working in a professional environment under the supervision of trained technicians has given students valuable lessons both on technical skills as one personal skills how to communicate with, and learn from, technicians who may not share their academic level, yet are their superiors on technical skills. The teaching assistants supervising the students, who on average have followed the course themselves only a few years before the current students, were asked to reflect on the impact of the Makerspace on the education of our students. Some selected quotes:

– The Makerspace is a place where students encounter unexpected problems they have to solve in a manner they are not familiar with in their education: fixing things that break or do not work requires a different approach from getting stuck in a theoretical assignment.
– Students often enter the Makerspace with an idea, but don't know how to realize that idea: for example: "we need a hole in this bucket.[2]" They learn by first being instructed and then doing it for themselves that you have to properly fix something before drilling. They also are introduced to the limits of their knowledge, as in that one time where a rather arrogant student was instructed to get an iron-saw from the toolbox and realized he had no idea

what an iron-saw was. You don't get this type of (life)lessons in other courses [within our curriculum].
– The Makerspace increases the sense of ownership in students by giving the tools to turn an idea into a physical thing. This triggers the students to step out of their theoretical bubble and become more pragmatic when looking for solutions to the problems they encounter.
– As Teaching Assistant I notice that since we have the Makerspace, students are more enthusiastic about the course in general and their project in particular because the makerspace allows them to more rapidly test if their ideas work, speeding up the design cycle. Sometimes this happens in the "oh shit, this doesn't work → back to the drawing board" way, sometimes it is "we can do this much simpler than we thought on paper → update the design".

7   The Presentation of the Final Project

Students present their demonstrations during a science fair, where their former physics teacher and staff from the university is invited to join. To ensure that this is a happy occasion that students look back upon positively, only teams that have a working setup a few days before the final presentation are allowed to partake. Demonstrating a working product prior to the event shifts the moment of assessment to a few days before the final presentation. Since the criteria for passing failing are very clearly communicated to the students ("you only pass if it works") students always know themselves if they are doing ok.

The resulting science fair is a highlight of the academic year[3] where students proudly look back at how far they have come during their first year at university. The physics demonstrations range from well-known demonstrations like Chladni plates, cloud chambers and Gauss canons to more unique setups where students show liquification of sand. The diversity in topics shows that students exploit the given freedom. By showing their demonstration experiments in a science fair setting, not only to their teachers of DEPS but also to other teachers who teach classes in the first year, various teachers get to see whether the students are able to apply the theoretical knowledge they covered in their course not only on an exam, but also in a practical application, which is ultimately what we train our students for.

For both the version where students presented physically during the science fair, as well as two different versions for different lockdown situations because of the corona pandemic, short videos of the final event are available (Hut, 2018, 2020, 2021).

Acknowledgements

We thank teaching assistants Naoual El Yazidi, Gijs Vis and Emile Kooij for their input.

Notes

1 Note that during the COVID related lockdown, the designs were cut out and mailed by post to the students. It should be noted that the flat nature of laser-cut designs is ideal for this type of "work at home" situations.
2 This is an example that really happened, not a reference to the song.
3 Personal opinion of the teacher of the course (and author of this chapter).

References

Deci, E. L., & Ryan, R. M. (2012). Self-determination theory. In P. A. M. Van Lange, A. W. Kruglanski, & E. T. Higgins (Eds.), *Handbook of theories of social psychology* (pp. 416–436). Sage Publications Ltd. https://doi.org/10.4135/9781446249215.n21

Hut, R. (Producer). (2018). *DEPS1 final presentation on campus.* https://www.youtube.com/watch?v=Xp6SUXFNXtM

Hut, R. (2020). *2DEPS1 final assignment full lockdown: Online Rube Golberg machine.* https://www.youtube.com/watch?v=BBpUrAcd5QA

Hut, R. (Producer). (2021). *DEPS1 final assignment half lockdown (build at home, demonstrate on campus).* https://www.youtube.com/watch?v=pL6k4J-xBpk

Hut, R. W., Pols, C. F. J., & Verschuur, D. J. (2020). Teaching a hands-on course during corona lockdown: From problems to opportunities. *Physics Education, 55*(6), 065022.

Pols, C. F. J. (Producer). (2020). *Opening makerspace TN.* https://youtu.be/bWuhHjvBFtI

PART 3

Thematic Reflections

∵

CHAPTER 10

Maker Pedagogy

P. John Williams

Abstract

This chapter examines the pedagogy of the makerspace case studies through a framework which discusses the rationale, aims, content, activities, resources, teachers role, collaboration, where and when, and assessment. The conclusion is that there is significant diversity across all these aspects of makerspaces, but what fundamentally unites them is concrete action learning.

Keywords

maker education – pedagogy – makerspaces – learning

1   Introduction

Maker education pedagogy is grounded in a long- and well-established history of thinking about how children learn and grow, epitomized in the philosophies of constructivism and constructionism (see Chapter 12 in this book by Fox-Turnbull).

Papert's (1987) learning theory of constructionism could be considered the foundation of maker education pedagogy. Building on earlier educational theorists such as Rousseau, constructionism holds that pedagogies should derive from student interests, and they learn through embodied and making experiences.

Piaget's notions of constructivism developed from Dewey's emphasis on experiential and social learning, the idea of self-knowledge, inquiry based and self-directed learning. Piaget advocated a focus on what children are interested in, and what they are able to achieve at various levels of development, and what influences them to change their ideas.

These various elements of learning theory come together in the contemporary phenomena of maker movements, which started to become widespread in the early 2000s. This is however a coming together of convenience, as it was not learning theory which provided the impetus for the development of the maker movement, it was a more mundane desire people felt to take over some control of their environment, and react to a society based in consumerism, developing out of the "Do It Yourself" (DIY) culture.

A definitive history of the maker movement is yet to be articulated, but its social characteristics of community-building and collaboration distinguished it from previous versions of people simply making things (Burke, 2014). It has evolved from general community based approaches and become embraced by educators in museums, libraries and schools because of the synergies with educational theory.

However, some would argue that making and using tools is a defining characteristic of humanity, and consequently has been a significant and longstanding element of civilization. Debate remains about when humans first began using tools, but the evidence is that it was a long time ago. The modern maker movement is the most recent iteration of this very human activity, reinforced by a social community dynamic and by prevailing learning theory.

2   Pedagogical Themes

The basic characteristics of makerspaces provide some clues as to what pedagogies may be appropriate in this context, when the makerspace is an element of formal educational institution. These characteristics include:
– Learning is meaningful (Smith, 2019)
– Exploration and learning is self-directed and personal (Blikstein, 2018)
– The environment is open
– Failure is accepted (Smith, 2019)
– Skill development is collaborative (Sheffield et al., 2017)
– Thinking is activity based (Bevan, 2017)
– Learning derives from hands on activity (Peterson and Scharber, 2017)
– Learner has ownership over decisions (Smith, 2019)
– Playing with ideas through tinkering (Becker, 2019)

These characteristics can be framed as a 'Maker Pedagogy', which is the enactment of the principles inspired by the maker movement grounded in design, artistic creation, ethical hacking, and adapting old devices for new uses (hack, adapt, design, and create) (Bullock & Sator, 2015).

A number of authors have rationalized the employment of making as an important pedagogy because of its efficacy in achieving broader education goals for student participants. Jay Silver (2016) references the concept of

'Invention Literacy' as the ability to look at how the human made world works and have the technical and understanding skills to invent new things by solving problems of everyday life. 'Creator Literacy' (Zhu & Luo, 2015) has been defined as the ability to creatively use various technical and non-technical means to identify problems, deconstruct them, find solutions through teamwork, and form creative artifacts through continuous experimentation, which is related to learners' abilities in interpersonal communication, teamwork, creative problem solving, critical thinking, and professional skills, and also determines the learners' ability to adapt to society and work and achieve self-fulfilment in the future.

A significant and recurring pedagogical theme in the makerspace literature relates to Design and Innovation. Maker spaces provide an ideal environment for the enactment of innovation in schools, including innovative pedagogy. Becker and Jacobsen (2020) identified four design decisions that emerged in the cycles of their research, which were determined to have the greatest impact on the teacher in terms of pedagogical growth:

a. student choice of topic and materials which led to more meaningful learning, choice of material and more flexible thinking;
b. students engaging in research to support making;
c. students and teacher implementing structured feedback; and
d. students and teacher modelling risk-taking; teacher risk-taking constitutes stepping back, students exercise more control over their learning and need the teachers less.

Evidence of these recurring design decisions and their influence on pedagogy are woven throughout the makerspace case studies in this book. The case in Kenya (Westerhof et al., Chapter 6) experienced a shaky beginning because there was little opportunity for student choice, an approach which is somewhat antithetical to the philosophy of makerspaces. The Delft University case (Chapter 9) indicates how the nature of the students final projects changed when students and teachers worked and researched together. The maker education community in Korea (Kwon, Chapter 7) illustrates the advances that can be made when teachers take risks together then implement feedback from those experiences.

3 Analytical Framework

Van den Akker (2013) developed a framework of ten components to address questions related to planning for student learning, illustrated in Figure 10.1. It

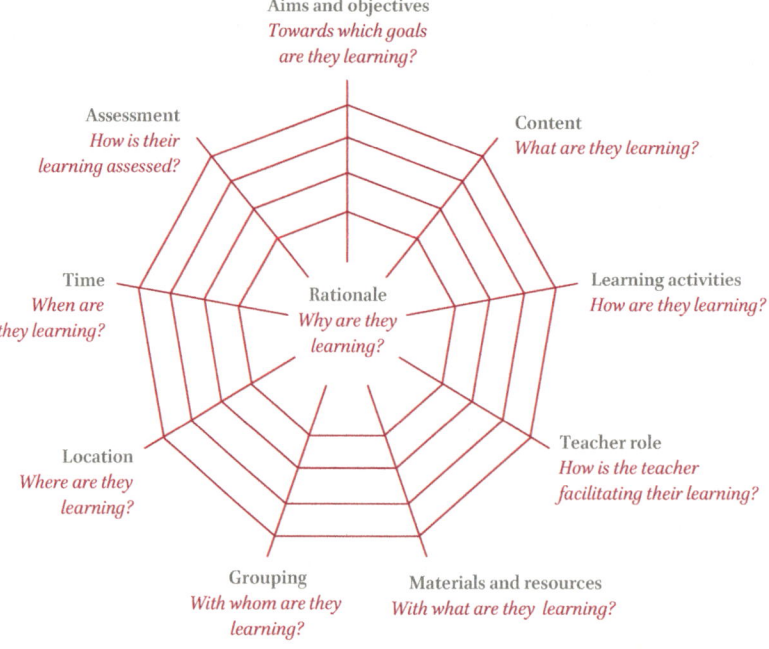

FIGURE 10.1   Framework of Makerspace Pedagogy (Van den Akker, 2013)

was used by Van den Akker as an elaboration of various typologies related to curriculum development. In this chapter, I want to adopt the framework as a structure for the analysis of makerspace pedagogies, drawing exemplars from the case study chapters and related literature.

While not all the elements of the framework are directly related to pedagogy, they are all indirectly related and combine to form a structure that supports the pedagogical approach. Hence, in the consideration of makerspace pedagogy, all these elements are relevant.

The structure of the framework has an intent – the spiderweb indicates many inter-connections, which are necessary in order to maintain the integrity of the structure. The status of Makerspaces in schools is a relatively new phenomena, and in order for them to be sustainable, this framework implies that all the connections need to be maintained. Just like a spiderweb, the effectiveness of the web in functioning successfully is dependent on the balance between the connections. It can still work with missing connections, but not as effectively. So it is with Makerspaces, to be as effective and sustainable as they are capable of being, all the components need to be functionally linked and in tension.

Derived from this structure, the following are the suggested components of a Makerspace pedagogy for learning:

1.   Rationale or Vision: Why are they learning?
2.   Aims & Objectives: Towards which goals are they learning?
3.   Content: What are they learning?
4.   Learning Activities: How are they learning?
5.   Teacher Role: How is the teacher facilitating learning?
6.   Materials & Resources: With what are they learning?
7.   Grouping: With whom are they learning?
8.   Location: Where are they learning?
9.   Time: When are they learning?
10. Assessment: How to measure how far learning has progressed?

The following discussion will utilize these components as a structure for discussion, drawing on the case studies as illustration.

4   Rationale or Vision: Why Are They Learning?

The vision of the effects of makerspaces is varied and in some instances grandiose, but generally relates to either social or personal development of the participants. The goal of the case study in Kenya (Westerhof et al.), which involved culture-sensitive design and development of appropriate toys, was seen as a medium to support the participants social development. The initial concept was to create marketable toys to sell and use locally.

The Mexico case study (Núñez-Solís et al., Chapter 5) also had a social sustainability goal by applying Circular thinking to the problems generated by e-waste from obsolete electronic products. Eco maker kits were used to stimulate curiosity while at the same time developing technical skills. The notion of Invention Literacy was employed as a goal which refers to the ability to look at how the human made world works and have the technical and understanding skills to invent new things by solving problems of everyday life.

One of the rationales for the maker education case study in Korea (Kwon) was to demonstrate the true value of Technology Education, so in this case this goal is unrelated to personal development. In Korea, maker education has been introduced into the school curriculum, and the many similarities between maker Education and Technology Education have been recognized by technology teachers as an opportunity to reinvigorate and promote their subject.

The iCentre maker space in China (Gu and Yang, Chapter 8) is committed to the very lofty goal of making students dreams come true, fully unleashing their creative potential and creating a good atmosphere of creativity, innovation, and entrepreneurship. This makerspace is situated in a higher education context to support the achievement of various course goals, but also actively develops courses and instructional tools for primary and middle school students, and provides consulting services for the construction of Makerspaces for primary and middle schools. This Maker Education in higher education has the basic vision of cultivating students' spirit of innovation, entrepreneurial consciousness, and entrepreneurial ability, reflecting the national strategy of innovation and entrepreneurship.

The library makerspaces established throughout the Netherlands (Pijls, Van Eijck & Bredeweg, Chapter 4) had a dual rationale of providing activities which allowed children to experience new social roles, and also to develop their creative and technological skills. It targeted lower socio-economic areas in order to provide experiences which may otherwise not be accessible. The programs comprised digital fabrication and tinkering, designing, community-art and programming/coding; each of these often based on a theme.

The rationales for makerspaces are varied and context dependant. When the makerspace is located within an institution, they tend to be curriculum related and when they are community based, they include a social rationale which may relate to personal development or relate to the broader community.

5   Aims & Objectives: Towards Which Goals Are They Learning?

Many maker spaces have unclear learning objectives because they are not aligned with the curriculum, but are extracurricular. The free, designerly, self-discovery, tinkering characteristics of makerspaces do not lend themselves to be compatible with a structured school experience, when learning goals are more likely to be specified and assessed.

The Korean case study (Kwon) is an exception to this because the government is promoting maker spaces in school and Technology teachers have seen this as an opportunity to promote their subject. The core concepts of the Technology curriculum: efficiency, communication, adaptation, innovation and sustainability can be strongly related to Maker education.

The learning goal of the EcoMakerKits, utilized as the focus of the development of Circular Thinking in the Mexican case (Nunez) was to practice the 21st century skills of creativity, collaboration, communication, and critical thinking, while at the same time encouraging responsible citizenship through circular thinking. These were achieved by developing digital tools to create a melody played through a constructed Bluetooth loudspeaker and an electric ventilator using e-waste, then test the Bluetooth loudspeaker and the electric ventilator and reflect on their learning.

The extracurricular and after school library makerspaces in the Netherlands (Pijls et al.) had quite general personal development goals for their activities, for example digital skills and creativity.

In some instances the Makerspace experience is recognized to complement discipline curriculum studies, by encouraging activities which would be difficult to structure within the timetabled school day. For example the Applied Physics case (Pols) in which students encountered unexpected problems they have to solve in a manner they are not familiar with in their education: fixing things that break or do not work requires a different approach from getting stuck in a theoretical assignment. In this case the Makerspace increases the sense of ownership in students by giving the tools to turn an idea into a physical thing.

An indication of the diversity of learning goals which can be achieved through Makerspace activities is clear from the case studies in this book, and is supported by the research of Emm and Hawkins (2020) which introduces a Bauhaus Makerspace design experience as a means of integrating multiple literacies and disciplines. Language literacy is developed through design and CAD activities through a multiliteracies pedagogy.

Many of the goals which are generally associated with makerspaces are evident in most of the cases presented in this book: creativity, technological literacy, collaboration. The specific goals of each makerspace are related to the rationale for their existence, and tend to be different depending on whether the location is in-institution or out-of-institution.

6   Content: What Are They Learning?

Because of the often high-tech focus of maker spaces, typified by ubiquitous 3D printers (for example the Korean case study), many tend to think that the goal of maker education is for pupils to learn how to operate digital technologies and produce tangible artifacts, but the design process and collaborative learning that takes place along the way are also important. Maker spaces can be places for collaboration, creativity and design, but also for critical reflection on how technology is currently transforming society. Through a range of activities, students can develop understanding about how the designed world came into existence, an important element of technological literacy.

Much maker education literature proposes that participants develop problem solving and creative thinking skills, attributes that all students need regardless of the vocation they pursue. This implies the easy transferability of such skills, but research indicates that these skills generally develop in context –

contexts of domain knowledge and practical environments, so transferability is not inevitable (Becheikh, Ziam, Idrissi, Castonguay, & Landry, 2010). This issue is exacerbated by the nature of many makerspaces – places where people can come and go and pursue their own interests – so there is an absence of any structure that may be able to facilitate transferability.

On the other hand, it is a challenge to design and implement maker activities characterized by innovative pedagogies and projects while working within the constraints of a standardized curriculum. A true makerspace offers student-driven opportunity for open-ended exploration (Fleming, 2018). The maker mindset (Jaatinen & Lindfors, 2019) of exploration, design thinking, action, human centred and collaborative is not entirely supported by many school structures.

While the library makerspaces in the Netherlands (Pijls et al.) specified goals related to technological skills and creativity, it was recognised that engagement by children resulted in the development of motivation, confidence and self-worth.

The Kenyan case study (Westerhof et al.) focuses on seven key design skills that are considered the most relevant for primary school pupils (Klapwijk, 2018):

- thinking in all directions (divergent thinking),
- developing empathy,
- making productive mistakes (early and frequent iteration),
- making ideas tangible (convergent thinking),
- sharing ideas (communication),
- defining your direction, and
- making use of the process (meta-cognitive skills).

The Applied Physics program described in the case study by Pols and Hut is an example of using makes space activities to supplement mandatory courses which are included in the applied physics bachelor programme. The aim is to provide students the opportunity to develop skills in the combination and application of the content knowledge gained in the formal classes, in designing solutions to given problems.

The university based iCentre in China (Gu and Yang) includes activities related to metal processing technology, electronic technology, explosion-proof demining robot design, 3D printer design and production, intelligent home design and production, photovoltaic power generation, with the stated goal of supporting the popularization of science both within the university, and also as a resource for primary and secondary schools.

Even in those makerspaces which are focussed on a final product, it is recognized that the important learning that takes place during the process, the design and problem solving journey, is paramount.

7   Learning Activities: How Are They Learning?

A tension within the methods of learning in makerspaces is epitomized by the experience of the case study in Kenya, where it was noted that students 'initial curiosity towards what the design educator could teach them dwindled once it became clear that these [maker] workshops followed a strict task-based structure that felt like formal schooling' (Chapter 6, this volume, in Westerhof et al.).

The tension here was between the expectations of a makerspace, a place where playful creativity, tinkering, adapting and personal problem solving take place in an unstructured environment, and the need for structured activity based learning in order to ensure equity of experience and specific externally established goal achievement. Unlike the Kenya case, these differences are particularly evident when a makerspace is encompassed within a school curriculum; when there are set goals to be achieved by the students in a makerspace, then structures are invariably introduced to help ensure the achievement of those goals.

An answer to this question: how students are learning?, may reflect a point of differentiation between a social makerspace, a general makerspace in a school and a technology education workshop. In Technology Education, activities are structured in order to facilitate student achievement of particular learning goals. Not that all students are necessarily following the same path to goal achievement, but an essential element is the constructive alignment of goals, pedagogy, activity and assessment. In a free and open school makerspace, no such alignment is necessary, although the elements of goals, pedagogy, activity and assessment may exist in some form. In a social makerspace (for example a community library) this alignment may not exist at all, and engagement may constitute the major goal.

The response to the problem of student disinterest in the toy making activity in Kenya was to restructure the makerspaces 'to be inviting, have exciting relatable topics for the children, be fun to partake in, and give the children a sense of accomplishment'. Tangible design goals were set that were feasible to reach in a single workshop, assignments were relatable and interesting to a diverse group of boys and girls.

In the Kenya case, the emphasis of the workshop shifted over time from the end-product (available, affordable, sustainable toys) to the playful learning experience of the creation of the toys. This transition reflects a focus on learning which may be detracted from if the end product is perceived as the main goal, for example a smartly produced, precise laser cut or engraved product. Learning occurs throughout the process, as the maker experiments with materials, learns from mistakes and reflects on experiences. When the end product is prioritized, less attention is directed toward learning.

In some instances, the nature of the makerspace determines the necessary pedagogy. For example, if the equipment available for use within the space includes sharp or powerful tools, or machines which are not intuitive (3D printers, laser cutters, welders, etc) then some form of structured pedagogy is necessary in order for the participants to effectively use the equipment. This form of tool and equipment learning maybe preparatory to engagement in a creative design process.

The characterization of makerspaces as collaborative communities of playful creativity, tinkering, adapting and personal problem solving is not reflected in all of the cases presented in this book. The focus on these characteristics very across different types of makerspaces, for example they are common in men's sheds (Golding & Carragher, 2015) types of makerspaces which tend to be less structured and goal oriented.

8   Teacher Role: How Is the Teacher Facilitating Learning?

The teacher as learning maker (van Dijk et al., 2020) has a fluid role in makerspaces. A student centred approach with little intervention from the teacher, is sympathetic to both a constructivist and constructionist philosophy in maker spaces. However, if the maker education experiences are in-school and in-curriculum, then there may be a tension related to teacher pedagogy. This may require teachers to gain new knowledge about pedagogical strategies, such as Design Thinking, in order to implement new practices. Teachers must also develop knowledge about the technology and tools in the space, including how the tools function and how to troubleshoot when there are issues (Oliver, 2016).

The Kenya case study provides insight into how the teachers facilitated learning. It was recognized early that a culture-sensitive design approach (Van Boeijen & Zijlstra, 2020) was key to success. Constant dialogue was established between the education developer in Netherlands and local facilitator and organizer in Kenya, and because of this, all stakeholders could suggest changes or specific additions or omissions from the workshops.

Learning by doing through play was the focus of the educational developer in producing the digital instruction materials. Through play, the children explored and acquainted themselves with the rules and symbols of their communities, and the adults guided them with 'joyful, engaging, iterative and socially interactive play experiences'. The goal here was to loosely scaffold the children through a design/play process with narrowly defined topics at the beginning, then as the children developed their design skills through successive workshops, less structured support was provided within a freer design space.

The Applied Physics support makerspace case study involved an iterative process, where students quickly build a prototype version, test it, make adjustments and then produce a better prototype. To support students in this process they had a mandatory meeting with a teaching assistant once a week. In this meeting they reported on progress made, tasks completed and how insights from the past week influenced future actions. The technical assistants were trained to push the students towards an iterative planning instead of a single production run.

Because the context in Korea includes government support for makerspaces in schools, and technology teachers have been proactive in maximising these opportunities, the strategies of the makerspace teachers are similar to technology education: exploring problems and implementing the process of solving problems using a range of materials, tools and equipment.

Teachers who participate in the development of a makerspace culture have indicated that their regular classroom culture has been impacted, with a consequent development of design thinking, and a focus on problem solving and brainstorming (Shively et al., 2021) within their non-makerspace classrooms.

Community based makerspaces may not employ teachers, but supervisors or coaches, so the basic assumptions related to teacher skills (pedagogy, behaviour management) may not be evident. The library makerspace coaches employed in the libraries of the Netherlands were librarians who underwent courses in pedagogy, maker education, digital fabrication and design, and needed continuous professional development.

Some maker teachers utilize competitions to achieve their educational goals because of the motivational aspects of competing, and the creative and designerly focus of many competitions. For example the iCentre space in China incorporates the following competitions: Comprehensive Ability of Engineering Training Competition, the Mechanical Innovation Design Competition, the Electronic System Design Competition, the Virtual Instrument Competition, the Construction Manufacturing Competition, the Energy-Saving Vehicle Competition, the Hardware Design Competition and the Digital System Innovation Design Competition.

The pedagogy of the makerspace teachers varies from those in a school setting where formal pedagogical training is an assumed prerequisite, to community makerspaces where the leaders or guides have had no pedagogical training and may require professional development education in order to ensure the makerspace achieves its objectives.

9   Materials & Resources: With What Are They Learning?

Although the perception of makerspaces include a predominance of digital resources such as 3D printers and laser cutters, the case studies in this book reveal a much broader variety of materials and resources.

The Chinese iCentre Innovation Workshop case study reflects this common perception with its focus on science popularization projects and equipment which includes an explosion-proof demining robot, a 3D printer, a smart home, a Smart Arm, a photovoltaic power generation system and other projects to support science popularization.

The Netherlands library makerspaces had consistent equipment across all ten sites: two or three 3D-printers, a laser-cutter, a vinyl-cutter, fifteen laptops, glue guns, two sewing machines, and pencils, paint, paper, etc.

The maker activity described at the Tianyi middle school in China focused on the design of a lamp and functioned in a special room in the school equipped with a large common tool section (pincer workbench, grinding wheel, polishing machine, drilling machine, wire saw, pistol drill, illuminator and other common equipment); a small tool section, requiring at least one group set (sharp-nosed pliers, diagonal pliers, scissors, straight screwdrivers, cross screwdrivers, large files, hobby knifes, tweezers, small files, internal heating type electric contact irons; and multi-meters.

The design and construction of toys in the Kenya makerspace began with the initial concept to create toys to sell and use locally, using local and found materials. When it became clear that found materials would not enable this, the pedagogies became flexible and focused less on the toy end product and more on creative and designerly making processes.

The EcoMakerKits case study also had a focus on sustainability by developing tangible solutions and alternatives and integrating Circular Thinking into the development of new sustainable products. The approach was project-based, to create artifacts made out of reused, repurposed or repaired objects.

The Applied Physics support maker education program arose from a perceived deficiency of student wasted time because of jury rigged solutions which improperly used everyday tools such as scissors, knives and miles of 'duct tape'. The result was a perception that dedicated rooms (makerspaces) with tools and equipment readily available to students were needed. As a result, three rooms were found – a Maker room for quick production of prototypes using the latest tools such as 3D printers and a laser cutter, a Machine room dedicated to more conventional and heavy machinery such as CNC and drills, and an Assembly room for the assembly of the prototypes with hand-craft equipment available to the students.

The makerspace facilities and equipment are either structured in such a way as to facilitate achievement of the goals of the makerspace, or if the facilities and equipment pre-exist, then they may have a deterministic effect on both the activities within the makerspace and the outcomes achieved.

10   Grouping: With Whom Are They Learning?

The element of the constructivist underpinnings of makerspaces relevant to this component of the framework is that students construct knowledge based on their experiences and their interactions with others. This was a common theme of the case studies, particularly as it related to the development of pro-cedural knowledge. Makerspace participants played and developed design knowledge together. However in those cases where the focus was on a final product rather than the process, some students worked individually rather than together. For example the lamp in China, the EcoKits in Mexico, the libraries in the Netherlands and the play produced artefacts in Kenya.

The only case which specifically addressed the nature of collaboration was the makerspaces which supported the university physics courses (Pols and Hut, Chapter 9, this volume). The students were given a lecture to help them develop strategies to work successfully together which focussed on effective communi-cation (the content – process – relationship model). The students subsequently had to collaboratively draft a code of conduct, which was referred to (and reflected upon) when troubles in the functioning of the team arose.

11   Location: Where Are They Learning?

Fleming (2018) concluded that a great makerspace has six key attributes: it is personalized, deep (allowing deeper learning), empowering, equitable, inten-tional, and inspiring. It also needs to be a safe environment in which partici-pants feel free to experiment and ask questions. These attributes provide no guidance in determining location, the location of a makerspace is determined by issues such as access, equipment, funding and availability.

Many makerspaces have developed as spaces for innovation within tradi-tionally structured schools, but timetabling a single makerspace in a school for equitable access can be problematic (Shively et al., 2021) particularly when attempting to be innovative (Becker & Jacobsen, 2020). This is because it may not fit in with the teachers programme, may not permit adequate blocks of time for action oriented design education and will increase student traffic around the school environment. For these reasons many school based maker-spaces are open to students after school or during lunch periods.

The location for the toys makerspace in Kenya was a community centre, which does not provide formal education, and children are free to come and go as they wish. This suited the purposes of the maker teachers. The makerspaces in libraries in the Netherlands were open to participants after school, and were often perceived by participants to complement the school curriculum by pro-viding alternative activities not available at school.

The dual goals of the iCentre makerspace at Tsinghua University were to provide an interdisciplinary platform for innovation and entrepreneurship education for the university students, and a real engineering environment for primary and secondary school students. This has resulted in the development of an innovation workshop, a mechanical workshop and an electronic craft work-shop, facilities which directly support the goals of the makerspace activities.

In the other university based case in this book, the makerspace supporting the Applied Physics program at Delft (Pols and Hut), specialized rooms were also developed to house the maker activities: a Maker room, a Machine room and an Assembly room.

Makerspaces can be affective if they are purposely designed to support the anticipated activity (such as in a university or school) but can also be effective if an existing setting is repurposed or adapted to makerspace activities (such as a community centre or a library).

12   Time: When Are They Learning?

The timing of learning in makerspaces is not a significant element in the anal-ysis of maker pedagogy. This is confirmed by the fact that none of the case studies considered the issue of when the participants were learning in their discussion of their experiences. Institutionally based makerspaces are open within predetermined times, community based makerspaces tend to be oper-ational outside of school times.

13   Assessment: How to Measure How Far Learning Has Progressed?

Assessing students' learning requires opportunities for students to share prod-ucts (Jaatinen & Lindfors, 2019), reflect upon processes (Bevan et al., 2015; Shively et al., 2018), and demonstrate what has been learned (Christensen,

Hjorth, Iversen, & Smith, 2019). Because of the significant diversity which exists in makerspaces and maker activities, not all of these elements are necessarily present in all cases. In fact, a valid critique of many makerspace activities, because of their informal and extracurricular nature, is that the outcomes are not measured, so there is no understanding of whether the often laudable goals have been achieved. Participants will no doubt learn many things, but no one knows (or at least rarely documents) what they are.

For example in the case study from China, guidance is provided by the General Office of the State Council of the People's Republic related to the goals of innovative makerspaces:

– stimulate students' awareness of innovation and entrepreneurship,
– cultivate the mindset of creators, the entrepreneurial spirit of all students to think hard, question well, and dare to challenge authority,
– cultivate a culture of innovation,
– stimulate students' entrepreneurial motivation, entrepreneurial interest, and entrepreneurial ideas, and
– enhance students' market awareness, business awareness, and risk awareness.

Despite these goals, the Green Energy-saving Lamp project is evaluated based on the final product.

In the Applied Physics maker education support case study, the students had to make (build) the solution they proposed based on their design. Some of the goals were to

– cooperate and work effectively in groups
– report and present a design
– make 2D (vector) and 3D models

The students are assessed as normal for the physics courses which the makerspace supports, but the teachers have found that since the inclusion of the Makerspace, students are more enthusiastic about the course in general and their project in particular, they have an increased sense of ownership, because the makerspace allows them to more rapidly test if their ideas work, speeding up the design cycle.

The goals of the Mexico case study were to foster sustainability awareness and stimulate circular thinking. A final activity in this case study was for the participants to evaluate and self-assess their understanding and knowledge based on the rubrics from the first self-assessment activity and to reflect on their learning by answering the questions:

– What did you learn?
– What made you curious?
– What worked well?

– What did not work?
– What else would you like to learn?

This enabled the maker teachers to understand the perceived effectiveness of the project from the students. They concluded that the combination of all activities helped to raise awareness of Circular Thinking, grasp the concept of e-waste and develop technical skills that could help them to expand their Maker Mindset.

The library makerspaces in the Netherlands also depended on participant self-reflection for assessment, and while this was invariably positive, it did not indicate if the goals of the program related to personal and social development, creativity and technological literacy were being achieved.

It is difficult to assess those goals often associated with makerspaces such as creativity, cooperation and innovation; and consequently they are not assessed in the majority of cases. In addition, because of the informal nature of many makerspaces, particularly those which are community based, and the lack of assessment literacy of the makerspace coordinators, little attention is given to assessment.

14   Conclusion

In all of the elements of the pedagogical framework discussed above, there is no single consistent conclusion to be made because of the fundamental diversity of approaches: rationales, objectives, pedagogies, content and activities, locations and assessment are all diverse. Those readers seeking a pedagogical template for a successful makerspace will be disappointed. This diversity is a strength of the makerspace movement; the only fundamental commonalities seem to be active learning through concrete material (see Chapter 11 on Materiality by Mehto & Kangas) experiences.

References

Becheikh, N., Ziam, S., Idrissi, O., Castonguay, Y., & Landry, R. (2010). How to improve knowledge transfer strategies and practices in education? Answers from a systematic literature review. *Research in Higher Education Journal, 7*, 1.

Becker, S. (2019). *Becoming makers: A designed-based research study investigating curriculum implementation through making.* [Dissertation, University of Calgary].

Becker, S., & Jacobsen, M. (2020). Becoming a maker teacher: Designing making curricula that promotes pedagogical change. *Frontiers in Education, 5*(83). https://doi.org/10.3389/feduc.2020.00083

Bevan, B. (2017). The promise and the promises of making in science education. *Studies in Science Education, 53*, 75–103. https://doi.org/10.1080/03057267.2016.1275380

Bevan, B., Gutwill, J. P., Petrich, M., & Wilkinson, K. (2015). Learning through STEM-rich tinkering: Findings from a jointly negotiated research project taken up in practice. *Science Education, 99*(1), 98–120.

Bullock, S. M., & Sator, A. J. (2015). Maker pedagogy and science teacher education. *Journal of the Canadian Association for Curriculum Studies, 13*(1), 61–87.

Burke, J. J. (2014). *Makerspaces: A practical guide for librarians* (Vol. 8). Rowman & Littlefield.

Christensen, K. S., Hjorth, M., Iversen, O. S., & Smith, R. C. (2019). Understanding design literacy in middle-school education: Assessing students' stances towards inquiry. *International Journal of Technology and Design Education, 29*(4), 633–654.

Emm, A., & Hawkins, D. (2020). From Bauhaus to makerspace: Meaning design and computer-aided design in introductory German. *Die Unterrichtspraxis/Teaching German, 53*(2), 138–150.

Fleming, L. (2018). Pedagogy, not passing trend. *School Library Journal, New York, 64*(5): 33.

Golding, B., & Carragher, L. (2015). Community men's sheds and informal learning. In J. Ostrouch-Kamińska & C. C. Vieira (Eds.), *Private world(s)* (pp. 103–118). Sense Publishers.

Jaatinen, J., & Lindfors, E. (2019). Makerspaces for pedagogical innovation processes: How Finnish comprehensive schools create space for makers. *Design and Technology Education, 24*(2).

Klapwijk, R. M. (2018). Formative assessment of creativity. In M. J. De Vries (Ed.), *Handbook of technology education* (pp. 765–784). https://doi.org/10.1007/978-3-319-44687-5_55

Oliver, K. M. (2016). Professional development considerations for Makerspace leaders, part one: Addressing "What?" and "Why?" *TechTrends, 60*(2), 160–166. https://doi.org/10.1007/s11528-016-0028-5

Papert, S. (1987). *A critique of technocentrism in thinking about the school of the future.* http://www.papert.org/articles/ACritiqueofTechnocentrism.html

Peterson, L., & Scharber, C. (2017). Learning about makerspaces: Professional development with K12 inservice educators. *Journal of Digital Learning in Teacher Education, 34*(1), 43–52. https://doi.org/10.1080/21532974.2017.1387833

Sheffield, R., Koul, R., Blackley, S., & Maynard, N. (2017). Makerspace in STEM for girls: A physical space to develop twenty-first-century skills. *Educational Media International, 54*(2), 148–164. https://doi.org/10.1080/09523987.2017.1362812

Shively, K., Stith, K., & Rubenstein, L. (2021). Ideation to implementation: A 4-year exploration of innovating education through maker pedagogy. *The Journal of Educational Research, 114*(2), 155–170, https://doi.org/10.1080/00220671.2021.1872472

Silver, J. (2016). *Invention literacy.* https://medium.com/startup-grind/invention-literacy-5915a411e29d

Smith, S., Wakefield, A., & Talley, K. (2019). *Facilitating makerspace adoption: Professional development for university faculty in making techniques and pedagogy* [ASEE conference paper 25151].

Van Boeijen, A. G. C., Daalhuizen, J. J., & Zijlstra, J. J. M. (Eds.). (2020). *Delft design guide: Perspectives, models, approaches and methods* (2nd ed.). BIS Publishers.

Van den Akker, J. (2013). Curricular development research as a specimen of education design research. In T. Plomp & N. Nieveen, (Eds.), *Educational design research* (pp. 52–71). Netherlands Institute for Curriculum Development.

Van Dijk, G., Arjan van der Meij, A., & Savelsbergh, E. (2020). Maker education: Opportunities and threats for engineering and technology education. In P. J. Williams & D. Barlex (Eds.), *Pedagogy for technology education in secondary schools.* Springer. https://doi.org/10.1007/978-3-030-41548-8_5

Zhu, Z. T., & Luo, L. (2015). From maker movement to maker education: Cultivating mass innovation culture. *Research on Audio-visual Education, 3*(7), 5–13.

CHAPTER 11

Dynamic Roles of Materiality in Maker Education

Varpu Mehto and Kaiju Kangas

Abstract

Maker education is often fundamentally material in nature; makers use material means to transform their design ideas into various tangible forms and to explore the properties and possibilities of their designs. Material making employs and shapes the material world around that making and also provides versatile learning opportunities. This chapter examines the case chapters of the present book from the perspective of materiality by exploring the role of various material design representations in maker education and discussing the learning opportunities that material making may offer. The dynamic and active roles of materiality are highlighted to enrich practitioners' and researchers' understandings of what matters in learning.

Keywords

material making – design – learning opportunities

1   Introduction

Making in maker education refers to a broad range of activities, such as creating, designing, building, tinkering, crafting, engineering and programming (Kangas et al., 2022; Ryan et al., 2016). Many of these activities are fundamentally materially mediated and embodied in nature. The iterative interaction between thinking and doing is essential (Kimbell & Stables, 2007) as students transform their ideas into various material, tangible forms and seek feedback through experimentation with materials, tools and technologies.

In maker education, students are often addressed with complex, open-ended design tasks that require them to engage in the creation and elaboration of design ideas and analysis of design constraints. Through various open-ended maker projects, students gradually learn to employ design principles to address design challenges and to use technological and material means to express, test and further elaborate their design ideas (e.g., Riikonen et al.,

© KONINKLIJKE BRILL NV, LEIDEN, 2023 | DOI:10.1163/9789004681910_011

2020). Hence, materiality concretizes the iterative nature of the design process. Materialization of design ideas makes them visible for evaluation and development (Binder et al., 2011), and material representations can be tested and further refined (Welch et al., 2000).

However, the materiality of making has effects beyond intentional design solutions, for example, by providing inspiration and surprise and by altering the nature of the thinking process towards slow and detailed elaboration or playful creation. Further, materiality can support collaboration and affect opportunities for participation. Simultaneously, making is materially connected to social and ecological issues, which awaken questions of responsibility. Materially embedded learning can provide means to situate these far-reaching questions in locally meaningful practices.

In this chapter, we examine the case chapters of the present book by focusing on the materiality of making, that is, making that employs and shapes the surrounding material world. Our own research and development work has focused on open-ended maker projects in formal education, which has affected our understanding of materiality and oriented our reading of the case chapters. With materiality, we refer not only to the tangible objects created and used during designing and making but also to the material surroundings inspiring and constraining those activities either intentionally or unintentionally.

First, we explore design representations in maker education, focusing especially on the material forms of representation. Second, we examine the learning opportunities that material making provides. These opportunities take place at various connected levels: individual maker thinking with materials, collaboration and participation in making, and global issues situated in local making practices. Third, we consider pedagogical, theoretical and methodological implications of materiality in maker education by discussing how practitioners and researchers could attune themselves towards materiality. We argue that acknowledging the active and dynamic roles of materiality could enrich understanding on what matters in learning.

2   Design Representations in Maker Education

In designing, various means are used to give abstract ideas a visual or material form. Two- and three-dimensional design representations are used for visualizing, externalizing and storing design ideas; for thinking, reflecting, and elaborating on ideas; and for communicating and creating a shared vision of ideas (Laamanen & Seitamaa-Hakkarainen, 2014; Mehto et al., 2020a, 2020b; Pei et al., 2011). In the following paragraphs, we first discuss the function and significance of design representations in general and in maker education. Then, we focus more specifically on material design representations and explore their nature and role in maker education contexts.

2.1   *Function and Significance of Design Representations*
According to the taxonomy created by Pei et al. (2011), designers use four distinct types of design representations: sketches, drawings, models and prototypes. A sketch is a preliminary, rough representation, which is produced freehand to present key elements of a design. A drawing, in contrast, 'is a formal arrangement of lines that determine a particular form and are highly structured to formalize and verify aspects of the design' (Pei et al., 2011, p. 67). Models are used in the early stages of the process for problem solving and idea generation to explore and explain the function, performance and aesthetic aspects of a design in a rough three-dimensional form. Prototypes are used in later stages to evaluate and verify the function, performance and aesthetics of the designed product. In professional design, these four main types can be further divided into 32 distinct types of design representations, each serving a different purpose in the design process (Pei et al., 2011).

Although these various representations and the detailed definitions of their purposes are not necessary in maker education contexts, the practices related to them can inform makers and their facilitators in several ways, especially in open-ended maker projects. Firstly, the vast number of different representations illustrate that designing is an iterative process, and design ideas are developed through sustained and repeated efforts (see Kangas & Seitamaa-Hakkarainen, 2018). Second, design representations underline that generating ideas and solutions to a complex design challenge requires collaboration; therefore, design ideas need to be externalized and communicated in one way or another (Mehto et al., 2020b). Third, the design process is shaped by the means of representation; that is, the materials, tools and technologies used for representing inspire and constrain the process (Mehto et al., 2020a).

The various representations are essential for professional designers; however, research within the field of Design & Technology education has shown that the function and significance of these representations may not be evident for young makers learning design (Hope, 2005; MacDonald et al., 2007; Welch et al., 2000). Creating design representations entails the risk that they become prioritized at the expense of participation and learning if the purpose and advantages of using them as design tools are not understood (Murphy & Hennessy, 2001). In maker projects focusing on design, it should be explicitly addressed how various representations provide means for the generation and elaboration, not just the execution, of design ideas (MacDonald et al., 2007).

To achieve this, young makers should be involved in several projects in which they can practice externalizing with different types of media. Understanding various representation methods, recognizing how they are used to construct explanations and negotiating the meaning of different representations are crucial to learning design in maker education (Campbell & Jane, 2012).

2.2 *Nature and Role of Material Design Representations*

In this chapter, we focus especially on three-dimensional, tangible design representations that students create in maker-centred learning projects. These can be models or prototypes from various phases of the process as well as material explorations used for examining the properties and possibilities of materials. Novice designers, such as school students, often prefer working with three-dimensional representations (Hope, 2005) because children's experiences are based on direct exploration of the physical world (Anning, 1997). Further, two-dimensional representations are often inadequate for exploring three-dimensional attributes of a design, and tangible models and prototypes support both novice and expert designers in understanding and addressing these attributes (Kangas et al., 2013; Pei et al., 2011).

In maker education, students use a wide variety of materials, tools and technologies, ranging from low tech (e.g., art and craft tools and materials) to high tech (e.g., rapid prototyping and programming technologies), to give their ideas a material form and to test and experiment with their design solutions. In the early design phases, sketch models can be used to capture the key characteristics of the form and/or to test and experiment with functional properties (Pei et al., 2011). Students usually build sketch models with affordable materials that are easy to manipulate, for example, cardboard, playdough or construction kits. Recycled materials are also often used, as illustrated in the chapters by Gu and Yang (see Figure 8.3 of this volume) and Núñez-Solís et al. (Chapter 5, this volume). In addition, maker projects can employ materials collected from nature, such as clay and twigs, as described by Westerhof et al. (Chapter 6, this volume). Sketch models can be used for exploring visual design elements and principles, such as shapes, patterns or colours, and for technical designing, for example, experimenting with structures and functionalities. As sketch models are relatively easy to make, they can be used for iterative generation and elaboration of design ideas; students can construct several sketch models to develop their design ideas further. However, as noted by Westerhof et al. (Chapter 6, this volume), maker education can also put more emphasis on the pure joy of building instead of often time-consuming iterations.

Maker projects typically also involve material resources that enable exploration with more advanced functionalities. For example, electronic tinkering kits (see Chu et al., 2015; Gu & Yang, Chapter 8 in this volume), e-textiles (see Kafai et al., 2014; Litts et al., 2017), programmable robotic kits (see Leonard et al., 2016) and microcontrollers (see Mehto et al., 2020a) have been used for building functional models and prototypes as well as final products. Additionally, rapid prototyping tools, such as 3D printers and laser cutters, are commonly used in maker education contexts (see Chan & Blikstein, 2018). These technologies enable multiple iterations of testing and making models because they allow elements of a design to be easily changed and manipulated. However, especially with younger makers, they are more commonly used for making the final outcomes of a project rather than models and prototypes, as illustrated by Gu and Yang (see Figure 8.1 of this volume).

The small maker technologies described above can be used in almost any kind of classroom or workshop; however, maker education can also employ machinery and materials that require dedicated spaces. As described by Pols and Hut (Chapter 9, this volume), iterative model making and prototyping in higher education also requires heavy machinery (e.g., milling machine, lathe) and workstations for assembly. In some countries, such as Finland, machinery and workstations for both hard and soft materials are common at lower levels of education (see Jaatinen & Lindfors, 2019). More commonly, however, these are available at specific maker spaces, which are expensive to establish and maintain, as noted by Holm Kanstrup et al. (Chapter 3, this volume). Pijls et al. (Chapter 4, this volume) underline that maker spaces also require personnel, who support the makers in using the facilities; training and salaries for them requires resources. Due to limited financial or other resources (e.g., time, skills) of many maker education contexts, the boundaries between design representations and final products are not, in fact, clear-cut in maker education, especially at lower levels of education. Quite often, models or prototypes are the final outcomes of a project.

As many makers' designing and making skills are still developing, models and prototypes function both as tools for idea refinement and as practical training of making (Yrjönsuuri et al., 2019). In addition, material making provides many other opportunities for learning, as is described below.

3   Learning Opportunities in Material Making

Materiality inspires and constrains designing and making in multiple ways; thus, material making also provides versatile opportunities for learning. In the following sections, we explore these opportunities at three levels. First, we focus on the individual makers thinking with materials. Second, we zoom out from individual makers to the opportunities that materiality provides for collaboration and participation. Third, we consider the role of material making in addressing global issues in local practices.

3.1   *Opportunities for Thinking with Materials*

Various material representations and explorations assist makers in identifying issues in their designs, discovering novel opportunities and recognizing promising solutions by providing feedback on functional and structural aspects of makers' ideas (Binder et al., 2011). By providing examples of how materials can be used to test design decisions, Pols and Hut (Chapter 9, this volume) emphasize the importance of iterative model making. The immediate feedback that materials provide can allow inexperienced makers to work more independently (Kangas et al., 2013), although more experienced makers with deep material knowledge can imagine more potentials of a certain material than novices (Ramduny-Ellis et al., 2010). These design skills can be elicited in the embodied experiences with materials, which emphasize the role of the body as knowledge provider in embodied cognition (Groth, 2016). For example, as Pols and Hut illustrate, encountering unexpected problems in making can push students to the limits of their knowledge, thus exemplifying the need to learn embodied and material skills. Instead of being isolated in the mind, the process of making appears more as constant interaction between the maker and matter.

However, the effect of materials reaches beyond intentional or pre-planned design and making activities, such as modelling or prototyping. Materials do not rely on human rationalization, and thus they can surprise makers, prevent obvious solutions and encourage novel ideas (Ramduny-Ellis et al., 2010). This includes the materiality of the space, which can shape the learning opportunities (Keune & Peppler, 2019). Various artefacts and materials involved in the processes and places of making affect which questions can be asked during making (Mehto et al., 2020b). In their chapter, Núñez-Solís et al. (Chapter, 5, this volume) describe how dwelling upon the technological details of a design can even result in deeper scientific curiosity on how electronics function. Further, the enabling constraints created by materials affect not only the content of the design but also the nature of thinking and learning (Mehto et al., 2020b). As Pols and Hut (Chapter 9, this volume) describe, due to issues raised by material experimentation, students have to step out of a 'theoretical bubble' and become more pragmatic when looking for solutions to emerging problems. Moreover, working with materials can be slow from time to time, and the goal to make a functioning product requires focus on detail (Yrjönsuuri et al., 2019). This slowness allows time for thinking and can lead to profound idea refinement. The role of materiality in making cannot be explored only from the perspective of human intentions, since materials transform situations as well.

Making challenges the assumption that learning is merely a mental process with predetermined objectives. Clapp et al. (2016) stated that the tangibility of making can be engaging and stimulating, owing to, for example, the multi-sensorial qualities of physical materials. Open-ended and unscripted material practices can enable makers to act on their own terms regardless of their age (Thiel, 2015). Further, making can allow experiences of being knowledgeable and competent, even if one struggles with more academic learning practices, such as writing (Toohey & Dagenais, 2015). In maker education, learning activities do not focus merely on fulfilling external requirements but also highlight the importance of play and the joy of building, as emphasized by Westerhof et al. (Chapter 6, this volume). The authors describe how the process of making a toy becomes more important than the finalized toy itself. In other words, making has more than instrumental value.

3.2   *Opportunities for Collaboration and Participation*

Material making offers fruitful grounds for supporting students' active participation and collaboration. Externalizing ideas into material forms makes them accessible to others, even without verbal interactions (Mehto et al., 2020a); these materialized ideas can then be jointly evaluated and developed (Ramduny-Ellis et al., 2010). Unlike fleeting verbal expressions, materials and artefacts remain constantly available and can thus stabilize dynamic interactions (Day & Wagner, 2014). Materiality can support students in creating a common ground for shared understanding of the design task and design ideas (Lahti et al., 2016). Further, materials can invite students to look, touch and tinker, and they can encourage even division of labour and shared making activities (Mehto et al., 2020a; Yrjönsuuri et al., 2019). Even if students are working on individual projects, material making provides a natural ground for helping each other (Pijls et al., Chapter 4, this volume). Making provides material anchors for design activity and interaction that focus on shared design efforts.

Materiality can also shape opportunities for participation; materials and artefacts can be used, for example, for taking turns at talk (Day & Wagner, 2014). However, materiality can allow for a means of contribution beyond language and verbal discussion, which can in some situations be uncomfortable for some. Rich material resources allow multiple makers to work simultaneously; in contrast, limited material resources, such as a singular laptop for a team of makers, can hinder opportunities for participation (Mehto et al., 2020a). Materiality also affects the division of labour, as possession of a particular tool can give authority to a single maker to affect the course of the design process (Buchholz et al., 2014). Therefore, when designing collaborative making projects, special attention must be given to the material resources to ensure equal learning opportunities for all students.

The potentials of making as a social mediator reach beyond collaborative small teams. For example, Kwon (Chapter 7, this volume) describes how shared interest in certain technologies offers teachers a common ground for collaboration in developing maker practices. Holm Kanstrup et al. (Chapter 3, this volume) explains how hands-on activities are a useful way to facilitate shared understanding between stakeholders. They utilized a participatory design approach in workshops to sustain makerspace initiatives, where participants (e.g., teachers, directors of school departments and principals) worked together in a hands-on manner. Further, makerspaces can be materially embedded in local communities. Pijls et al. (Chapter 4, this volume) described how collecting waste from local vendors offers makerspaces free and interesting materials, creating a mutually beneficial relationship between the makerspace and local community. The materiality of makerspaces requires resources and careful infrastructure in order to be sustainable. Securing such material practice requires collaboration across organizational levels.

3.3   *Opportunities for Addressing Global Issues*

Maker-centred learning offers opportunities to address wide-reaching societal, ecological and political issues. Materiality can play a role in connecting far-reaching questions to situated practices, thus unravelling the dichotomies between the global and local. Although socio-political and ecological questions have been addressed in the field of maker education, there is very little research specifically focused on how the materiality of making provides opportunities for learning to cope and act amidst these issues. An important aspect is the choice of material resources, which can already in itself provide a framework for the contents of learning. Núñez-Solís et al. (Chapter 5, this volume) describe how the concept of the circular economy was addressed using electronic components that would have otherwise become waste. Further, researchers have discussed the importance of including various materials, such as textiles, into coding practices to make learning inviting for students traditionally excluded from technical domains (Buchholz et al., 2014; Kafai et al., 2014), thus enhancing, for example, gender equality in maker education.

The choice of material resources should not, however, be universally determined because local practices and resources can provide unique opportunities for maker education. Westerhof et al. (Chapter 6, this volume) provide an example of how using materials that are widely available in local surroundings, such as sticks and rocks, allow making workshops to be less dependent on external contributors. Barajas-López and Bang (2018) argued that limited perspectives on which materials are considered for maker projects run the risk of reproducing and strengthening settler colonialism. They proposed that reclaiming traditional forms of making, such as clay work, can centre indigenous knowledge systems and thus support equity in making. Altogether, the effects that the chosen materials have on learning are not limited to supporting thinking and social interaction. The selection of making materials, tools and techniques requires consideration of their wider connections so that learning advocates for the intended values.

Whether it is intentional or not, material resources introduce global issues into local spaces (Bennett, 2010; Latour, 2005). When making tasks involve complex digital technologies that are provided by commercial corporations, their interests and presence in maker projects can become highlighted. For example, Paakkari et al. (2019) illustrated how global commercial actors gained a foothold in classrooms through students' own smartphones. Further, Vossoughi et al. (2016) cautioned that adapting maker practices without considering the entangled socio-political questions poses the risk of blindly reproducing neoliberalist values. They highlighted the importance of explicitly analysing the underlying pedagogical philosophies and practices in maker education. In addition to how technologies and materials are used, attention should be paid to the materials themselves. For example, by analysing child labour in cobalt mining, Gallagher (2019) illustrated how childhoods are globally connected by the minerals found in digital media devices. Following the material, cobalt, he bridged together local and global perspectives and shed light on the politics of specific material practices. In pedagogical practices, considering similar far-reaching connections of technologies through making can shift the focus from an external abstract phenomenon to tangible details at hand.

The situated nature of making frames learning as embedded, embodied, and affective (Mehto et al., 2020b). Students do not learn about phenomena as outside observers; instead, they engage with them in an embodied manner. The embedded nature of material making can help to situate wide social and ecological questions into locally meaningful practices. Such tangibility makes action possible, even without the certainty provided by right or wrong answers. Further, creating functional artefacts with the available materials compels the maker to listen to the material world. The artefact emerging from designing and making must fulfil multiple requirements, such as technical, economical, aesthetic and ethical, while simultaneously balancing resources with the maker's skills and motivations, the available materials and time. Performing such a balancing act shifts the aim of learning from mastering the world to being part of it (Ingold, 2013). Finding ways to support learning with the world is a crucial challenge for future education (Common Worlds Research Collective, 2020). The two key opportunities for addressing far-reaching questions through making are firstly the situated embeddedness, which allows action without certainty, and secondly the persistent requirements of materials, which invite learners to acknowledge their positions as part of the world.

4   Discussion and Conclusions

In this chapter, we examined the maker education cases of the present book from the perspective of materiality. As the case examples and previous research illustrate, the activities of designing and making rely upon and are strongly shaped by various material resources and surroundings. Furthermore, inspirations and constraints produced by materiality provide versatile opportunities for learning at three levels which illustrate how material making has more than instrumental value.

First, making process is not isolated in the mind, but makers think with materials through embodied actions. Materials provide tangible feedback on ideas, inspire novel ideas through surprises, and provide opportunities for engaging play. Second, material resources in maker projects can enable or hinder active participation and collaboration in designing and making. Material representations can make ideas that are hard to verbalize accessible to others and provide means of participation beyond language. Third, materiality provides a means to address complex, global issues through locally situated practices and resources, which can support makers in seeing themselves as active shapers of the world. However, instead of searching for universal pedagogical structures, careful attention should be paid to wide-reaching connections of situated materialities.

In conclusion, we must consider the pedagogical, theoretical and methodological implications of materiality in maker education. From a pedagogical perspective, materiality challenges traditional, academic ways of learning, and therefore, it requires active and careful consideration. As the emphasis of future-oriented learning should be on developing students' and teachers' abilities to navigate in undetermined contexts (Organisation for Economic Co-operation and Development, 2019), learning should take place in such contexts and utilize the emergent social and material affordances those contexts offer rather than focusing only on predefined objectives. Material making often goes in unanticipated directions and creates space for learning through hands-on, playful exploration without a pre-structured plan. Simultaneously, materiality demands halting with practicalities by anchoring nonlinear, often messy processes to tangible objects at hand. Materials and associated practices offer various kinds of prompts for problem solving, investigation and discovery. Through materials, students can express personal ideas and meanings, and mistakes can be embraced as learning opportunities.

However, to promote and utilize learning opportunities provided by materiality, maker-centred learning should not be seen as unconstrained exploration. Students need freedom to construct their own ideas and expertise, but this should take place within the boundaries of attentively formulated tasks with appropriate constraints and carefully selected material resources (Sawyer, 2018). Making requires facilitation that embraces the learning opportunities that the partly unpredictable nature of materiality offers; teachers should simultaneously provide purposeful structures and address students' emergent needs (Sawyer, 2021). The learning opportunities in material making may disrupt the notion of 'right' answers and the ideal of measurable achievement (Kafai et al., 2014).

In addition to paying attention to materiality in pedagogical practices, the active role of materials for co-constituting learning should be acknowledged in research. The effect of materials is not reliant on merely their physical properties nor their intentional human activities (Bennett, 2010); instead, research needs to tune into the relations and entanglements of makers and matter. These relations are constantly changing, and amidst far-reaching connections, it is not always evident who or what are parts of certain activities (Latour, 2005). Thus, taking material approach requires methodologies that embrace the messiness of practices. Researchers who aim to understand the role of materiality need theoretically grounded thinking to support their situated findings, patient focus on mundane practices and fleeting details and a readiness to follow even surprising trains of thought. For example, Bennett (2010) could steer the researcher's gaze to the affective forces of materials. Latour's (2005) ideas could help with sensitizing makers to more-than-human strings of actions connecting the local context of making to other times and places. In addition, mundane activities, such as practices of cleaning up and sorting the materials, might turn out to be interesting in terms of research.

Making brings together multiple fields of knowledge and ways of knowing. These multiple realities co-exist and can even enhance each other. For example, materials can inspire makers to tinker and play, and these embodied explorations can deepen material knowledge and even inspire technical solutions the maker could not have imagined in their mind. Simultaneously, materiality may reveal non-working or half-baked solutions that require deliberation, patient iterations and careful rationalization in order to ensure functional technical features. Thus, making unravels dichotomies between playing and learning or being and knowing.

However, the practical skills needed in making, such as computational thinking and technical building, are not separate from questions of responsibility. Far-reaching social and ecological issues are also material and local in nature (Latour, 2005). Even though the maker may not intentionally consider the material effects of their actions, such as the recycling opportunities of the product, origins of raw materials, political histories of the artefact or underlying commercial interests, those effects still take place materially. Not all aspects need to be verbally addressed or explained, and embodied practices are a means to grapple with such material connections. Therefore, it is essential that researchers and organizers of maker projects foster their ability to attune to these responsibilities.

Making provides a feasible way to act amidst these complex issues. While the limits of theoretically analysing the connections and effects of one's actions are endless, the materiality of making provides tangible boundaries. Instead of creating universal solutions, making focuses on acting with local surroundings, including materials, skills and time. Engaging with these material boundaries instead of merely pushing through one's intentions can help makers spot issues that call for response, requiring the makers themselves to change. Thus, the maker not only learns about the material world but is also taught by it (Ingold, 2013). The material perspective enriches the understanding of what matters in learning. The original focus on individual capacities and theoretical knowledge expands to finding ways to live well within the world by generating responsible situated changes.

References

Anning, A. (1997). Drawing out ideas: Graphicacy and young children. *International Journal of Technology and Design Education, 7*(3), 219–239. https://doi.org/10.1023/A:1008824921210

Barajas-López, F., & Bang, M. (2018). Indigenous making and sharing: Claywork in an Indigenous STEAM program. *Equity & Excellence in Education, 51*(1), 7–20. https://doi.org/10.1080/10665684.2018.1437847

Bennett, J. (2010). *Vibrant matter: A political ecology of things.* Duke University Press. https://doi.org/10.2307/j.ctv11hjh6w

Binder, T., De Michelis, G., Ehn, P., Jacucci, G., Linde, P., & Wagner, I. (2011). *Design things.* MIT Press.

Buchholz, B., Shively, K., Peppler, K., & Wohlwend, K. (2014). Hands on, hands off: Gendered access in crafting and electronics practices. *Mind, Culture, and Activity, 21*(4), 278–297. https://doi.org/10.1080/10749039.2014.939762

Campbell, C., & Jane, B. (2012). Motivating children to learn: The role of technology education. *International Journal of Technology and Design Education, 22*(1), 1–11. https://doi.org/10.1007/s10798-010-9134-4

Chan, M. M., & Blikstein, P. (2018). Exploring problem-based learning for middle school design and engineering education in digital fabrication laboratories. *Interdisciplinary Journal of Problem-Based Learning, 12*(2). https://doi.org/10.7771/1541-5015.1746

Chu, S. L., Quek, F., Bhangaonkar, S., Ging, A. B., & Sridharamurthy, K. (2015). Making the maker: A means-to-an-ends approach to nurturing the maker mindset in elementary-aged children. *International Journal of Child-Computer Interaction, 5*, 11–19. https://doi.org/10.1016/j.ijcci.2015.08.002

Clapp, E., Ross, J. O., Ryan, J., & Tishman, S. (2016). *Maker-centered learning: Empowering young people to shape their worlds.* Jossey-Bass.

Common Worlds Research Collective. (2020). *Learning to become with the world: Education for future survival.* UNESCO. https://unesdoc.unesco.org/ark:/48223/pf0000374032

Day, D., & Wagner, J. (2014). Objects as tools for talk. In T. Heinemann & M. Rauniomaa (Eds.), *Interacting with objects: Language, materiality, and social activity* (pp. 101–124). Benjamins Publishing. https://doi.org/10.1075/z.186.05day

Gallagher, M. (2019). Childhood and the geology of media. *Discourse: Studies in the Cultural Politics of Education, 41*(3), 372–390. https://doi.org/10.1080/01596306.2019.1620481

Groth, C. (2016). Design and craft thinking analysed as embodied cognition. *FORMakademisk - Forskningstidsskrift for Design Og Designdidaktikk, 9*(1), 1–21. https://doi.org/10.7577/formakademisk.1481

Gu, J. & Yang, Q. The case studies of maker education in China. In R. M. Klapwijk, J. Gu, Q. Yang & M. J. de Vries (Eds.), *Maker education meets technology education: Reflections on good practices* (Chapter 8, this volume). Brill.

Holm Kanstrup, K., Iversen, O. S., Van Mechelen, M., Dindler, C., & Wagner, M. L. A. Participatory design approach to sustaining makerspace initiatives. In R. M. Klapwijk, J. Gu, Q. Yang & M. J. de Vries (Eds.), *Maker education meets technology education: Reflections on good practices* (Chapter 3, this volume). Brill.

Hope, G. (2005). The types of drawings that young children produce in response to design tasks. *Design and Technology Education: An International Journal, 10*(1), 43–53. https://ojs.lboro.ac.uk/DATE/article/view/Journal_10.1_2005_RES3

Ingold, T. (2013). *MAKING: Anthropology, archaeology, art and architecture.* Routledge. https://doi.org/10.4324/9780203559055

Jaatinen, J., & Lindfors, E. (2019). Makerspaces for innovation learning: How Finnish comprehensive schools create space for makers. *Design and Technology Education: An International Journal, 24*(2), 42–66. https://openjournals.ljmu.ac.uk/DATE/article/view/1325

Kafai, Y., Fields, D., & Searle, K. (2014). Electronic textiles as disruptive maker activities in schools: Supporting and challenging maker activities in schools. *Harvard Educational Review, 84*(4), 532–556. https://doi.org/10.17763/ haer.84.4.46m7372370214783

Kangas, K., & Seitamaa-Hakkarainen, P. (2018). Collaborative design work in technology education. In M. J. de Vries (Ed.), *Handbook of technology education* (pp. 597–609). Springer. https://doi.org/10.1007/978-3-319-44687-5

Kangas, K., Seitamaa-Hakkarainen, P., & Hakkarainen, K. (2013). Design thinking in elementary students' collaborative lamp designing process. *Design and Technology Education: An International Journal, 18*(1), 30–43. https://doi.org/10.17763/ haer.84.4.46m7372370214783

Kangas, K., Sormunen, K., & Korhonen, T. (2022). Creative learning with technologies in young students' STEAM education. In S. Papadakis & M. Kalogiannakis (Eds.), *STEM, robotics, mobile apps in early childhood and primary education* (pp. 157–179). Lecture Notes in Educational Technology. Springer. https://doi.org/10.1007/ 978-981-19-0568-1_9

Keune, A., & Peppler, K. (2019). Materials-to-develop-with: The making of a maker-space. *British Journal of Educational Technology, 50*(1), 280–293. https://doi.org/ 10.1111/bjet.12702

Kimbell, R., & Stables, K. (2007). *Researching design learning: Issues and findings from two decades of research and development.* Springer. https://doi.org/10.1007/ 978-1-4020-5115-9

Kwon, H. Connecting maker education to secondary school technology education. A case of the technology teachers' learning community in Republic of Korea. In R. M. Klapwijk, J. Gu, Q. Yang & M. J. de Vries (Eds.), *Maker education meets technology education: Reflections on good practices* (Chapter 7, this volume). Brill.

Laamanen, T. K., & Seitamaa-Hakkarainen, P. (2014). Constraining the open-ended design task by interpreting sources of inspiration. *Art, Design and Communication in Higher Education, 13*(2), 135–156. https://doi.org/10.1386/adch.13.2.135_1

Lahti, H., Seitamaa-Hakkarainen, P., Härkki, T., Kangas, K., & Hakkarainen, K. (2016). Textile teacher students' collaborative design processes in a design studio setting. *Art, Design & Communication in Higher Education, 15*(1), 35–54. https://doi.org/ 10.1386/adch.15.1.35_1

Latour, B. (2005). *Reassembling the social: An introduction to actor-network-theory.* Oxford University Press. https://doi.org/10.17323/1726-3247-2013-2-73-87

Leonard, J., Buss, A., Gamboa, R., Mitchell, M., Fashola, O. S., Hubert, T., & Almughyirah, S. (2016). Using robotics and game design to enhance children's self-efficacy, STEM attitudes, and computational thinking skills. *Journal of Science Education and Technology, 25*(6), 860–876. https://doi.org/10.1007/s10956-016-9628-2

Litts, B. K., Kafai, Y. B., Lui, D. A., Walker, J. T., Widman, S. A. (2017). Stitching codeable circuits: High school students' learning about circuitry and coding with electronic textiles. *Journal of Science Education and Technology, 26*(5), 494–507. https://doi.org/10.1007/s10956-017-9694-0

MacDonald, D., Gustafson, B. J., & Gentilini, S. (2007). Enhancing children's drawing in design technology planning and making. *Research in Science & Technological Education, 25*(1), 59–75. https://doi.org/10.1080/02635140601053500

Mehto, V., Riikonen, S., Hakkarainen, K., Kangas, K., & Seitamaa-Hakkarainen, P. (2020a). Epistemic roles of materiality within a collaborative invention project at a secondary school. *British Journal of Educational Technology, 51*(4), 1246–1261. https://doi.org/10.1111/bjet.12942

Mehto, V., Riikonen, S., Seitamaa-Hakkarainen, P., & Kangas, K. (2020b). Sociomateriality of collaboration within a small team in secondary school maker centered learning. *International Journal of Child-Computer Interaction, 26.* https://doi.org/10.1016/j.ijcci.2020.100209

Murphy, P., & Hennessy, S. (2001). Realising the potential – and lost opportunities – for peer collaboration in a D&T setting. *International Journal of Technology and Design Education, 11*(3), 203–237. https://doi.org/10.1023/A:1011286331859

Núñez-Solís, A., Madahar, S., Eskue, N. & Silva-Ordaz, M., Using "EcoMakerKits" to stimulate maker mindset and circular thinking in Mexico. In R. M. Klapwijk, J. Gu, Q. Yang & M. J. de Vries (Eds.), *Maker education meets technology education: Reflections on good practices* (Chapter 5, this volume). Brill.

Organisation for Economic Co-operation and Development. (2019). *OECD learning compass 2030: A series of concept notes.* Author. https://www.oecd.org/education/2030-project/contact/OECD_Learning_Compass_2030_Concept_Note_Series.pdf

Paakkari, A., Rautio, P., & Valasmo, V. (2019). Digital labour in school: Smartphones and their consequences in classrooms. *Learning, Culture and Social Interaction, 21*(January), 161–169. https://doi.org/10.1016/j.lcsi.2019.03.004

Pei, E., Campbell, I. R., & Evans, M. A. (2011). A taxonomic classification of visual design representations used by industrial designers and engineering designers. *Design Journal, 14*(1), 64–91. https://doi.org/10.2752/175630610X12877385838803

Pijls, M., Van Eijck, T. & Bredeweg, B. Informal learning in a public library makerspace for youth in the Netherlands. In R. M. Klapwijk, J. Gu, Q. Yang & M. J. de Vries (Eds.), *Maker education meets technology education: Reflections on good practices* (Chapter 4, this volume). Brill.

Pols, F. & Hut, R. Maker education in the applied physics bachelor programme at Delft University of Technology. In R. M. Klapwijk, J. Gu, Q. Yang & M. J. de Vries (Eds.), *Maker education meets technology education: Reflections on good practices* (Chapter 9, this volume). Brill.

Ramduny-Ellis, D., Dix, A., Evans, M., Hare, J., & Gill, S. (2010). Physicality in design: An exploration. *Design Journal, 13*(1), 48–76. https://doi.org/10.2752/146069210X12580336766365

Riikonen, S., Seitamaa-Hakkarainen, P., & Hakkarainen, K. (2020). Bringing maker practices to school: Tracing discursive and materially mediated aspects of student teams' collaborative making processes. *Journal of Computer Supported Collaborative Learning, 15*(3), 319–349. https://doi.org/10.1007/s11412-020-09330-6

Ryan, J., Clapp, E., Ross, J., & Tishman, S. (2016). Making, thinking and understanding: A dispositional approach to maker-centered learning. In K. Peppler, E. Halverson & Y. Kafai (Eds.), *Makeology. Makers as Learners* (Vol. 2, pp. 29–44). Routledge. https://doi.org/10.4324/9781315726496

Sawyer, R. K. (2018). Teaching and learning how to create in schools of art and design. *Journal of the Learning Sciences, 27*(1), 137–181. https://doi.org/10.1080/10508406.2017.1381963

Sawyer, R. K. (2021). The iterative and improvisational nature of the creative process. *Journal of Creativity, 31*, 1–6. https://doi.org/10.1016/j.yjoc.2021.100002

Thiel, J. J. (2015). Vibrant matter: The intra-active role of objects in the construction of young children's literacies. *Literacy Research: Theory, Method, and Practice, 64*(1), 112–131. https://doi.org/10.5840/envirophil2011817

Toohey, K., & Dagenais, D. (2015). Videomaking as sociomaterial assemblage. *Language and Education, 29*(4), 302–316. https://doi.org/10.1080/09500782.2015.1006643

Vossoughi, S., Hooper, P. K., & Escudé, M. (2016). Making through the lens of culture and power: Toward transformative visions for educational equity. *Harvard Educational Review, 86*(2), 206–232. https://doi.org/10.17763/0017-8055.86.2.206

Welch, M., Barlex, D., & Lim, H. S. (2000). Sketching: Friend or foe to the novice designer? *International Journal of Technology and Design Education, 10*(2), 125–148. https://doi.org/10.1023/A:1008991319644

Westerhof, M. B., Gielen, M., Van Boeijen, A. G. C., & Jowi, J. O. Playful learning by design in Kenya: Remote development of design education workshops for rural Kenya. In R. M. Klapwijk, J. Gu, Q. Yang & M. J. de Vries (Eds.), *Maker education meets technology education: Reflections on good practices* (Chapter 6 this book). Brill.

Yrjönsuuri, V., Kangas, K., Hakkarainen, K., & Seitamaa-Hakkarainen, P. (2019). The roles of material prototyping in collaborative design process at an elementary school. *Design and Technology Education: An International Journal, 24*(2), 141–162. https://openjournals.ljmu.ac.uk/DATE/article/view/1315

CHAPTER 12

Social Learning

Does Cooperation Contribute to the Learning of the Makers?

Wendy Fox-Turnbull

Abstract

This chapter explores the scope and nature of social learning evident in the Maker-space movement as identified by the cases studies presented previously. The makerspace movement is clearly situated within a constructionist paradigm, placing the learner centrally in the construction of artefacts. Because of its collaborative nature and the need for learners to become critical thinkers and makers Makerspace is well situated to ensure learners today are equipped with the necessary skills and dispositions essential to life in the 21st century.

This chapter draws on literature on three learning theories particularly relevant to makerspace philosophy. The first, Kolb's Experiencing Learning theory, providing an excellent mechanism for teaching and learning design-based activities while placing learners at the centre of learning. The second, Social Learning Theory, describes the process of collaborative practice in a common activity with the aim of reaching an intended goal. Bandura suggests that Social Learning theory emphasises synthesis of behavioural events and human cognitive processes. This is relevant to makerspaces through the collaborative nature of design and development of artefacts-technological products and systems. The third theory is Social Partication Theory and draws together both learning through experience and learning socially and is therefore most pertinent to the Makerspace movement as it gives equal emphasis to working collaboratively and learning through doing.

To identify and discuss the scope and nature of social interaction, a modfied version of Bronfenbrenner's Ecological Systems Theory is applied. This Ecological Systems Model is modified to organise a discussion on the social interaction within the Makerspace case studies. Selected for its layering and spheres of influence the model gives a framework for the types of social interaction evidenced in the cases. In this section the cases presented are organised according to The Ecological Systems Model and categories in relation to their influence on learners.

Keywords

social learning – collaboration and cooperation – makerspace – ecological systems model

1   Introduction

This chapter provides reflection on the case studies in the previous section in relation to aspects of social learning. Makerspaces are workshops that facilitate creative and technical endeavour for individual tinkering, social learning and group collaboration on innovative technological projects (Schrock, 2014). They are extremely collaborative environments, modelling the practice of scientistist and technologists. Often the true benefit of makerspaces is in the process, rather than the product (Harrington, 2019). The makerspace phenomenon draws on and facilitates a number of aspects critical to success in education in the 21st century (Hatzigianni et al., 2021; Rayna & Striukova, 2021), three of which inform this chapter: learning through participation in concrete experiences- experiential learning (Kolb, 1984), the role social interaction plays in the learning process- social theory (Bandura, 1977) and Social Partication Theory (Zewde, 2010). This last theory draws together learning through experience and learning socially. Thus an explanation of Social Partication Theory and its relevance to the makerspace movement is presented leading onto commentrary about role of and aspects of social learning evident in the provided case studies. Due to the collaborative nature of makerspace social interaction plays a significant role in learning.

2   Social Interaction in Educational Activity

Social interaction is a vital component of participating in collaborative projects. Vygotsky's (1978) Constructivist Learning Theory suggests that students learn through interaction with others and their environment. According to Vygotsky there are two critical but opposing tendencies at work in social interaction- Intersubjectivity and Alterity. Intersubjective dialogue occurs between novice and expert, with the aim to reach a shared definition to assist the novice to a state of independence. In the makerspace context an expert may be an assisting adult or alternatively it may be one of the particpants who is particularly knowledgable and skillful in aspects of the project. It is therefore feasible to imagine the 'expert' role shifting within and across participants and projects.

Alterity occurs when discrepancy or conflict occurs between participants ideas, views and understanding, thus it is concerned with the distinction between one's thoughts and that of others'. In collaborative practice, common in Makerspaces participants, if they are to successfully design and develop outcomes with peers need to share common understandings of their way forward. When there are conflicting ideas, change must occur for some or all particpants, thus sparking cognitive development (Babrow & Kuang, 2022; Daniels, 1996b).

Intersubjectivity and Alterity go hand-in hand in the Makerspace context because understanding of others' thinking and knowing during collaborative practical engagement in developing designed solutions is absolutely nesessary. In this space the immediacy of talk and resulting cognitive restructuring is highly desirable.

Interaction between people is a central aspect of cognitive, social and cultural development within a constructivist paradigm. As people interact, they construct their world. Joint problem solving uses debate as a major force in cognitive development (Daniels, 1996a). Constructionism Theory builds on Constructivist Theory by suggesting that deepest learning occurs if learners are constructing something that others will see, critique, and perhaps use (Papert & Harel, 1991). Hence 'doing and talking together' facilitates the potential for powerful learning. Makerspaces are intentionally designed constructionist spaces where young people can design and share projects using 'high tech' and 'low tech' resources and materials while working alongside others (Halverson & Sheridan, 2014; Peppler et al., 2016; Sheridan et al., 2014).

Discussion that takes place during educational activities is dialogue. Dialogue is complex and dynamic, often involves very different cultures, perspectives, ideas and people, and therefore is much more than just talk (Shields & Edwards, 2005). It generally involves the use of words and requires engagement with people (Mercer & Hodgkinson, 2008). During dialogue, the speaker considers the listener's response giving insight into potential variability of meaning. When listener's response aligns with the speaker, understanding in the conversation is enriched (Babrow & Kuang, 2022; Barnes & Todd, 2021). However, when the listener's understanding differs (alterity), the speaker may sense resistance. Beliefs, values and attitudes inform the way people act and interact, however these are not static but change as people read, experience, observe and adapt to new situations. When people collaborate in problem solving situations they 'inter-think' and are able to combine shared understandings, skills and knowledge in creative ways often reaching outcomes well above the capability of each individual (Mercer & Dawes, 2008; Mercer & Littleton, 2007). Problem solving situations involve a dynamic engagement of ideas with dialogue as the principle means to establish shared understanding, testing solutions and reaching agreement or compromise. Dialogue and thinking together are important aspects of life-long learning. Given the collaborative nature of problem solving required to develop technological outcomes designed in makerspaces, the implications are clear. Social dialogue coupled with concrete experiences have a huge potential in assisting people to learn and flourish.

3   Experiential Learning Theory

The Makerspace movement is practical in nature and is a space and an approach where participants can go to design and make, not always using digital tools (Hatzigianni et al., 2021). Although the makerspace movement is a reasonably recent phenomenon, the idea of learning through doing is not. It has its roots in the understanding that experiences facilitate learning and assists the learner to transform themselves and their environment (Durkheim, 1956, 1984). Abdulwahed and Nagy (2009) suggest that Kolb's experiential learning model provides an excellent mechanism for teaching and learning design-based activities. Kolb (1984) promoted experiential learning as a successful pedagogical model within which the learner passes through a series of four stages of a learning cycle. Zewde's (2010) modified version of Kolb's experiential learning cycle (Figure 12.1) begins with the learners' participating in conceptualising and understanding the issues at hand- Abstract Conceptualisation (AC), then subsequently engage in concrete experiences- Concrete Experience (CE). Students move freely into experimentation with new ideas-Active Experimentation (AE) and either accept or reject key ideas. This involves reflection, observation and registration – Observation and Reflection (OR) of the key ideas gleaned from participation in the concrete experience leading to full conceptualisation and accepting – Abstract Conceptualisation (AC) of new ideas developing participants with richer and more advanced knowledge and

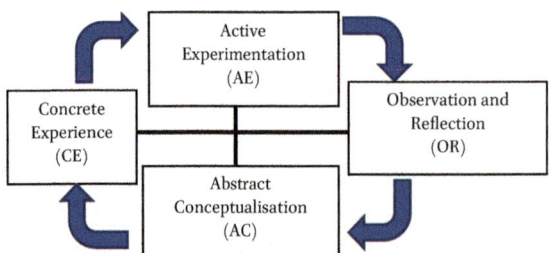

FIGURE 12.1   Zewde's modified version of Kolb's experiential learning model

skills, including the adoption of new materials and technologies. Models are designed to be simple and represent a clean version of reality. In Makerspace as within any technological practice reality is messy as participants revisit and jump forward as their thinking develops. To add to this complexity the cycle may be used multiple times on one or different aspects of a single project.

4   Social Learning Theory

Social learning is defined as the process of collaborative practice within which participants work and learn together through participation in a common activity or process with the aim of reaching an intended goal (Rosenthal & Zimmerman, 1978). This is hardly surprising; humans are instinctively social beings, and can attribute their success as a species on their ability to work and learn together to achieve common goals such as when hunting for food or building shelter. Collective survival depends on society's ability to learn and adapt to our changing environment (Zewde, 2010). Social Learning Theory emphasises a synthesis of behavioural events and the human cognitive process while paying particular attention to social variables (Bandura, 1977). Dunn (1971) states "social learning is an essential component of the absolute goal of life" (p. 181). Social learning theory recognises that socioeconomic development is a cummulative evolutionary process that builds on lessons from each practical experience (Zewde, 2010). Dewey (1951) states that the social process consists of all activities by any of a group's members.

Social participation in projects goes beyond the using of materials, and receiving and following of instructions- this is complying. Participation centers and engages people as learners, thus enabling and empowering them to learn, to conceptualise and undertake a range of related tasks. Bandura (1977) identified that cognitive development and external stimuli operate in a reciprocal relationship within an ever-changing environment. Human behaviour is contingent of individuals' response to their environment and to others. This is constantly changing as a result of the actions of all those involved (Babrow & Kuang, 2022; Rosenthal & Zimmerman, 1978). Experience is a critical part of social learning, thus the two theories are linked. Due to the physical and collaborative nature of makerspace both the above theories go someway to assisting our understanding of the programme's success. However, Participatory Social Learning Development (PSLD) theory appears to combine both the above theories and is also well situated to help us understand the makerspace phenomenon.

5 Participatory Social Learning Development Theory

PSLD theory emerged in the early 1970s as social learning theory as described above. It views socioeconomic development as a continuous process of experimenting by doing and learning both individually and collectively (Zewde, 2010). Zewde (2010) added 'participatory' to ensure that participants are the agents of their own development. Through experiences, reflecting, absorbing new ideas and technologies, concepts are tranformed into purposeful action, providing meaning, which facilitates constructive use of ideas in the interest of individuals and society's social and ecomonic needs (Zewde, 2010). PSLD offers a valuable merging of both experiential learning and social learning theory as it situates learning within social activity.

6 Participatory Social Learning Development in Makerspace Cases

In makerspaces, Kolb's concrete action would be manifest in designing and making technological outcomes, sometimes digital in nature and working collaboratively with peers and experts. This is evident in each of the cases as identifed below.

Westerhof and colleagues in Chapter 6 describe a series of workshops undertaken by elmentary students in rural Africa. Although the students worked individually to design and create their own outcomes social interaction and collaboration were particularly obvious in the first and third phases of each workshop. In the first phases the students explored the topic and their ideas through the asking of questions of the workshop facilitator (expert), leading into student discussion about key ideas of the identified context for each workshop. In the third and final phase of each workshop the students presented their designs to each other, thus identifying, and celebrating diversity of ideas.

Gu & Yang in Chapter 8 describe two cases, the first case a makerspace facility situated within a university that caters for primary and secondary school children as an 'outreach' facility and the second makerspace activity taught in a middle school specialist facility. Both cases aim to focus on social development of the whole child, thus facilitate opportunities for students to be innovative and creative and to solve real-life problems. The role of social interaction is implied both cases. In the university case student teachers are trained to work with students thus developing their interpersonal skills. In the second case set in Tianyi Middle School students again work and are assessed individually, however communication with teachers plays a large role in the activity of designing and developing LED lamps.

In Chapter 5 Núñez-Solís and colleagues' recount of maker education using e-waste to stimulate the maker mindset and circular thinking in a Mexican context provided opportunity for young children to build their technical skills and act on a global issue: electronic waste, thus highlighting the importance of reusing, repairing and repurposing technology and materials. Students aged 10 to 13 worked with a retired engineer (expert) who was the workshop facilitator and undertook series of five activities based on the 5E (Engage, Explore, Explain, Elaborate, and Evaluate) model. The first, second and fifth activities were done individually and focused on grasping the conceptual understanding of what 'Circular Economy' is with the assistance of the expert. Critical thinking and communication skills were practiced in this workshop. The third activity focused on creative and tinkering skills to create an original outcome representing the concept of 'Circular Economy'. The learning goal of the activity series was to practice the 21st century skills of creativity, collaboration, communication, and critical thinking. Throughout the five activities students worked in self-selected sex-based teams of two and with their 'expert' facilitator to meet the session goals. Of particular note in this chapter is the prominence of discussion facilitated by the 'expert'.

Pijls, Van Eijck and Bredeweg in Chapter 4 present a number of vignettes all of which show evidence of collaboration. The first five describe a safe community space in public libraries for children, aged from 8–12, from low socio-economic families to design and make both digital and material outcomes. Although children frequently work on individual projects a number of them talked about sharing ideas and getting assistance from both the makerspace coaches and other children in the programme and sharing their new learning with their families. Pijl et al.'s chapter also reports on the setting up and support of this makerspace movement (Maakplaats021). This involved the development of a training programme for library staff to become the makerspace coaches, mentoring of student teachers to assist the makerspace coaches, developing both technical and pedagogical skills of the coaches and collaboration within the community to establish and maintain this library based programme.

In Chapter 9 Pols and Hut's case is situated in the tertiary space bachelor's programme at Delft University, The Netherlands. Their first-year learning outcomes include student success in the design, realisation and testing a physical apparatus or manufacturing or measuring process and the ability to cooperate and work effectively in groups. In their second year, learning outcomes also indicate collaborative design as successful students will be able to design and devise an instrument that measures and digitally stores or displays a physical quantity, make 2D (vector) and 3D models, and work effectively in small groups.

Kwon's Chapter 7, situated in South Korea, presents an investigation into the technology teachers' professional learning community for maker education. The four themes drawn from the study clearly illustrate the social and participatory nature of the Makerspace movement from a teachers' perspective. These are:

- *sharing and communication*, technology teachers are makers, and practitioners who share ideas and learn from each other,
- *diffusion and movement*, technology teachers' professional learning community is focused on sharing and communication of ideas,
- *experienced makers and collaboration,* thus presenting a balanced interest and practical ability in both hardware and software parts,
- *active,* teachers are active in practicing and spreading the philosophy and practice of maker education and technology education.

In Chapter 3 Holm Kanstrup et al., focus on the participatory aspect of the Makerspace movement. They indicate that participatory design aims to give voice to those affected by the result of the design and that they benefit. This chapter also focuses on empowering technology teachers and principals to set up and sustain a makerspace practice within their school or communities. The study identified six steps to this process within which social participation is obvious.

The first involved the participants understanding the complex nature of the makerspace initiative. An existing makerspace manager (expert) outlined ongoing initiatives, facilitated a discussion about makerspace gave a tour of an existing facility enabling participants to talk to existing teachers. This activity culminated in the collaborative design of a community-based training facility shared within and across schools and their local communities. In the second step teachers participated in a collaborative makerspace activity, thus facilitating their undertaking of design process which focused their understanding of the central role collaborative learning plays in this space. This session culminated with a facilitated discussion of the role of teachers in the makerspace movement. The third step presented a state-of-the-art overview of research followed by a facilitated discussion to situate maker education within the broader political landscape from a macro perspective. The fourth step involved school staff and external partners and represented a shift into the micro space within which participants reflected on and design the ideal makerspace, share with colleagues from the same school community collaboratively developed a strategy for implementation. In this session, participants also learned to communicate convincingly their initiatives. The fifth step involved each group presenting the implementation plan to other groups present and a higher ranked education official aimed at local policy and obtaining structural support. The sixth and final stage involved receiving practical insight by the visiting of another makerspace focusing on the practical, such as equipment purchased, safety and maintenance, relevant regulations, challenges and opportunities experienced by the makerspace. This visit concluded with a few practical activities aimed to help participants' evaluation of resources. The session concluded with a collaborative representation of their implementation plans, with adjustments made and collaboratively identified how their plan could be applied to their initiative.

7 Types and Levels of Social Learning across the Cases

The above section identifies the social and collaborative aspects within Makerspace and in each of the cases. Now let's look closely at the nature and scope of social learning evident across the cases. Using Rosenthal and Zimmerman's (1978) definition of social learning as the process of collaborative practice within which participants work and learn together through participation in a common activity with the aim of reaching an intended goal, this section explores specific aspects of social learning evident in the cases. A modifed version of Bronfenbrenner's (1979) Ecological Systems Theory (Figure 12.2) is used to frame this section. This model was originally developed to show how each aspect of a child's environment influences their development and how aspects impact each other. It is modified for this chapter to organise discussion related to social interaction with the makerspace movement. The learner is the central component in both Bronfenbrenner's Ecological Systems Theory and the participatory and social learning theories mentioned previously this chapter.

Four of the cases presented: Chapter 6 by Westerhof et al., Chapter 5 by Núñez-Solís et al., Chapter 4 by Pijls et al. (vignettes 1–4) and Gu and Yang's second case in chapter 8 are situated within classroom or community training programmes for school-aged children. They sit within Bronfenbrenner's microsystem of influence because the children are the primary learners who have numerous layers of influence encompassing them including their teachers, makerspace coaches, community hubs such as libraries and schools and the wider system that educates them including education policy makers. The case from Delft, Chapter 9 by Pols & Hut, is set in a tertiary setting and also occurs in Bronfenbrenners' microsystem of influence with science and engineering students. It is somewhat unusual to apply Bronfenbrenner' Ecological Systems Theory to tertiary students as it usually refers the development of younger child, however the students in this case study are the 'primary learners' who also have other layers of influence on them- their lecturers, the university and the wider tertiary education system, just like their primary and secondary school aged counterparts.

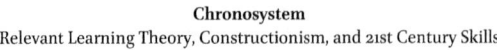

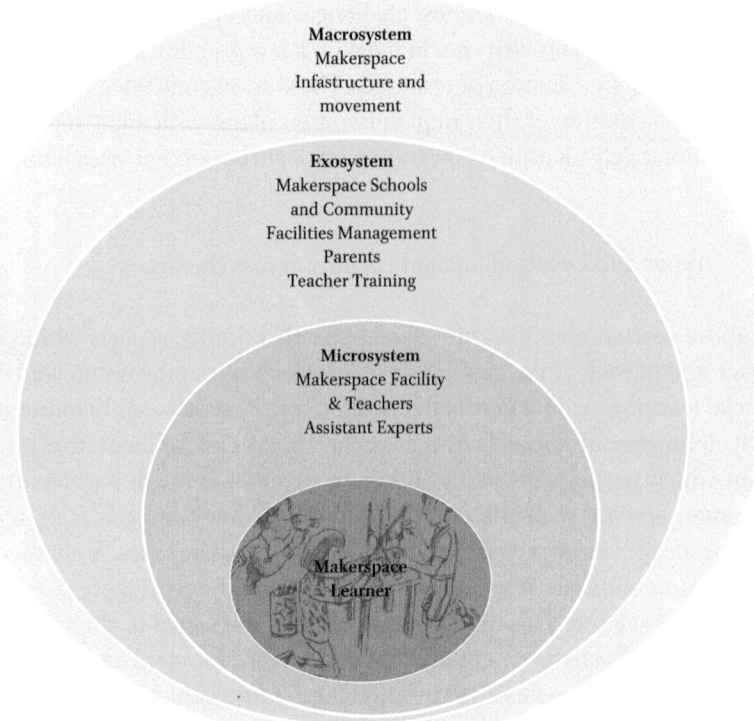

Chronosystem
Relevant Learning Theory, Constructionism, and 21st Century Skills

Macrosystem
Makerspace
Infastructure and
movement

Exosystem
Makerspace Schools
and Community
Facilities Management
Parents
Teacher Training

Microsystem
Makerspace Facility
& Teachers
Assistant Experts

Makerspace
Learner

FIGURE 12.2   Makerspace through a Modified Bronfenbrenner's Ecological Systems Theory

The Kwon chapter, Chapter 7 and Pijls et al. vignettes 6–8 are set in the makerspace teachers and coaches professional learning community, thus situated in the Exosystem. Kwon's chapter describes technology teachers as maker practitioners and Pijls et al. discuss the training of their makerspace coaches along with some student teachers who complete a practicum in their makerspaces thus both sitting just beyond the microsystem. Gu & Yang's Chapter 8 – first case is interesting. On the one hand it is situated within the Exosystem as it provides teacher support to teach students in makerspace activity, thus outside the immediate circle of influence for primary learners. However, students are also present in this case study as they are brought into the facility to participate in makerspace activity, thus situating it in the Microsystem. Thus illustrating that cases may not be situated exclusively in one of Bronfenbrenner's systems, but span across them.

In Chapter 3, Holm Kanstrup et al. presents a model for establishing and sustaining the makerspace infastructure and is situated within the macrosystem of influence as it founded on common overarching values and beliefs about makerspace education. Chapter 2 Gu & Yang describe the makerspace developments within China and is also situated within Bronfenbrenner's macrosystem as it discussed the movement development in China, however it could also be situated in the Chronosystem. The Chronosystem is defined as life transitions and sociohistorical events, and is relevant as it recognises the need for nations to have all citizens well equipped for life and economic development in the 21st century and beyond, which drives the makerspace movement. In Chapter 2, Gu & Yang link the makerspace movement to China's historical and political ideology, thus stradling between the two outer systems. Another relevant aspect of the Chronosystem is education theory that underpins action and practice of the maker movement, thus discussion and consideration of relevant learning theories discussed earlier in this chapter are also situated within Bronfenbrenner's Chronosystem.

7.1   *Social Interaction in the Makerspace Microsystem*

This section draws on the case studies of Westerhof et al., Pijls et al., Núñez-Solís et al., Gu & Yang and Pols & Hut. The first three involved children in community makerspace facilities. In the cases of Gu & Yang Case 1 occurs in community facility situated in a university. Case 2 is situated within a school programme. Pols & Hut investigated the maker approach in a university setting for tertiary students.

At the Microsystem the social learning characteristics underpinning teaching and learning occur from the simple transmission of information such as when giving instructions to a higher level thinking and engagement such as when students design, construct, reflect and evaluate their performance and achievement. As Einarsson and Hertzum (2020) suggested makerspace activity starts with the tranmission of information, which is usually structured around the giving of detailed instructions. In our cases transmission of information occured for the giving of instructions. This usually occured face to-face but in some cases via video, thanks to the COVID-19 global pandemic. Safety instructions were also given via transmission in the Pols & Hut case. In their study Rayna and Striukova (2021) identified the teaching of safety skills were the only skills specifically mentioned by all their partipants. Explanations of the status-quo and the setting up of the authentic context to be studied also occurred through direct transmission of information in all five cases within the microsystem. Some of the students in these case studies were also involved in listening to explanations of recognised experts. The transmissive phase of the process assists with Abstract Conceptualisation stage of Zewde's (2010) modified version of Kolb's Experiential Learning Model.

Once underway activity involved collaborative play, tinkering and designing and making for the students some of which was quite structured and others more iterative. This approach saw the participants agents of their own learning in line with PSLD (Zewde, 2010). In both the Gu & Yang cases students are involved in creative problem solving to develop a range of outcomes. In the Núñez-Solís case students were encouraged to become agents of change through consideration of Circular Ecomony thinking. Their groups consisted of people with varied skills. Aligned with constructionist theory (Papert & Harel, 1991), students collaboratively designed, explored and developed artefacts to meet the identifed issue or problem. In Pols & Hut case time was spent developing a collaborative culture to ensure students were able to work successfully together. In Pijls et al. case vignettes 1–4 students worked individually however they also interacted with their peers for assistance and feedback. Rayna and Striukova (2021) state that a range of collaborative and cooperative skills are developed through the makerspaces, however conscious effort is needed to do so. In this phase the Concrete Experience and Active Experimentation stages of Kolb's experienctial learning model were met.

Continuing the Active Experientation stage, another key aspect to students' social learning in the makerspace in the microsystem involves a higher level of thinking through teacher questioning, critical debate between students and with their teachers to facilitate critical problems solving and developing empathy of those who are impacted on the issue in hand. In the Pols & Hut case teachers took a socratic approach to their questioning, encouring students' critical thinking about their own and other's ideas. In Núñez-Solís et al. students explored circular thinking in relation to environmental issues. Snape and Fox-Turnbull (2013) and Fox-Turnbull (2003) identifed the importance of authentic contexts within technology education to enhance students' learning.

Aligning with Kolb's Observation and Reflection stage, the final phase identifed in each of the cases at this level involved the students presenting their outcomes and reflecting on their process and practice. In PSLD reflection is considered a critical component of social learning (Zewde, 2010). Even when students work as individuals as in this phase, there is a social element to it. The very nature of presenting design ideas and outcomes to others is social. When working collaboratively this is obvious. Teams need to work together to identify what and how to present their outcomes. They may well share the task. When working individually aspects of social learning are less obvious, however as in Gu & Yang's cases presenting to others needs consideration of audience. Individuals also need to be aware of and acknowledge those who have assisted them and or are impacted by their designed outcomes, such as stakeholders. In constructionism the sharing of designs and design ideas plays a pivotal role in students' learning. The sharing and talking about designed artefacts that are personally meaningful facilitates a deeper understanding of materials, ideas and construction possibilities (Keune et al., 2019).

7.2   *Social Interaction in the Makerspace Exosystem*

This section draws of the case studies of Kwon, aspects of Gu & Yang's first case and Pijls et al.'s vignettes 6–8 as they are situated in the teacher professional space, one level removed from the individual students' learning. In Kwon's case cooperation and sharing are two foundational beliefs that underpin maker education in South Korea. Teachers in the learning community at the focus of this study played a leading role in the field of maker education in Korea. The case is situated in a movement aimed at spreading the making culture. In the initial stages this group held regular meetings, seminars, and lectures. This involved transmission of knowledge as in the microsystem above and also situated the Abstract Conceptualisation stage in Zewde's (2010) version of Kolb's Experiential Learning Model. Participants were assisted in the identification of a common understanding and purpose for makerspace education.

In these meetings teachers were given opportunities to talk about issues and difficulties encountered and explore and develop solutions together. This provided opportunity for learning not available at universities or teacher education institutions and illustrates at shift to Kolb's Concrete Experience stage as teachers explored concrete ideas and solutions to their issues and difficulties. The open sharing in this phase motived participants to reciprocate the assistance recieved. Teachers reported that they became makers themselves in their communities by designing, developing and conducting workshops and voluntary professional development sessions for others, thus moving through to Active Experientation of learning shared and gained at the seminar series. Subsequent meetings also provided teachers opportunities to reflect on and share their experiences both from classroom teaching and their assistance of others (Observation and Reflection phase). Aspects of Gu & Yang's first case are also situated in the Exosystem as it describes a team of people who provide a platform for training tertiary students in makerspace education. At this level the team at the Tsinghua makerspace facility worked collaboratively to design and develop skills training, plan and implement 'creater marathons', develop tools for brainstorming and facilitate the use of expert guests to share their ideas to broaden their students' horizons. In addition they have incubated many projects for students. In providing this range of activities and tools they facilitate a journey through Kolb's Abstract Conceptualisation, Concrete Experience and Active Experimentation stages for the school and tertiary students who come into their centre. They also engaged in observation and reflection when evaluating and critiquing their programme for future improvements. The Pijls et al.'s latter vignettes have an underlying theme of pedagogy as they focus on developing professional skills and knowledge of the maker coaches and student teachers. Coaches used reflection and experimentation to consider and develop effective strategies for facilitating their workshops, thus they were also situated across Kolb's Abstract Conceptualisation, Concrete Experience and Active Experimentation stages. Harrington (2019) suggests that when some people participate in maker communites their main motivation is to be and for others just to make. In these cases collaboration and the formation of learning community are emphasised. Collaboration and communication amongst participants leads to improved outcomes and increased capability.

7.3   *Social Interaction in the Makerspace Macrosystem*

This section draws on the case studies reported by Holm Kanstrup et al. Chapter 3, and Gu & Yang's Chapter 2. Both are situated in Bronfenbrenner's macrosystem. Holm Kanstrup et al. propose a framework for the development of a sustained robust makerspace infastructure in Denmark with a focus on the sustainability of makerspace infastructure. This case used the Scandinavian Participatory Design approach to makerspace development which emphasises direct and continuous involvement and voice to stakeholders. The case describes a six step framework leading towards sustainability of the makerspace initiative used in eleven workshops in eleven municipalities. Gu & Yang's chapter explores and describes the makerspace movement in China and its underpinning philosophy and purpose.

The paragraphs below use the Holm Kanstrup chapter to illustrate Kolb's steps within the Macrosystem. Unlike the preceding two systems, where transmission of information in the early stage played a critical role in establishing a context, activity in the Holm Kanstrup et al. case began with a brief explanation of vision and objectives, followed by discussion. The Abstract Conceptualisation stage continued with a sharing of knowledge and experiences within and between makerspaces and other infastructural levels such as makerspace managers, school principals, municipal and govenment personel. Movement into the Concrete Experience stage began with a tour of existing makerspaces where they interacted with teachers and students. The makerspace manager also shared meaningful student experiences along with technical and organisation requirements of running a space. After the tour participants collaboratively planned and shared a community-based training programme for their local makerspaces (Active Experientation stage). This activity was situated within the constructionist paradigm as participants drew on their experiences to construct their plans. Keune et al. (2019) and Papert (1993) state that projects within a constructivist paradigm must be meaningful and present evidence of learning. The makerspace plans were both. The Active Experientation stage continued through the second step presented in this case. Staff from participating schools who were not at the first workshop and from a range of disciplines experienced collaborative hands-on makerspace activity with the aim to developing their understanding makerspace's educational potential.

The third step in the framework moved into Kolb's Observation and Reflection phase as particpants were presented with 'state-of-the art' overview of international research on maker education' followed by discussion aimed at situating maker education with a political, economic and social context and developing shared understanding of makerspaces.

Step Four took all participants except the director of education through an activity asking individuals to reflect on their dream facility as individuals and then in small school/community based groups share, identifying, and discuss ideas. This included identifying existing and required resources, exploration of avenues of assistance and ultimately visually presenting ideas to other groups and their Director of Education. The fourth to sixth steps ensured participants were able to implement their planned makerspace within managerial, polical, local, practical and physical constraints of each situation.

As we know PSLD states that participants must be agents of their own development (Zewde, 2010). Participants in this case study were agents of change within the macrosystem as each was assisted to action their planned makerspaces. There is little doubt that learning undertaken in this case was social in nature. Learning occured within and across varied groups and levels of people

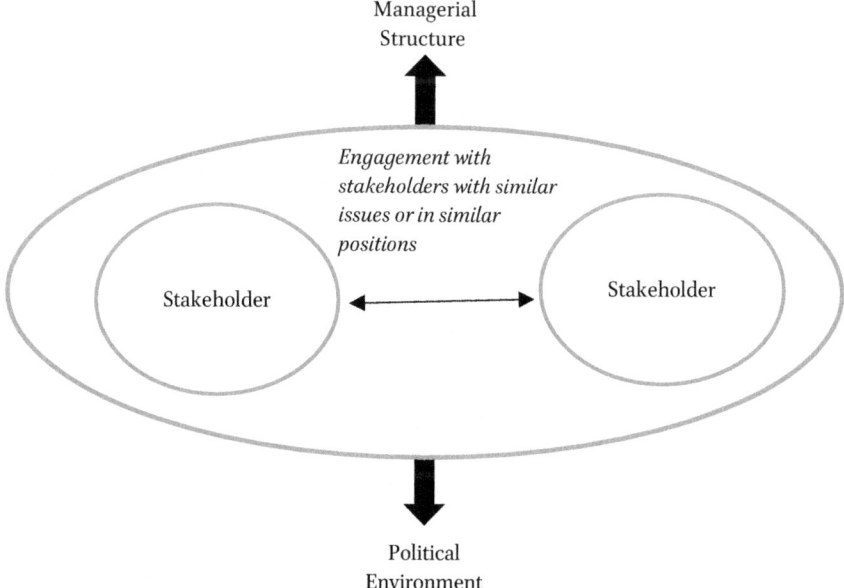

FIGURE 12.3   A macrosystem for makerspaces

as illustrated in Figure 12.3. Groups of stakeholders shared with each other, but also they were able to understand the political and managerial possibilities and constraints, thus ensuring a deeper understanding of developing and sustaining the maker movement.

8   Conclusion

All cases illustrated were examples of PSLD and involved learning aligned to experiential learning theory following Zewde's (2010) modified version of Kolb's Experiential Learning Model. The cases presented in this book clearly illustrate that cooperation and collaboration contribute to participant's learning and sense of ownership, not just within Bronfenbrenner's microsystem, at the classroom or makerspace level, but also across the exo and macrosystems. Learners at all levels were agents of their own learning. Working collaboratively, sharing ideas with others, presenting developed artefacts and reflecting on their own and others' outcomes.

All cases involved participants in designing, making and modifying outcomes, most collaboratively starting with Abstract Conceptualisation. It was interesting to find that most cases involved some direct transmission of information. Although not commonly associated with constructionist principles knowledge transmission played an important role in these cases. This is a timely reminder that constructionist learning does not occur organically without preparation and planning in makerspace facilities. Initial stages of any project within all systems requires transmission of instructions to assist the setting of the scene and has an important role in keeping particpants safe. However it is clear from the cases that early transmission of information and instructions did not diminish partipicants agency or sense of empowerment; in fact it possibly enhanced it as transmission of information ensured all participants had the necessary information to be empowered learners and agents of change.

When undertaking makerspace activities particpants were also engaged in the Concrete Experience and/or Active Experientation stages, however the nature of activity differed across Bronfenbrenner's systems. In the Microsystem children and tertiary students designed and made artefacts. The Exosystem saw teachers engaged in makerspace activity with the aim of developing a shared understanding of, planning and implementing the makerspaces in their school or develop opportunity for professional development. Finally in the Macrosystem concrete experiences and active experimentation occurred to ensure the design and development of sustainable maker movement infastructure and policy.

Sharing outcomes and reflecting on outcome success and failure was common to all cases, across all levels. In most cases aspects of observation and reflection were undertaken orally, through discussion and sharing, however in one case it was in the form of a written report. Observation and reflection enables participants to engage in dialogue through articulating their processes, artefacts and learning, thus talking together facilitates the potential for powerful learning.

In conclusion the cases presented in this book strongly indicate the important role social interaction has in the makerspace movement at all levels of particpation and structural organisation. The nature and purpose of the social interaction changed across Bronfenbrenner's systems of influence on the learners central to the movement- our children. However what did not change is the impact social engagement had on motivation, empowerment and engagement for particpants. This acts as a timely reminder of the value of social interaction has on practical learning and reminds us that rich opportunities for social interaction must be embedded in the foundations of all makerspace facilities, programmes and the movement as a whole.

References

Abdulwahed, M., & Nagy, Z. K. (2009). Applying Kolb experiential learning cycle for laboratory education. *Journal of Engineering Education, 98*(3), 285–292.

Babrow, A. S., & Kuang, K. (2022). Problematic integration theory. In D. O. Braithwaite & P. Schrodt (Eds.), *Engaging theories in interpersonal communication: Multiple perspectives* (pp. 64–75). Routledge, Taylor & Frances.

Bandura, A. (1977). *Social learning theory*. Prentice Hall.

Barnes, D., & Todd, F. (2021). *Communication and learning revisitied: Making meaning of talk*. Taylor & Francis.

Bronfenbrenner, U. (1979). *The ecology of human development: Experiments by nature and design*. Harvard University Press.

Daniels, H. (Ed.). (1996a). *The genesis of higher mental functions*. Routledge.

Daniels, H. (1996b). *An introduction to Vygotsky*. Routledge.

Dewey, J. (1951). *Democracy and education: An introduction to the philosophy of education*. The McMillan Printing Company.

Dunn, E. (1971). *Economic and social development: A process of social learning*. The Johns Hopkins University Press.

Durkheim, E. (1956). *Education and sociology-translated and introduction by S.D. Fox.* The Free Press.

Durkheim, E. (1984). *The division of labour in society.* The McMillan Company.

Einarsson, A. M., & Hertzum, M. (2020). How is learning scaffolded in library maker-spaces? *International Journal of Child-Computer Interaction, 26.* https://doi.org/10.1016/j.ijcci.2020.100199

Fox-Turnbull, W. (2003). *The place of authentic technological practice and assessment in technology education* [Master of Teaching and Learning thesis, Christchurch College of Education].

Halverson, E. R., & Sheridan, K. (2014). The maker movement in education. *Harvard Educational Review, 84*(4), 495–504.

Harrington, E. G. (2019). *Academic libraries and public engagement with science and technology.* Chandos Publishing, Elsevier.

Hatzigianni, M., Stevenson, M., Falloon, G., Bower, M., & Forbes, A. (2021). Young children's design thinking skills in makerspaces. *International Journal of Child-Computer Interaction, 27,* 1–11. https://doi.org/10.1016/j.ijcci.2020.100216

Keune, A., Peppler, K., & Wohlwend, K. (2019). Recognition in makerspaces: Supporting opportunities for women to "make" a STEM career. *Computers in Human Behaviour, 99,* 368–380.

Kolb, D. (1984). *Experiential learning: Experience as a source of learning and development.* Prentice Hall.

Mercer, N., & Dawes, L. (2008). The value of exploratory talk. In N. Mercer & S. Hodgkinson (Eds.), *Exploring talk in school* (pp. 55–71). Sage Publications Ltd.

Mercer, N., & Hodgkinson, S. (Eds.). (2008). *Exploring talk in school.* Sage Publications Ltd.

Mercer, N., & Littleton, K. (2007). *Dialogue and the development of children's thinking: A sociocultural approach.* Routledge.

Papert, S. (1993). *The children's machine: Rethinking school in the age of the computer.* Basic Books.

Papert, S., & Harel, I. (1991). *Constructionism.* Ablex Publishing Corporation.

Peppler, K., Halverson, E., & Kafai, Y. B. (2016). *Makeology: Makerspaces as learning environments* (1st ed.). Routledge. https://doi.org/10.4324/9781315726519

Rayna, T., & Striukova, L. (2021). Fostering skills for the 21st century: The role of Fab labs and makerspaces. *Technological Forecasting and Social Change, 164.* https://doi.org/10.1016/j.techfore.2020.120391

Rosenthal, T. L., & Zimmerman, B. J. (1978). *Social learning and cognition.* Elsevier Science & Technology.

Schrock, A. R. (2014). Education in disguise: Culture of a hacker and maker space. *Inter-Actions: UCLA Journal of Education and Information Studies, 10*(1). https://doi.org/10.5070/D4101020592

Sheridan, K., Halverson, E. R., Litts, B., Brahms, L., Jacobs-Priebe, L., & Owens, T. (2014). Learning in the making: A comparative case study of three makerspaces. *Harvard Educational Review, 84*(4), 505–531.

Shields, C., & Edwards, M. (2005). *Dialogue is not just talk: A new ground for educational leadership*. Peter Lang Publishing Inc.

Snape, P., & Fox-Turnbull, W. (2013). Perspectives of authenticity: Implementation in technology education. *International Journal of Technology and Design Education, 23*(1), 51–68. https://doi.org/10.1007/s10798-011-9168-2

Vygotsky, L. S. (1978). *Mind in society: The development of higher psychological processes* (M. Cole, V. John-Steiner, S Scribner, & E. Souberman, Eds.). Harvard University Press.

Zewde, A. (2010). *Sorting Africa's developmental puzzle: The participatory social learning theory as an alternative approach*. University Press of America.

CHAPTER 13

Reflecting on Maker Education as a Potential Context for the Development of Spatial Ability

Jeffrey Buckley

Abstract

Based on significant evidence of the benefit of increasing learners' levels of spatial ability, its development has become a focal agenda for many educators, educational researchers, and educational policy makers. While to date spatial ability has received little attention in research surrounding maker environments, maker education has the potential to be a particularly auspicious context for its development within learners. In this chapter, the seven case studies of maker education in this edited volume from Kenya, Mexico, China, the Netherlands (×2), Denmark, and South Korea are reflected upon through this specific lens. Each case study provoked a different dimension to this reflection, with questions of how spatial ability relates to "making", how it's development should be prioritised against other already noted aims of maker education, and what could be the implications of making spatial ability development an explicit goal of maker education inductively arising. These questions are unpacked, and it is envisioned that this reflection will underpin ensuing advances on if and how spatial ability development should be further examined or integrated into maker education environments.

Keywords

maker education – spatial ability – visualisation – cognitive development – goals of education – spatialisation of curricula

1   Introduction

Over the last decade, the "maker" label has become attached to a broad range of educational activities associated with craft and construction (Godhe et al., 2019). These range from formal to informal activities, include "make" elements that are both physical (e.g., kit assembly) and virtual (e.g., 3-dimensional modelling), and involve the use of a spectrum of tools from basic hand-tools through to rapid prototyping and automation. Maker education as a concept has to a degree grown in ambiguity, and consideration of this is an important preface to the statement that a direct relationship between maker education and spatial ability has not been the subject of much, if any, empirical investigation to date. To illustrate this, a search on Google Scholar for "maker education" AND "spatial ability" at the time of writing this chapter (19th of February, 2022) returned only 23 unique manuscripts. Unfortunately, of these, two were book chapters which I could not get access to, and two were articles published in Korean and one was an edited book published in Italian which are languages I cannot read. Of the remaining 18 published works,[1] only 4 described an empirical link between spatial ability and maker related activities, of which 3 were qualitative observations (Bhaduri et al., 2021; Boyle, 2019; Simpson & Kastberg, 2022) and 1 was a quantitative post-test only boxplot from an undescribed instrument purporting to measure "spatial thinking skills" (Akshay et al., 2018).

Investigating this potential relationship could be particularly fruitful given the significant evidence underpinning the relationship between spatial ability and Science, Technology, Engineering, and Mathematics (STEM) in general (Wai et al., 2009) and the growing evidence of its specific importance in technology education (Buckley et al., 2022), a subject area with much commonality with maker education. While a direct association between maker education as a concept and spatial ability has been speculated, theorised, qualitatively observed, and identified as desirable, it has not yet been the focal subject of any formal investigation. That said, there is much empirical evidence associating spatial ability and signature activities of maker education such as craft (Bailey & Sims, 2014) and design (Lin, 2016) in non-maker specific contexts, a notable distinction given the importance of context and environment both in and for learning. Before delving into a reflection on the maker education case studies in this volume through the lens of spatial ability development, as spatial ability has not been extensively studied in this context it is worth framing what spatial ability is as an intelligence construct so as its potential place in maker environments can be better considered.

2 Framing Spatial Ability

Schneider and McGrew (2018), who together for the last decade have been leading the development of the Cattell-Horn-Carroll (CHC) model of intelligence – the current most comprehensive framework of cognitive abilities – lay out that among other criteria the qualification of a cognitive ability requires that it is both plausibly linked to functions that evolve to help humans survive and reproduce and that it should have practical use or validity. From an educational perspective the core focus has been on defining spatial ability as a psychometric construct and investigating its predictability and explanatory power for desirable outcomes such as performance and retention. It is here where this chapter will centre and how the practical use and validity of spatial ability will be discussed. However, it is worth acknowledging the evolutionary lens offered by Geary (2022) who comments that "from an evolutionary perspective, spatial abilities are an aspect of folk physics that is supported by brain and cognitive systems that enable organisms to engage in the physical world". In discussing the evolutionary functions of spatial ability, Geary (2022) predominantly focuses on navigation and wayfinding, movement detection, and closure, which relate closely to Schneider and McGrew's criterion that spatial abilities can be linked to helping humans survive and reproduce. Geary's (2022) comments on multiple facets of spatial ability also offers a nice introduction to how spatial ability is understood today. It is a broad cognitive domain constituting of several narrow and discrete cognitive factors associated with the processing of spatial information.

The construct of spatial ability as an intellectual factor was first described by Sir Francis Galton lein in the late 1800s. Specifically, Galton referred to a "visualising faculty" and even at this early stage Galton's observations were that spatial ability was multidimensional (Galton, 1880). For example, Galton described his visualising faculty as encompassing capacities such as being able to recall a clear and complete mental image of any recently examined object – a skill which today relates to the spatial factor of imagery – and to being able to mentally visualise that object freely from any perspective – a skill which, depending on whether egocentric or allocentric reasoning is involved and whether the object is simple or complex, would today relate to either the visualisation, mental rotation, or spatial orientation spatial factors. Since Galton's pioneering work, the construct of spatial ability was evolved during the 1900s through a series of seminal empirical psychometric studies, with each adding to or refining its dimensions. Three central research questions guided this period of inquiry (Eliot & Smith, 1983). Initial focus was placed on examining whether spatial ability had incremental validity beyond a general intelligence (g) factor, i.e., was there a cognitive ability associated with the processing of spatial information that was independent from and practically useful beyond general intelligence. Next, after this was established, emphasis shifted to determining the sub-components of spatial ability. Finally, following the identification of a series of these sub-components, known as "spatial factors", efforts were invested into determining the extent to which these related to each other and to other cognitive factors not associated with spatial ability. Significant contributions in this time, for example and chronologically, came from Thurstone (1936), Holzinger and Harman (1938), Guilford and Lacey (1947), French (1951), Guilford, Fruchter and Zimmerman (1952), Zimmerman (1953), Lohman (1979), Lohman, Pellegrino, Alderton, and Regian (1987), Horn (1988), and Carroll (1993). These works illustrate how the language associated with spatial ability changed over time and how, depending on the nature of the testing instruments used, different spatial factors were observable.

Today, within the CHC theory, spatial ability is formally termed "visual-processing" and is described as "the ability to make use of simulated mental imagery to solve problems — perceiving, discriminating, manipulating, and recalling nonlinguistic images in the 'mind's eye'" (Schneider & McGrew, 2018, p. 125). Others have described spatial ability as "the ability to generate, retain, and manipulate abstract visual images" (Lohman, 1979, p. 126), the "innate ability to visualise that a person has before any formal training has occurred" (Sorby, 1999, p. 21), and as "the ability to visualise, manipulate and interrelate real or imaginary configurations in space" (Gaughran, 2002, p. 3). In contrast to a broad descriptor, Sutton and Allen (2011, p. 5) describe spatial ability relative to specific task performance in saying that it is "the performance on tasks that require: (a) the mental rotation of objects; (b) the ability to understand how objects appear in different positions; and (c) the ability to conceptualise how objects relate to each other in space". Additionally, Wai et al. (2009, p. 827) define spatial ability through a predictability lens, referring to it as "a salient psychological characteristic among adolescents who subsequently go on to achieve advanced educational and occupational credentials in (Science, Technology, Engineering, and Mathematics) STEM".

Given these different definitions, it is important to consider Meehl's (2006) noting of two issues in the context of intelligence constructs in that verbal definitions such as those just cited are neither sufficiently comprehensive nor do they command consensus. The previous descriptions, while not incorrect, are not complete. Instead, Meehl's (2006) recommendation is to define such constructs empirically, with verbalisations instead being considered as descriptive. To this end, spatial ability is currently best defined through empirical frameworks such as the CHC theory. In this framework, spatial ability is defined as a second-order (broad) cognitive factor, reflective of a number of first-order (narrow) spatial factors. In the most currently iteration of the CHC theory (Schneider & McGrew, 2018, pp. 126–128), 12 narrow spatial factors are listed and described as:

1. Visualisation: The ability to perceive complex patterns and mentally simulate how they might look when transformed (e.g., rotated, twisted, inverted, changed in size, partially obscured).

2. Speeded rotation: The ability to solve problems quickly by using mental rotation of simple images.

3. Imagery: The ability to voluntarily mentally produce very vivid images of objects, people, or events that are not actually present.

4. Flexibility of closure: The ability to identify a visual figure or pattern embedded in a complex distracting or disguised visual pattern or array, when one knows in advance what the pattern is.

5. Closure speed: The ability to quickly identify and access a familiar, meaningful visual object stored in long-term memory from incomplete or obscured (e.g., vague, partially obscured, disguised, disconnected) visual cues of the object, without knowing in advance what the object is.

6. Visual memory: The ability to remember complex images over short periods of time (less than 30 seconds).

7. Spatial scanning: The ability to quickly and accurately survey (visually explore) a wide or complicated spatial field or pattern with multiple obstacles, and identify a target configuration or identify a path through the field to a target endpoint.

8. Serial perceptual integration: The ability to recognize an object after only parts of it are shown in rapid succession.

9. Length estimation: The ability to visually estimate the length of objects (without using measuring instruments).

10. Perceptual illusions: The ability not to be fooled by visual illusions.

11. Perceptual alternations: Consistency in the rate of alternating between different visual perceptions.

12. Perceptual speed: The speed and fluency with which similarities or differences in visual stimuli can be distinguished.

To operationalise this definition in empirical investigations (which is important as it is operational definitions that evidence of the importance of spatial ability directly relate to), spatial ability can be modelled as a latent variable. It is itself not directly measurable or observable. Instead, data is collected through the administration of psychometric tests to a cohort of participants which are indicative of a number (usually at least three) of first-order spatial factors (listed above). These narrow spatial factors are directly measurable and through factor analytic methods the "shared" variance is defined as spatial ability (cf., Buckley, 2020).

In practice, studies examining the relationship between what they describe as spatial ability and an educational outcome such as performance or retention often are not this comprehensive. Instead, one spatial factor is usually the subject of investigation which is often the visualisation factor when participants are adolescents or older. Other factors have also been studied, just to a lesser extent and for this chapter the visualisation factor will be a focus (cf. Buckley et al., 2018). The visualisation factor is the strongest loading first-order spatial factor on the broader second-order factor of spatial ability (Ebisch et al., 2012; Schneider & McGrew, 2018). In other words, it is the most characteristic factor for describing spatial ability more broadly. Like spatial ability itself, it is best described empirically rather than verbally. However, as this is a directly observable cognitive ability its empirical definition is not through a framework, but it is defined based on the instruments used as indicators of it. As described above, the visualisation factor involves the mental manipulation of complex geometries, where complex often means 3-dimensional, and this manipulation can involve mental rotations, mental cutting, mental folding, etc. Good practice would involve the use of a number of instruments, each of which involving a different one of these mental operations, and visualisation would be defined as a composite score across each of these. Figure 13.1 provides an example item from one common psychometric test of visualisation, the Purdue Spatial Visualisation Test: Visualisation of Rotations (PSVT:R: Guay, 1977). In the PSVT:R, participants are shown a stimulus geometry in an initial state (top left) and an end state (top right). The end state is derived by the rotation of the object by up to three 90° rotations. In Figure 13.1, one 90° rotation clockwise about the y-axis brought the stimulus geometry from its initial state to the end state. A different geometry is then provided (centre) and the task is to apply the same rotation(s) that the stimulus geometry moves through to it, in this case one 90° rotation clockwise about the y-axis. Five possible solutions are then provided (bottom) and one of these is the correct end state. The participant must indicate which they believe it to be. In Figure 13.1 the correct answer is "D".

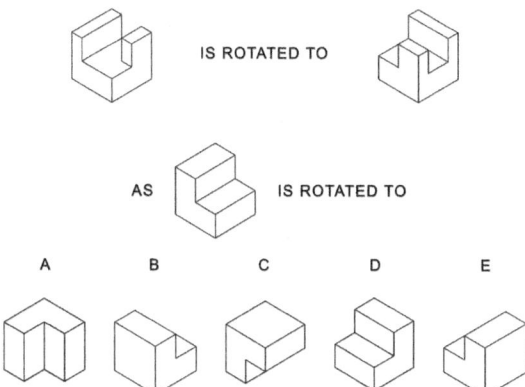

FIGURE 13.1   Example item from the instructions of the Purdue Spatial Visualisation
Test: Visualisation of Rotations (PSVT:R: Guay, 1977)

While there are multiple tests which can serve as operational definitions for spatial ability, the PSVT:R is a common example and one which has been used previously in technology education (Buckley et al., 2019; Julià & Antolì, 2018; Julià & Antolí, 2016; Lane & Sorby, 2021; Šafhalter et al., 2022). It is performance on this test and other similar tests (see also Figure 13.2) that is used to indicate learners levels of spatial ability, and this cognitive ability is particularly useful to education researchers, educators and education policy makers as it (1) is predictive of STEM outcomes such as educational performance and the attainment of advanced qualifications (Wai et al., 2009), (2) can be developed through "spatialised" pedagogical approaches (Newcombe, 2017) and dedicated interventions (Uttal et al., 2013), and (3) the development of spatial ability has been found to transfer back to improved STEM education performance (Sorby et al., 2018). Interestingly and also usefully, evidence is emerging that spatial ability itself can be developed through the teaching of specific subjects such as mechanics (Munoz-Rubke et al., 2021). Now, through a series of case studies, the role of spatial ability in maker education can start to be theorised more formally, and given the lack of consideration it has been given to date in this context, spatial ability could potentially become a new and important dimension of maker education agendas.

3   Review of Maker Education Case Studies

The seven case studies on the implementation of maker education in this volume formed that basis of this reflection. These case studies come from Kenya, Mexico, China, Denmark, South Korea, and, two from The Netherlands, and provide rich first-person accounts of maker education in context. A challenge in reading these while thinking about how maker education could provide a context for the development of spatial ability was presented when I noticed that spatial ability was not directly mentioned from any perspective in any of the chapters. This, given the previously described literature search, was not surprising but it is important to note that the discussion herein is not a synthesis of the case study authors explicit commentary around spatial ability. Further, and exciting from my perspective, is that while there was overlap each case study provoked me to think about spatial ability and maker education in a new way. It is very likely that more case studies would have resulted in even more dimensions to this reflection, suggesting that a grounded theory-based inquiry to extend this reflection could have significant merit. While each case study provided a unique perspective on how spatial ability could relate to maker education, three broader themes stood out which given the nature of this reflection seem most appropriately framed as questions: (1) how does spatial ability relate to "making"? (2) how should spatial ability be prioritised within maker education? and (3) what are the implications of spatial ability development being an explicit intended goal of maker education? Each of these questions is unpacked in the next sub-sections.

3.1 *How Does Spatial Ability Relate to "Making"?*

Perhaps the most obvious question to ask regarding the place of spatial ability within maker education is how it relates to "making" in maker environments. Dougherty's (2016, p. 143) definition that making is "the process of realising an idea and making it tangible" is useful to keep in mind in this regard. Making was naturally a core thread across each case study, however two in particular – those from Kenya and Mexico – framed making in ways that the place of spatial thinking became more apparent.

In their chapter (Chapter 6), Westerhof, Gielen, van Boeijen and Jowi describe a maker workshop delivered by the Sustainable Rural Initiatives (SRI) through a local community centre in Kisumu County in Kenya. Developed in collaboration with the Industrial Design Engineering school at TU Delft, the workshop centred around children making "appropriate toys" from free local materials and was designed around the three phases of exploring, building, and presenting. In their chapter, two figures are provided which show the toys in the process of being made and then being presented. One shows what appears to be a house with a bamboo internal support structure and clay walls and roof. The final artefact, at least as a hazy idea, would have needed to be visualised before the building process. It also seems reasonable to infer that the thinking about how the materials would work together, such as using clay to hold the bamboo in place and positioning the bamboo in such a way that it would support the clay, would benefit from imagining multiple possible solutions which is an inherently spatial thought process. In the second image, finished toy cars made from clay are presented. While of course trial and error could have been used in this and in the previous house example, thinking spatially about the proportions of components such as the wheels and how to assemble them seems more efficient, suggesting a benefit from spatial ability.

Núñez-Solís, Silva, Madahar, and Eskue provide a very different perspective on making in their chapter. In relation to their case study (Chapter 5), which centres around upcycling and the circular economy, they discuss how the Mexican company Recicla Electrónicos México S.A de C.V. created "EcoMakerKits" which they provide to schools as educational materials. Their "EcoMakerStore" provides a wider variety of kits – sets of components which can be assembled into a working product – but they focus on the Bluetooth speaker and ventilator kits in their chapter. I visited their website[2] to see the kits on offer in more detail and was immediately reminded of Gaughran's (2002) conference paper where he discusses a continuum of spatial factors using the analogy of a plug-top being mentally disassembled and reassembled. While scholarship around spatial factors has progressed since Gaughran's (2002) publication, kit assembly as an activity seems very much reflective of spatial tests such involving visual puzzles – indicators, like the PSVT:R, of the visualisation spatial factor. Figure 13.2 shows what the items in these types of spatial tests look like (with actual test items being more difficult). Here, a puzzle is provided (top) and a selection of 6 "pieces" (bottom) are provided. The problem involves identifying which pieces are required to make the full puzzle, and a specific number of pieces must be selected. In Figure 13.2, for example, pieces 5 and 6 are sufficient but the task is to identify three pieces so the correct solution would be pieces 1, 2, and 6.

Assembling a kit is a similar activity where the puzzle from Figure 13.2 represents the assembled product and the pieces from Figure 13.2 represent the kit's components. However, it is possible that spatial reasoning could be circumvented (cf. Buckley et al., 2022). Núñez-Solís, Silva, Madahar, and Eskue provided a video tutorial to accompany their kits which, depending on how it is used, could remove the need to think about how the components go together.

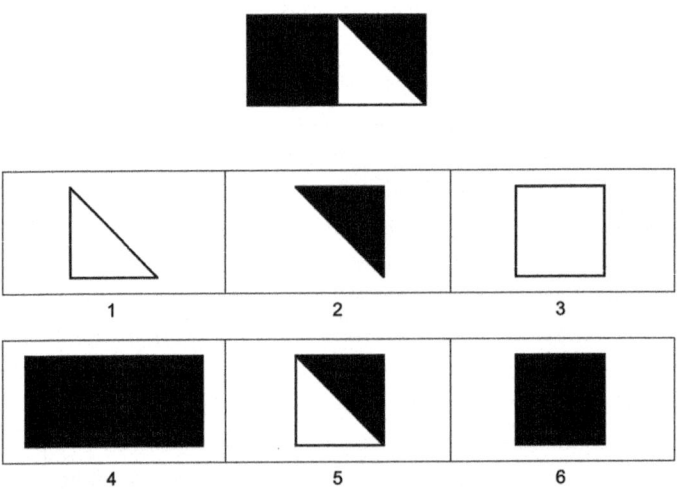

Which 3 of these pieces go together to make this puzzle?

FIGURE 13.2   Example of the item structure for the Visual Puzzles subtest of the 4th edition of the Wechsler Adult Intelligence Scale (WAIS-IV; adapted from Pearson Assessments, 2022)

With a video showing step-by-step how to assemble each piece, learners do not need to think about how components fit together either physically and within a system of moving parts. The use of kits could be both an aspect of maker education which elicits spatial thinking or even develops it, but pedagogical decisions need to be taken into account in terms of how they are used.

3.2 How Should Spatial Ability Be Prioritised within Maker Education?

Considering that spatial ability seems aligned with capability in terms of making or building and that also, such as through the use of kits, maker education could be an environment where spatial ability could be developed, the question of how it should be prioritised relative to other goals needs to be asked. With this in mind, I was particularly intrigued by Pols and Hut's case study (Chapter 9) on maker education in the Netherlands. In their chapter, they describe the development of a makerspace for use by students in two mandatory courses in an applied physics programme in Delft University. As a brief note, it is worth pointing out that the learning outcomes in these courses highlight another dimension to making in maker education that spatial ability has been empirically linked with, those of "use simulation software" and "make 2D (vector) and 3D models" (Basham & Kotrlik, 2008; Dilling & Vogler, 2021; Lei et al., 2009; Shavalier, 2004; Storey Vasu, & Kennedy Tyler, 1997). What was of particular interest was that the authors stated a lot of time was "wasted" on simple "jury rigged" solutions. They provided a photograph of such a prototype, which included a lot of duct tape, cork, and string, and while it was a prototype and less polished it was reminiscent of the activity from the Kenyan case study where toys were made from clay. Maker spaces were introduced in the case study to facilitate moving beyond such prototypes in the applied physics courses by streamlining activity so that iterative prototyping and testing and the development of specific advanced technical skills could be more feasible. From a technical perspective, advanced manufacturing skills are now more likely to be developed and the students will progress through more of a design process that is contextually relevant. However, if the development of spatial ability were to be an explicit goal in this environment, I would hypothesise that it is the initial prototyping activity where solutions need to be conceived and basic materials need to be creatively imagined into a model where this development would be fostered more (although this would need to be empirically evidenced). A balance between disciplined learning and general spatial development would require considered pedagogical decisions.

Building on this idea, Gu and Yang's chapter (Chapter 8) in which they describe a case study of maker education in China highlights another pedagogical dimension to spatial ability development. Gu and Yang, similar to

Núñez-Solís, Silva, Madahar, and Eskue in Mexico, discuss maker kits, however the real emphasis was on a 5-week (10 classroom hour) design task where children had to make a desk lamp. Much like in Westerhof, Gielen, van Boeijen and Jowi's case study from Kenya, the children were tasked with using locally available material (although could spend up to ¥15, which is approximately €2) which they had to source themselves. Gu and Yang provided a photograph of the students finished work and the 10 lamps shown were made from a variety of materials such as paper cups, a woven wooden basket, a shuttlecock, and what appear to be parts of various toys. They really are quite innovative and personalised. Interestingly, as part of the case study, the authors listed the problems the children faced with the task. To paraphrase, they included electronic components such as wires or batteries not being correctly installed and the joining of different parts not being strong enough and requiring, for example, more glue. The problems faced were not spatial, and on reflection it is not clear that the task required spatial thinking. If it did it was trivial. The main learning outcomes were associated with electronics and "creative literacy". This highlights an important point that just because designing and making have been linked with spatial ability, it does not mean that merely including these activities within an educational task will elicit a cognitively spatial response. If an educator intends for a task to require spatial ability or in particular to develop it, the task needs to be designed accordingly. This includes, for example, "spatialising" the task, making spatial reasoning an efficient strategy for learners when responding to the task, and ensuring sufficient cognitive demand of this nature. Designing such tasks, if spatial ability development was to be a goal, would also require both consideration of the actual artefact and building procedure (such as the use of a kit, the provision of instructions, the sourcing of materials, etc.), and consideration of pedagogical strategy where learners are encouraged to visualise problem solutions.

Finally in this theme is the case study offered by Pijls, van Eijck, and Bredeweg (Chapter 4), which also comes from The Netherlands. This chapter was particularly interesting from the perspective of spatial ability development, as the authors describe a series of interviews with makerspace coaches and children who attended a makerspace with one quote being "thinking is 3D is what everybody has to learn", and yet despite this I did not think it should be primarily part of the previous section on how spatial ability is related to making. I was instead struck by a series of comments about the importance of accessing makerspaces and their more general benefits for children which has instead made me reflect on whether spatial ability development should be a priority. For context, Pijls, van Eijck, and Bredeweg describe how the Amsterdam Public Library created a network of 10 makerspaces called Maakplaats021.

Each makerspace was located in a library location and contained 3D printers, a laser cutter, a vinyl cutter, laptops, glue guns, sewing machines, and various other small pieces of stationary (e.g., pencils, paints, etc.). Library staff were recruited as makerspace coaches. From the interviews, the authors identified a series of themes which related to skills development, the variety of potential learning opportunities, developing interest in programming, community collaboration, developing confidence, and developing spatial ability (referred to as "thinking in 3D"). There were more insights in the chapter that related to the makerspace coaches, but these are not described here. Of all the chapters, this was perhaps the most pointed in the series of benefits to young people from engaging with makerspaces, and it has caused me to reflect on whether developing spatial ability should be considered as a priority. Of course, it may be a very important effect of maker related activity – and it is clear how this can be from this and the other chapters – but it is something that should be a goal? Maybe, but in my opinion not at the expense of some of the other benefits of makerspaces. The chapter is filled with quotes from children who were proud of their creations, had developed skills (like sewing) enabling them to help their parents at home, learned basic social and hygiene skills, and proclaimed interest in technology and making due to exposure they may otherwise not have received. Most impactful (for me) was the following quote in the chapter:

> One week ago, we were sitting with the children, chatting a bit and I asked them 'Who feels happy now?' Many raised their hands.

In my opinion, spatial ability development can be a priority of makerspaces, but perhaps not the priority.

3.3   What Are the Implications of Spatial Ability Development Being an Explicit Intended Goal of Maker Education?

Across the previous case studies this reflection inductively provoked thinking around when, where, and how spatial ability manifests in maker environments and if it was to be a more explicit agenda how would this be balanced with disciplinary learning outcomes. On reading Holm Kanstrup, Iversen, Van Mechelen, Dindler, and Wagner's chapter, a potential value of the development of spatial ability being an explicit agenda of maker education became apparent. The authors present a framework for the establishment of sustainable makerspaces. They derived this from their experiences of 11 cases across Denmark and "sustainable" in this chapter relates primarily to funding sustainability for makerspaces. The problem, as the authors put it, is that makerspaces receive a form of development funding to get established and to operate in their first few years, but then struggle to secure and generate fundings to continue beyond this period. In response, the authors developed a six-step framework which they provided to stakeholders through workshops as a way of supporting their long-term planning. The six steps, or six objectives for stakeholders, involved:

1. Understanding the complexity of a makerspace initiative.
2. Hands-on introduction to makerspace education.
3. Establishing the grand narrative of a maker space initiative.
4. Developing the makerspace initiative within the existing municipality landscape.
5. Confirmation and articulation of management support for the maker-space initiative.
6. Choosing and purchasing technologies for the maker space.

In their chapter, the authors provide more detail on each of these, but the third step in particular is critical. The authors note a general aim of these makerspaces – effectively the "grand narrative" – as being to "[increase] children's interest in creating digital technologies and understanding how emerging technologies affects our everyday lives". This, based on the previously described case studies, is an aim generally mediated through make-based activity. As discussed, spatial ability could be developed through maker activity with purposefully designed activities and depending on other intended learning outcomes, this could be included without much disruption. Could the addition of spatial ability development, subject to qualifying this through empirical investigation, support the acquisition of further funding? I am remined of the work of Uttal et al. (2013) who through a meta-analysis of spatial training studies identify $g = .40$ as the "most conservative effect size" from their work for the effect of spatial training on improving spatial ability. To give context to this, they note that if spatial ability were to be improved by this much in a population of people, the number of people in that population who have the level of spatial ability associated with receiving a bachelor's degree in engineering would approximately double.[3] To have such a significant and tangible impact, in addition to the currently noted aims of maker education, would certainly aid efforts in securing funding through the explication of additional societal benefit.

4   Consolidation and Conclusion

A seventh case study relating to maker education in South Korea provided by Kwon provoked similar reflection to those previously discussed. An emphasis was placed on fun, making was contextualised in terms of 3D printing and programming, and the alignment of maker education and formal secondary education was discussed. Many considerations have been raised relating to the place of spatial ability in maker environments both empirically (e.g., how does it relate to building and craft?) and epistemologically (e.g., should spatial development be an explicit agenda?). What Kwon's chapter uniquely presents is how this conversation can, and perhaps should, now be continued. Kwon describes MAKERS (a pseudonym), a professional learning community (PLC) responsible for a technology teachers' association in Seoul. Through interviews with four technology teachers who are members of MAKERS, rich insight is gained into their thoughts about both maker and technology education in South Korea and the relationship between them. One specific comment from a teacher (Daehan, also a pseudonym) encapsulates my concluding thoughts. Daehan said

> There are many misconceptions about technology and technology education, including in schools. I was worried and upset about that. However, when technology teachers get together to share their concerns and discuss their own solutions, it miraculously leads to better practice.

Shared discourse from maker education stakeholders can lead to improved practice, and the nature of this improvement is defined by those stakeholders. Educators who are involved in maker education are perfectly placed to collaboratively consider intended outcomes. In terms of the development of spatial ability being one of these goals, existing research supports the view that it is possible and could have significant societal and individual learner impact. Dialogue between educators and researchers (and other relevant stakeholders) could advance this agenda in a meaningful and contextually appropriate way.

Notes

1   These included 11 articles published in academic journals, 4 articles published in conference proceedings, 2 Doctoral theses, and 1 conference proceeding published between 2015 and 2022, with most publications coming from 2019 (n = 3), 2020 (n = 3), and 2021 (n = 7).
2   https://ecomakerstore.com/
3   Based on data from Wai et al. (2009, 2010).

References

Akshay, N., Sugunan, N., Muraleedharan, A., Natarajan, A. P. A., & Bhavani, R. R. (2018). Design, observe and tinker: A constructionist approach to introduce maker skills in rural schools. *2018 IEEE 18th International Conference on Advanced Learning Technologies*, 293–297. https://doi.org/10.1109/ICALT.2018.00074

Bailey, S. K. T., & Sims, V. K. (2014). Self-reported craft expertise predicts maintenance of spatial ability in old age. *Cognitive Processing, 15*(2), 227–231. https://doi.org/10.1007/s10339-013-0596-7

Basham, K., & Kotrlik, J. (2008). The effects of 3-dimensional CADD modeling on the development of the spatial ability of technology education students. *Journal of Technology Education, 20*(1), 32–47.

Bhaduri, S., Biddy, Q., Bush, J., Suresh, A., & Sumner, T. (2021). 3DnST: A framework towards understanding children's interaction with Tinkercad and enhancing spatial thinking skills. *Interaction Design and Children 2021*, 257–267. https://doi.org/10.1145/3459990.3460717

Boyle, J. (2019). The butterfly brigade: MakeHer take flight and bring making into lower secondary school science. *Physics Education, 54*(5), 1–15. https://doi.org/10.1088/1361-6552/ab26c6

Buckley, J. (2020). The need to consider the predictive capacity of intelligence and its malleability within design and technology education research. *International Journal of Technology and Design Education.* https://doi.org/10.1007/s10798-020-09588-9

Buckley, J., Seery, N., & Canty, D. (2018). A heuristic framework of spatial ability: A review and synthesis of spatial factor literature to support its translation into STEM education. *Educational Psychology Review, 30*(3), 947–972. https://doi.org/10.1007/s10648-018-9432-z

Buckley, J., Seery, N., & Canty, D. (2019). Investigating the use of spatial reasoning strategies in geometric problem solving. *International Journal of Technology and Design Education, 29*(2), 341–362. https://doi.org/10.1007/s10798-018-9446-3

Buckley, J., Seery, N., Canty, D., & Gumaelius, L. (2022). The importance of spatial ability within technology education. In P. J. Williams & B. von Mengersen (Eds.), *Applications of research in technology education: Helping teachers develop research-informed practice* (pp. 165–182). Springer. https://doi.org/10.1007/978-981-16-7885-1_11

Carroll, J. (1993). *Human cognitive abilities: A survey of factor-analytic studies.* Cambridge University Press.

Dilling, F., & Vogler, A. (2021). Fostering spatial ability through computer-aided design: A case study. *Digital Experiences in Mathematics Education, 7*(2), 323–336. https://doi.org/10.1007/s40751-021-00084-w

Dougherty, D. (2016). *Free to make: How the maker movement is changing our schools, our jobs, and our minds.* North Atlantic Books.

Ebisch, S., Perrucci, M., Mercuri, P., Romanelli, R., Mantini, D., Romani, G. L., Colom, R., & Saggino, A. (2012). Common and unique neuro-functional basis of induction, visualization, and spatial relationships as cognitive components of fluid intelligence. *NeuroImage, 62*(1), 331–342. https://doi.org/10.1016/j.neuroimage.2012.04.053

Eliot, J., & Smith, I. M. (1983). *An international directory of spatial tests.* Humanities Press.

French, J. W. (1951). *The description of aptitude and achievement tests in terms of rotated factors.* University of Chicago Press.

Galton, F. (1880). Mental imagery. *Fortnightly Review, 28*(1), 312–324.

Gaughran, W. (2002). Cognitive modelling for engineers. *2002 American Society for Engineering Education Annual Conference and Exposition.*

Geary, D. C. (2022). Spatial ability as a distinct domain of human cognition: An evolutionary perspective. *Intelligence, 90*, 101616. https://doi.org/10.1016/j.intell.2021.101616

Godhe, A.-L., Lilja, P., & Selwyn, N. (2019). Making sense of making: Critical issues in the integration of maker education into schools. *Technology, Pedagogy and Education, 28*(3), 317–328. https://doi.org/10.1080/1475939X.2019.1610040

Guay, R. (1977). *Purdue spatial visualization test: Rotations.* Purdue Research Foundation.

Guilford, J. P., Fruchter, B., & Zimmerman, W. S. (1952). Factor analysis of the army air forces sheppard field battery of experimental aptitude tests. *Psychometrika, 17*(1), 45–68. https://doi.org/10.1007/BF02288795

Guilford, J. P., & Lacey, J. (1947). *Printed classification tests* (No. 5). Army Air Forces Aviation Psychology Program.

Holzinger, K. J., & Harman, H. (1938). Comparison of two factorial analyses. *Psychometrika, 3*(1), 45–60.

Horn, J. (1988). Thinking about human abilities. In J. Nesselroade & R. Cattell (Eds.), *Handbook of multivariate experimental psychology* (pp. 645–685). Academic Press.

Julià, C., & Antolí, J. Ò. (2016). Spatial ability learning through educational robotics. *International Journal of Technology and Design Education, 26*(2), 185–203. https://doi.org/10.1007/s10798-015-9307-2

Julià, C., & Antolì, J. Ò. (2018). Enhancing spatial ability and mechanical reasoning through a STEM course. *International Journal of Technology and Design Education, 28*(4), 957–983. https://doi.org/10.1007/s10798-017-9428-x

Lane, D., & Sorby, S. (2021). Bridging the gap: Blending spatial skills instruction into a technology teacher preparation programme. *International Journal of Technology and Design Education.* https://doi.org/10.1007/s10798-021-09691-5

Lei, P.-L., Kao, G. Y.-M., Lin, S. S. J., & Sun, C.-T. (2009). Impacts of geographical knowledge, spatial ability and environmental cognition on image searches supported by GIS software. *Computers in Human Behavior, 25*(6), 1270–1279. https://doi.org/10.1016/j.chb.2009.05.003

Lin, H. (2016). Influence of design training and spatial solution strategies on spatial ability performance. *International Journal of Technology and Design Education, 26*(1), 123–131. https://doi.org/10.1007/s10798-015-9302-7

Lohman, D. (1979). *Spatial ability: A review and reanalysis of the correlational literature* (p. 204). Office of Naval Research.

Lohman, D., Pellegrino, J., Alderton, D., & Regian, J. (1987). Dimensions and components of individual differences in spatial abilities. In S. Irvine & S. Newstead (Eds.), *Intelligence and cognition: Contemporary frames of reference* (pp. 253–312). Springer.

Meehl, P. (2006). The power of quantitative thinking. In N. Waller, L. Yonce, W. Grove, D. Faust, & M. Lenzenweger (Eds.), *A Paul Meehl Reader: Essays on the practice of scientific psychology* (pp. 433–444). Erlbaum.

Munoz-Rubke, F., Will, R., Hawes, Z., & James, K. H. (2021). Enhancing spatial skills through mechanical problem solving. *Learning and Instruction, 75*, 101496. https://doi.org/10.1016/j.learninstruc.2021.101496

Newcombe, N. (2017). *Harnessing spatial thinking to support STEM learning: OECD education working paper no. 161* (EDU/WKP(2017)10). OECD. https://www.oecd.org/officialdocuments/publicdisplaydocumentpdf/?cote=EDU/WKP(2017)10& docLanguage=En

Pearson Assessments. (2022). *Wechsler adult intelligence scale* (4th ed.). https://www.pearsonassessments.com/store/usassessments/en/Store/Professional-Assessments/Cognition-%26-Neuro/Wechsler-Adult-Intelligence-Scale-%7C-Fourth-Edition/p/100000392.html

Šafhalter, A., Glodež, S., Šorgo, A., & Ploj Virtič, M. (2022). Development of spatial thinking abilities in engineering 3D modeling course aimed at lower secondary students. *International Journal of Technology and Design Education, 32*, 167–184. https://doi.org/10.1007/s10798-020-09597-8

Schneider, J., & McGrew, K. (2018). The Cattell-Horn-Carroll theory of cognitive abilities. In D. Flanagan & E. McDonough (Eds.), *Contemporary intellectual assessment: Theories, tests, and issues* (pp. 73–163). The Guilford Press.

Shavalier, M. (2004). The effects of CAD-like software on the spatial ability of middle school students. *Journal of Educational Computing Research, 31*(1), 37–49. https://doi.org/10.2190/X8BU-WJGY-DVRU-WE2L

Simpson, A., & Kastberg, S. (2022). Makers do math! Legitimizing informal mathematical practices within making contexts. *Journal of Humanistic Mathematics, 12*(1), 40–75.

Sorby, S. (1999). Developing 3-D spatial visualization skills. *Engineering Design Graphics Journal, 63*(2), 21–32.

Sorby, S., Veurink, N., & Streiner, S. (2018). Does spatial skills instruction improve STEM outcomes? The answer is 'yes'. *Learning and Individual Differences, 67*(1), 209–222. https://doi.org/10.1016/j.lindif.2018.09.001

Storey Vasu, E., & Kennedy Tyler, D. (1997). A comparison of the critical thinking skills and spatial ability of fifth grade children using simulation software or logo. *Journal of Computing in Childhood Education, 8*(4), 345–363.

Sutton, K., & Allen, R. (2011). *Assessing and improving spatial ability for design-based disciplines utilising online systems* (No. 9781921856716; pp. 1–40).

Thurstone, L. L. (1936). The factorial isolation of primary abilities. *Psychometrika, 1*(3), 175–182. https://doi.org/10.1007/BF02288363

Uttal, D., Meadow, N., Tipton, E., Hand, L., Alden, A., Warren, C., & Newcombe, N. (2013). The malleability of spatial skills: A meta-analysis of training studies. *Psychological Bulletin, 139*(2), 352–402. https://doi.org/10.1037/a0028446

Wai, J., Lubinski, D., & Benbow, C. (2009). Spatial ability for STEM domains: Aligning over 50 years of cumulative psychological knowledge solidifies its importance. *Journal of Educational Psychology, 101*(4), 817–835. https://doi.org/10.1037/a0016127

Wai, J., Lubinski, D., Benbow, C. P., & Steiger, J. H. (2010). Accomplishment in Science, Technology, Engineering, and Mathematics (STEM) and its relation to STEM educational dose: A 25-year longitudinal study. *Journal of Educational Psychology, 102*(4), 860–871. https://doi.org/10.1037/a0019454

Zimmerman, W. S. (1953). A revised orthogonal rotational solution for Thurstone's original Primary Mental Abilities Test battery. *Psychometrika, 18*, 77–93. https://doi.org/10.1007/BF02289029

CHAPTER 14

Making in Informal and Formal Settings

Gerald van Dijk and Elwin Savelsbergh

Abstract

The maker movement is increasingly finding its way into informal and formal educational settings. This chapter welcomes that trend and reflects on the cases in this book through five lenses, whereby informal and formal settings are contrasted. The first lens focuses on the development of a maker identity. In the formal setting in Delft (The Netherlands), for instance, students are expected to develop a professional engineering identity, which calls for certain task characteristics and a learning environment that differs from informal settings. The second lens focuses on what in being learnt: maker skills can be a learning objective in itself but making can also be a vehicle to learn other things. The third lens is about 'what drives learners, what is motivating?' The fourth lens is concerned with the value of working with tangible objects, and the use of different types of materials. Lastly, ways to sustain 'making in education', for instance by means of collaboration between learners, teachers and stakeholders is a lens that is used to shed light on contrasts between formal and informal settings.

Keywords

formal maker education – informal maker education – maker identity – motivation – playfulness

1   Introduction

Chapter 1 in this book describes how maker education originated in informal settings and then made its way into schools. Schools, however, have their own responsibilities and this means that maker practices are often transformed. In this chapter we reflect on similarities and differences between the cases presented in this book, in terms of formal and informal maker practices. By formal practices we mean maker activities in schools and associated infrastructure, including a Friday afternoon maker class that is not compulsory (cases: Delft/ The Netherlands case, Mexico, China, Korea, Denmark). Informal practices, in our definition, are situated outside schools, in libraries, hobby clubs, etc. (Kenya, Amsterdam/The Netherlands). Another category would be non-formal settings, such as at home, but these are not part of the case studies in this book.

In order to analyze the cases in a more or less similar manner we use five lenses.
– Developing a maker identity.
– Learning (what?) through making.
– Motivating to make and learn.
– Learning and making with materials.
– Sustaining an infrastructure for making.

Each of these lenses will now briefly be explained.

As has been seen in the cases, be they formal or informal, *making* can have many faces and many purposes. We shape our environments, and we ourselves are shaped by the objects and technologies we create and by the things that we learn through making (Oosterbaan, 2021; Verbeek, 2005). Making not only serves to fulfill our practical needs, but also psychological needs for competence, autonomy, and relatedness (Ryan & Deci, 2000; Sennet, 2008). Foreshadowing our reflection on the cases, one can already see that an informal setting has different affordances in terms of for instance autonomy, because there are less obligations in terms of a strongly institutionalized curriculum. Beyond the levels of practical use and personal relevance, making can also be viewed from more societal and critical angles. As with technology in general, making is not neutral (Kranzberg, 1986). One may think of repair cafés where making is about saving cost and reducing waste, or of the Makers' Bill of Rights (Make: Magazine, 2006) and the maker ethics of sharing and giving people access to the means of production. In some subgroups, particularly in informal settings, making tends to be even more activist – as a rebellion against prevailing powers (big tech, capitalism, government). In discussing the case chapters in this book, we address whether those who are responsible for a specific maker setting take a stance on the kind of maker identity they would like to promote, and how that may be related to the formal or informal setting.

Next, we reflect on the objectives of making in formal and informal settings. In informal settings, the objectives tend to be relatively open: to offer a place where youngsters can pursue their interests, enjoy themselves, and develop positive attitudes. Nevertheless, the cases demonstrate that also there, one can identify a curriculum, even if it is more implicit. In formal settings, the educational agenda tends to be more directed: there will be an institutionalized curriculum and learning objectives that need to be attained within a set amount of time. In such a context, learning objectives tend to be more specific and operationalized. Some educators in the cases focus on the development of maker skills and knowledge (including properties of materials and mastery of tools), others focus on the quality of the creative process and the development of a maker mindset, whereas still others will use making as a means to attain conceptual understanding in their domain (cf. Papert, 1987; Janssen & Waarlo, 2010). The relation between making and foundational knowledge is an interesting one to explore in our reflection, especially since there can be tensions between knowledge-oriented functions of the curriculum and process-oriented views of making.

A next issue we address is motivation: what drives youngsters to engage in making, both in formal and in informal setting? In line with the previous paragraph and much of the literature about maker education (Van Dijk, Van der Meij, & Savelsbergh, 2020), it may be expected that for many people making is intrinsically rewarding. But oftentimes there are other drivers as well, such as an inspiring teacher, the needs of a client, or a competitive challenge. The cases in this book demonstrate that these factors can come into play in both formal and informal settings, but in different ways.

As we have mentioned maker activities will have an impact on the world. While this is true for all kinds of making, including software projects, in the case that material artefacts are being made (like in all case studies in this book), making also has a very specific impact in the sense that materials are being used and (future) waste is being created. Maker practices differ a lot in how they address this issue: repair cafés (informal, and not described in this book) operate with the explicit aim to reduce waste, and some makers collect scrapheap materials to build their projects. In contrast, some maker practices primarily rely on virgin materials and there is a constant influx of cheap electronic parts from marketplace sites such as Alibaba. In the educational context, budgets tend to be limited, and the numbers of participants working on similar projects can be substantial, which makes stock and supply of materials an interesting issue to address. The setting, formal or informal, also has an impact on this aspect of maker education, as we will show.

This brings us to the final perspective for our review: a maker space functions in a wider societal context. We have seen several enthusiastic attempts to start maker projects, in schools as well as in informal setting, that either never really took off, or ran out of steam after a while. A supportive organizational and institutional context will be needed in order to sustain educational maker initiatives. Some of the cases in this book describe such support, which is the final topic of our reflection, whereby we will tentatively show differences and similarities between formal and informal settings and ways to bridge these settings for the benefit of both.

2   Conceptions of Maker Identity

In both the formal and informal settings that are described in this book, we see children, teachers, engineers, school managers and politicians in action as makers. However, these practices come in highly varied forms: the Kenyan children are playfully molding clay into a shape of a car with minimal requirements, whereas the Dutch engineering students are (among other tasks) making a contraption to measure a physical quantity, and thereby spending much of their time on technical problem solving to meet a list of requirements. In both cases, however, there is a lot of openness in the task, and this central to most conceptions of 'maker identities' as usually perceived in maker education (Martinez & Stager, 2013). In this sense 'making' can be distinguished from 'designing', which is more goal oriented, and often focused on user requirements. Making, as in maker education, is also more of an open process than 'recipe style' constructing. The distinctions between making, constructing, and designing are fuzzy, but most of the cases in this book are testimony of this openness, and hence the agency of the maker as a central characteristic of a maker identity.

Leaving the age difference aside, it comes to no surprise that in the informal settings of the Kenyan and Amsterdam case, without strong curricular demands, the degree of openness is greater than in the Delft university setting. The Kenyan and Amsterdam children are almost 'making as artists', with only a few guiding questions to make them think about who would use (respectively) their type of car, or handbag. This artistic slant of making has been seen in informal settings a lot in the past years, and it is now finding its way into formal education settings, because it promotes a sense of autonomy and a feeling of (technical) competence (Martinez & Stager, 2013; Mersand, 2021). Moreover, often there is strong collaboration between makers, who generously share code, drawings and ideas on- and offline. Fulfillment of psychological needs such as relatedness, competence and autonomy (Ryan & Deci, 2000) bolsters motivation to learn and has been shown to lead to an identity as maker. Increasing motivation is a holy grail for education, which explains in part, why making has moved from the world of informal education to schools. The Chinese middle school case is interesting in this respect, because it combines an engineering conception of making (the circuit must work) with free artistic expression for the form of the lamp, beyond mere decoration. The different accents on making as artistic expressions, assembling (as in the Mexican case), or technical problem solving (Delft), can be seen in the other cases too.

Part of a maker identity can be a dedication to make the product work smoothly, to diligently perfect its shape, and to attain high standards of craftsmanship. In an age where learning has to be fast and effective, and where tangible things are replaced by virtual realities, development of such proud craftsman's identities is nothing to be frowned upon (Sennet, 2008). Whether that conception of a maker identity is being strived for in the cases isn't always clear. The Delft case with engineering students and the Amsterdam cases seem to incorporate this view to some extent. Having visited one of the maker settings described in the Amsterdam case, we can testify of those children's dedication to slowly craft their products in a dedicated way. And from our own observations and numerous talks with teachers in formal (and compulsory) maker classes we now start wondering whether the school context itself may sometimes hinder the development of this kind of (craftsmanship) maker identity. After all, in school we train students to get the assignment done, get a grade and move on to the next one. A sense of fast effectiveness may often prevail over slow dedication. This is a gross generalization, of course. Research into school makerspaces has not yet focused strongly on possible tensions between school curricula and slow and dedicated craftsmen-like learning in school-based maker spaces (Rouse & Gillespie Rouse, 2022). Sloyd education in Scandinavia, that strongly builds on traditional crafts and extends this to modern technologies, would be an interesting example in this respect. Also, art classes around the world and no doubt, some maker classes at schools, also succeed to develop this kind of maker identity.

None of the case descriptions in this book does take an explicit stance about normative aspects of being a maker, or the role of making in society. Participants do not engage in explicit reflection on 'what is good and bad' about the technology or (uses of the) product at hand, and messages about the values of making seem to be conveyed only implicitly, both in the practices themselves, and in the case descriptions in the book. This makes an interesting contrast, both to the explicit value-ladenness of the maker movement in general, and to the traditions of technology education, where explicit reflection has since long been recognized an essential component of technological literacy (e.g., NGSS, 2013). The maker movement for instance incorporates ethical hacking and artistic contributions to sustainability, with a political message. And in formal technology curricula students often do reflect on the the history of technology, the reciprocal impact of technology and society, about 'what things do to us' (Verbeek, 2005) and other philosophical aspects of technology (Petrina, 2020). The fact that explicit normative considerations are absent in the case studies in the book does not warrant any strong conclusions, but it does make us wonder about the development of critical maker identities in formal and informal maker education. Perhaps the fun-factor comes in the way of critical reflection? This would make sense as an explanation for schools, because there, maker education has often been introduced to boost interest in technology (careers).

And in informal settings there is no curriculum that prescribes such content, coaches are often hired because of their technical skills and their motivation to work with children, so we speculate that it is often left to chance whether they will talk about such content while coaching making activities.

3   Making as a Learning Activity

Across all cases we see an eagerness to teach children and students to make, in communities of teachers, researchers, teacher educators, politicians, and businesses. But to what end? For starters, maker education can be aimed at developing 'maker identities' (Blikstein, 2013), as we have already seen.

The limitations that the Kenyan team saw itself confronted with, left little room to make with anything more than very basic materials and tools. Nevertheless, some explicit 'teaching' of process, such as thinking about functions, looking at existing products for inspiration, bolstering creativity, presenting ideas, were present in the Kenya and Amsterdam case. This shows that playful making was not just an objective in itself, but a vehicle for learning.

In the Mexican (more formal) case, the engineers that developed the kit for the blue tooth speaker were makers, in the sense of designing an original solution for a very open problem. The task for the students was of a different nature: There was some room for creativity in programming a tune, but mostly the students followed instructions to assemble the product. Insofar as there has been a learning effect, it most likely pertains to fluency in following instructions. Of course, these could be valuable skills: In many circumstances, users and technicians need to be able to follow procedures from the manual, whether it is a nurse installing apparatus for blood transfusion or an IT professional creating a computer network. However, we do not see a strong maker orientation in the Mexican case study. And it comes as no surprise that assembly tasks are not described in the two informal cases (Kenya and Amsterdam). Assembling is probably deemed to be too prescriptive, lacking in creativity, for such informal settings.

The students in the formal Delft case are becoming engineers and *learning to make* is part of their education. However, they are also *making to learn* about analogue and digital electronics, coding, physics, 2D and 3D computer modelling, affordances of materials, and so on. So, in this case, making also serves as a means to attain conceptual learning objectives. Such learning is promoted by frontloading the process with product and process requirements that are not easy to achieve; a challenge that directs students on the path towards the desired science and technology learning outcomes.

A similar form of 'making' as a means to learn technology content is seen in the formal middle school Chinese case. There is lots of tinkering, and there is room for original solutions, but there are also constraints to create the right level of challenge and need for learning. This ensures a natural fit with objectives and pedagogies in engineering design studies. In the Chinese case, the making activities are also intended to contribute to entrepreneurial attitudes. In general, maker education promotes soft skills such as taking initiative, creativity, and collaboration, that align well with entrepreneurship. In general, one could say that the formal settings described in this book foreground substantive content more than the informal cases, but this can't be backed-up by research literature in general yet (Rouse & Gillespie Rouse, 2022). Attitudes and (21st) skills are foregrounded in both kinds of settings in this book, and the very name of the Amsterdam setting 'Maakplaats021' is an expression of the resolve of the teams to boost 21st century skills.

We have also commented on different conceptions of making and designing. Designing is often driven by purposes that are external to the designer. This takes shape in for instance a 'program of requirements', a morphological chart with different solutions for components of the design problem, user stories, mood boards, tests and all kinds of other design tools that enable communication between designers and users or customers, and that enable the individual designer to systematically advance from problem to design. Rudimentary use of such 'thinking steps' is seen in the Kenyan and Delft cases, but certainly to a lesser degree than in traditional 'design and technology' curricula, for instance in countries such as the UK or New Zealand. This should come as no surprise, given the origins of maker education. It originated in informal settings where purposes of making, and structures of learning processes are often loose. This looseness has also been advocated by proponents of maker education when it made its way into schools. Martinez and Stager (2013) for instance identified eight characteristics of a good project, one of them being 'purpose and relevance'.

> Is the project personally meaningful? Does the project prompt intrigue in the learner enough to have him or her invest time, effort and creativity in the development of the project? (Martinez & Stager, 2013)

These are great questions for any teacher to construct projects, but the purpose is located within the maker, and not in the needs and wants of users or customers. No wonder that projects such as 'hack a toy'[1] or 'make a useless machine' thrive in maker education, and that the cases in this book are rather lean on 'designing' in a more traditional sense. This means that making should not too easily be seen as a learning activity to promote designerly competences.

4   Motivations to Make and Learn

The very pleasure of making is what drives learners in many non-formal, informal and formal settings, as has been noted above. Resnick (2016) sees motivational aspects of maker education in its use of traditional and digital tools that are easily accessible (low threshold), that allow for creative and wide ranging solutions (wide walls) and the room to make it as challenging as the learner wishes (high ceiling). In this view, motivational drivers are located mostly within the learner, and tools are seen as vital to enhance motivation. Indeed, most likely, in all cases in this book, many learners had enjoyed themselves, from the Kenyan children playing with sticks and clay to the Delft engineering students making a 'measuring device'. And it's not just *wanting to have that self-made product* or playfulness that drives the process. Often, there's also curiosity involved: 'I wonder what would happen to the LED if I changed this code a little'. However, we have already seen that maker education isn't necessarily an individualistic educational innovation where external motivators aren't needed, and it's not just tool driven either.

In formal design education, there is often a client or potential user from outside school who acts as a driver for the process. Perhaps not accidentally, this is something that is scarce in the cases in this book, because the book is not about traditional forms of design education (Van Dijk, Van der Meij, & Savelsbergh, 2020). In the Amsterdam informal case (a library setting) the children are prompted towards an 'outsider orientation' to some extent. They make artefacts to be sold at a local market and they make the neighbourhood of the makerspace more beautiful. This orientation to needs and wants of people in the local community may be a natural fit with goals of a library. In maker classes at schools, we often see this in a different way, but coincidentally not so much in the cases in this book. Students in primary education may make a gift for Mother's Day, a cool Christmas card, in secondary education wearable electronics on a t-shirt for a festival visitor, etc. In this way, maker classes create opportunities for schools to strengthen their connections with parents and the neighbourhood, in a low threshold manner and at the same time boost students' motivation. Places like maker spaces in libraries (e.g., Amsterdam) do provide schools with concrete examples on how to bolster motivation by means of linkages with the community.

Another driving force, but one that we haven't seen explicitly in this book, is competition between teams or individuals in a 'making challenge' such as First Lego League or in a gamified making project. Obviously, these have their own pros and cons in terms of motivational aspects, that we won't elaborate upon, because they are a little less common (Hartmann & Gommer, 2021) and absent from this book.

And then there is the teacher or instructor as a motivator, of course. The case descriptions do not zoom into specific enactment of roles during making, but we know from our own research and from literature how crucial teachers and instructors are to set a motivating prompt, to get the making process going, to get students to improve on their work and to motivate them to persevere when the going gets tough, and lastly to be role models as makers. According to Martinez and Stager (2013) one of the most important roles of the teacher in maker education is to ask questions that 'revitalize a project', such as 'that is a beautiful square you made. What do you think would happen if you changed the angle to a different number?' (p. 78). This kind of responsive 'feed forward' with a focus on improvement requires a teacher with a sharp eye for the possibilities for learning within a project and for the capabilities and interests of his students. More often than not, such 'maker teachers' transgress the boundaries between informal and formal settings. We see these role models at maker fairs, hobby clubs in schools, and in formal teaching positions. They feel at ease in any of these worlds, it seems. But could this perhaps be a special breed of inspiring instructors and teachers? Again, research about this does not yet fully address best practices of 'maker teachers' (Rouse & Gillespie Rouse, 2022).

At schools, there may be teachers who are of that 'special breed'. However, a good engineering or physics teacher does not automatically make an inspiring 'maker teacher', and many teachers we encounter in formal maker education, at least in The Netherlands, aren't trained technology or maker teachers. Some do well, some don't, and to what extent schools require and facilitate training to become such a teacher, differs vastly between schools. In any case, the speed of innovation of digital manufacturing technologies, is hard to keep up with. Laser cutters, 3D-printers and robotics platforms can be hard to integrate with the digital infrastructure in the school. Digital hick-ups can be quite demotivating to novice users, and if the teacher has finally worked out a routine to make these devices work smoothly, an unexpected driver update can ruin the next lesson. It takes a lot of skills, specific pedagogical content knowledge, resilience and team work to keep motivating students in these settings.

In the informal setting in Amsterdam this is taken very seriously, and instructors receive serious training to become makers and a culture of ongoing learning has been established.

When talking about motivation, we should touch upon the issues of inclusion and diversity. In spite of the maker movement's emancipatory intentions, many maker fairs and fablabs tend to be populated mostly by members of the white middle class. In response, questions can be raised such as 'what counts as making'? And are students' home experiences with making sufficiently being recognised as valuable funds of knowledge (Vossoughi et al., 2016)? In our own research in an urban setting where elements of maker education have been introduced, we have observed that there are pitfalls of low expectations regarding students' technical capabilities and funds of knowledge (Fox-Turnbull, 2015), that may be unknown for their teachers who often live in another world. An awareness of the diverse maker experiences that students bring to the classroom could help to raise the teacher's expectations, and to attract interest from a wider diversity of students (Rouse & Gillespie Rouse, 2022). This may be no different in an informal setting, but in case a maker place is situated very close to a local community, instructors have an advantage. The Amsterdam (library) case, for instance, is (partly) situated in an urban, ethnically diverse community. The last picture in the case description illustrates how close the instructors are to the streets. They get to talk to the children's relatives who bring them to the library, they connect to local businesses (e.g., the market), so there are many opportunities to get to know the world the children live in. Therefore, it is probably not coincidental that they have found ways to tap into the children's funds of knowledge (e.g., working with textiles). This serves as a springboard for furthering motivation for learning about technology. This closeness to a diverse community, tapping into funds of knowledge as a means to bolster motivation, can be an inspiration to schools too, we assert.

5 Making in the Material World and Using Materials

As has become apparent in the previous paragraph and from literature, often the differences between cases within an (in)formal setting are larger than differences between settings (Mersand, 2021). This is true for the use of materials too. And similarities in the use of materials run across the different settings, as we will see. Nevertheless, some lessons can be learned in terms of formal and informal settings. Formal settings such as in Delft and Mexico oftentimes make use of materials that are aligned with curricular demands. The Delft case is exemplary in this respect. The first trials of the maker course were deemed unsatisfactory because the materials (and tools) used led to products that were considered mediocre in terms of an engineering curriculum, no matter how impressive it may have been that students managed to make a measuring instrument with only simple materials. The introduction of a maker space with machines and materials that match engineering practices led to better products and satisfactory learning outcomes. The Kenyan informal case describes the use of clay and sticks to teach about designing. Also in the Amsterdam informal case, materials that are readily available in the house, such as textiles are used. At first sight this may seem amateur-like and less suitable for formal engineering and maker settings, but that is not entirely the case. The use of cheap materials and tools is also common in professional design practices whereby in the early stages designers use these to 'think with their hands'. And indeed, the Kenyan use of materials is also reminiscent of the first steps in sophisticated pedagogies for design and technology. In Kimbell and Stables' APU approach (2008) rudimentary hands-on modelling with very simple materials is followed up by a series of well-planned teacher-led interventions, using more sophisticated materials. These aim to enhance levels of hands-on and minds-on work, up to a point where a working design is realized that meets specifications. So, in terms of the use of materials, the Kenyan case does align with early stages of some design processes. Indeed, their learning materials (including video's) explicitly refer to such practices. Of course, mainly due to a poorly resourced setting and the age of the children, the Kenyans didn't progress beyond the phase of rudimentary modelling, which would not be acceptable in formal curricula for engineering.

Gumbo (2020) advocates the use of locally available materials in any poorly resourced setting, including rural schools in Africa. Building materials, such as fabric, mesh wire, tin roofing, and so forth, are usually also available in such settings. To take this idea a bit further, and departing from our focus on the materials, Gumbo and others argue in favour of the use of locally available 'making knowledge, skills and wisdoms' in particular from elderly people in the community. It would be interesting to see if this has been the case in the Kenyan project.

A rationale for choosing materials can also be related to the functionality of the end product. Maker education, as it originated in informal settings, has a rich history of fun projects whereby functionality of the product is not paramount. The countless funny examples of 'useless machines' on the internet testify to that. In the Amsterdam makerspace for young children we also saw lots of products on display, that were made because they were fun to make, such as laser cut dragons. In the formal settings in this book such examples are mostly absent, and for good reasons. Functionality is a key concept in designing and engineering practices. And it can be problematic for formal settings to make (and use materials) just for fun, because sustainability is invariably a part of school curricula, which means that the use of materials needs to be justifiable. This does not mean that 'useless objects' have no place in formal education. We merely describe a tension that needs to be considered when making is taken to school curricula.

The issue of sustainability can be explored a bit further when we think about the digital age that children live in, and in which so much learning is about abstract notions and where content is delivered through virtual media. There is a risk there, namely that 'valuing materials and tangible things' is something that is 'taught about' in an abstract manner, or it is disregarded at all, and this is less of a pitfall in maker education. The children who participated in the Mexican project now own a Bluetooth speaker that they have assembled themselves. Making or repairing an artefact obviously results in bonding with the artefact, so it seems likely that many will treasure their speakers for a long time. The Chinese children have made a lamp that runs on old batteries. They have acquired knowledge about what it takes to design and make a lamp, how lamps differ from each other in interesting ways, and how discarded objects can still become useful. These children probably gave more attention to the object 'lamp', the materials and systems that it can be composed of, the effort that has been put into designing and making it, than ever before. And it is the formal setting with its associated infrastructure and curriculum, that has allowed a large number of students to start valuing the object and its materials in a new way. In a sense, the Chinese lamp, or the Mexican blue-tooth speaker are also objects that are 'put on the table by the teachers' for the students to study together, and without immediate need to apply this in the world outside school, such as a vocation. Masschelein and Simons (2013) argue that such attention to 'a common thing' (p. 10), without an *immediately-to-be-achieved goal'* (p. 39) deserves to be defended in schools. We need to protect the essence of schooling, which is a *'free time'* (Arendt, 1958) between home and work that enables young people to play, study and practice. Maker education, with its roots in playful informal practices, and with its attention to 'objects that are collaboratively studied and made' resonates with this idea, also when it is applied in schools. The essence of schooling as an autonomous 'free time' for study doesn't imply that schools can turn their back on needs that society as a whole may have. The Chinese and Mexican formal cases illustrate that maker education can help a school to transform itself for the greater good, to transmit a culture that we have yet to achieve: a culture of circularity and care for our planet. So, what materials are used in the cases and what does that tell us?

In the Chinese case, materials from broken and discarded objects were used. This can be called the 'scrap heap' or 'hacking' use of materials, which has been used in popular television shows and in informal maker spaces. The affordances of this method can be seen in the Chinese picture of a badminton shuttle that has become part of a lamp. This approach lends itself well to artistic and rather free expressions that are also at the heart of maker education and to early stages of modelling for a design. But obviously it would be too constraining to have to build a Blue Tooth Speaker (Mexico) or a 'device to measure physical quantities' (Delft) with badminton shuttles. In the Mexican case, materials from discarded objects or redundant industrial materials are used, but only after selection and pre-construction by professional engineers, who turned them into a neat assembly kit. The interference of the engineers (as developers of the construction kit) makes re-using materials less directly visible for the Mexican students, but it allows for fancy products to be made in terms of more precise forms and more sophisticated functions. With the aim of limiting the use of resources and waste and raising knowledge of the possibilities of circularity it is certainly worthwhile to consider using materials from nature, scrap heap and hacking and other forms of re-using and recycling, as has been done in for instance the cases in Kenya, Mexico and China. Making as a contribution to critical citizenship would involve explicit reflection on such issues: in which cases is such re-using and recycling a good solution for our problems, and how can you, as a citizen contribute to this? Such explicitness may however be easier to align with formal than informal settings, because sustainability is increasingly part of curricula, for instance for science, and therefore such content is not something that can easily be skipped (Tytler, 2012). Implicitly, sustainability can be and will be addressed in almost any case across formal and informal maker makerspaces, of course. However, for both formal and informal settings there are indications that tech savvy-ness, trying to keep track of the rapidly evolving technologies, can come at the cost of keeping up with circularity issues for specific materials and being explicit about sustainability (Kohtala & Hyysalo, 2015).

6   Ways to Sustain the Infrastructure and the Culture of Making

We now zoom out from concrete making practices and consider what it takes to sustain maker education. Collaboration is a key feature of the maker culture. Makers have been generous in sharing ideas, half products, and code, both in online communities, through events such as maker fairs, and on platforms such as instructibles.com. In a way, informal maker settings have shown the way for schools in this respect. Online coding platforms (such as Scratch) for students provide easy access to end-products and underlying code by other students around the world.

The cases also demonstrate that both formal and informal settings can benefit from the open maker culture in terms of professional development of teachers and coaches. In the Korean case, the professional development of teachers is a key element to embed high quality maker activities in the curriculum. The Korean teachers' ways to strengthen their practices are derivative of the spirit of collaboration that is inherent in the (informal) maker movement. One would wish to observe such events, because most likely these teachers help each other while tinkering, thereby becoming better makers themselves. And no doubt, they also discuss whether the technical problem they are working on, could be solved by their students, and which kind of teacher support some students would need, in that case. There is great strength in such forms of professional development by teachers, where knowledge and skills of content are developed hand in hand with pedagogical expertise. In many countries such forms of collaborative professional development seem to be more common in circles of teachers that embrace maker education than among teacher who don't. The latter group is more likely to be involved in programs that either focus on content or on pedagogy, but not always at the same time.

A similar form of professional development is organized in the Amsterdam informal case, where coaches are also trained in technical skills as well as in pedagogy. As the authors noted, pedagogical competences would deserve more attention in the Amsterdam case. This comes as no surprise, given the fact that instructors in informal settings are typically not qualified teachers. The researchers from Amsterdam even suggest how instructors could benefit from collaborations with schools and universities, for instance by having teacher trainees do an internship in informal maker spaces. This sounds like a very good idea indeed. Given the affordances of these different settings, and the different traditions, both the trainee and the maker coaches could benefit from such partnerships.

In the Danish case study, collaboration is described at the systemic and organisational levels. Maker spaces in and outside schools are vulnerable because they can be at the mercy of financing institutions. These may be good at helping to get trendy things started, but not so good at letting them thrive in the long run. The Danes have invested in development of lasting institutional infrastructures, with strong influence of teachers. They now have developed a system that may be useful in other countries too and we suggest that their efforts are broadly voiced. However, the Danish system may be rooted in a very strong local democratic culture, so this would surely have to be adapted to local circumstances.

7   Concluding Remarks

The cases in this book present seven examples of maker education in six countries, a little more about formal than informal settings. Nevertheless, some lessons can be learned by contrasting the cases.

Maker identities can strongly vary. They can be developed through playful designing with clay, artistically shaping a lamp, using a construction kit, or through making a fancy contraption to count physical quantities. And then there's the 'maker as a hacker' identity, that sometimes comes with awareness of the 'good and bad' of technology. Any of such maker identities could be developed in informal settings, but formal settings have their own responsibilities, affordances and strengths. Therefore, we call on researchers, curriculum developers and teachers who work in formal settings to think about the kind of maker identity that is a proper fit with 'what school is about', rather than just copy practices from informal maker places that seem trendy and inspiring. Making in schools needs to be part of a curriculum. That does not mean all activities should be fixed, or that there has to be a complete match with learning objectives of, for instance, STEM, art and economics. Some schools that we know about, have a rather traditional curriculum for subjects and they supplement this with a 'maker class' where students engage in playful, slow and dedicated making (Sennet, 2008), thereby developing maker identities. In a way, the Delft engineering department has also taken that route: a curricular add-on, without revolutionizing and perhaps compromising the entire curriculum. This kind of curricular thinking - what is school for and how can we improve it? - can be developed when stakeholders from formal settings learn from informal maker education settings. The paragraph about motivation shows a way to achieve closeness to the local community by means of maker activities that involve members of this community, with motivation of children as a result. The paragraph about the material world pinpoints the value of joint attention to a common tangible 'object on the table' (Masschelein & Simons, 2013), that is so natural in informal maker settings and that can easily get lost in schools with their tight curricula, particularly in the digital age. The case studies in formal settings, which were clearly inspired by informal maker education, demonstrate how lost ground can be regained in this respect. We have also seen how informal settings can learn from maker education in formal settings, for instance if maker instructors work side by side with experienced teachers (or teacher students) as a means to strengthen pedagogy (e.g., the Amsterdam case). Also, formal curricula can inspire informal settings to become clearer about 'what children could learn by making', because such curricula have usually been developed over time with input from teachers and other experts and objectives in formal education tend to be more concrete than the sometimes lofty ideals of informal maker initiatives. Learning aims with regard to sustainability provide a point in case: What knowledge, skills and attitudes can students develop by means of making, to sustain the world that we live in? This has already been codified to some extent in formal technology curricula (e.g., life cycle analysis) and maker education could borrow from such codification, while maintaining its strengths. Other promising ways to learn across settings are found in the case chapters, where teachers, school management, experts from informal maker settings, politicians and professional engineers work together to develop and consolidate 'learning to make' and 'making to learn'.

As we have seen in this chapter, there are many forms of maker education, and objectives and approaches can vary widely both between and within formal and informal contexts. Nevertheless, we also identified shared characteristics, and we saw opportunities for mutual learning and inspiration, such as aspects of 'value-ladenness' of technology and societal issues. Finally, across all settings, we saw the crucial role of the the teacher as a maker in creating inspiring and high quality (learning) experiences. Teacher training, both subject wise and pedagogically thus seems a key factor in mainstreaming maker education. The participants in the Korean case have taken this very seriously. Let us follow suit in many countries and give teachers the opportunities to develop themselves in 'teachers as makers', as many instructors in informal settings have done before them.

Note

1   Use these as search terms for examples.

References

Arendt, H. (1958). *The human condition* (2nd ed.). University of Chicago Press.

Blikstein, P. (2013). Digital fabrication and 'making' in education: The democratization of invention. In J. Walter-Herrmann & C. Büching (Eds.), *FabLabs: Of machines, makers and inventors* (pp. 203–223). Transcript Publishers.

Fox-Turnbull, W. (2015). Contributions to technology education through funds of knowledge. *Australasian Journal of Technology Education, 2*, 1–10.

Gumbo, M. T. (2020). Teaching technology in poorly resource contexts. In P. J. Williams & D. Barlex (Eds.), *Pedagogy for technology in secondary schools* (pp. 283–296). Springer.

Hartmann, A., & Gommer, L. (2021). To play or not to play: On the motivational effects of games in engineering education. *European Journal of Engineering Education, 46*(3), 319–343.

Janssen, F., & Waarlo, A. J. (2010). Learning biology by designing. *Journal of Biological Education, 44*, 88–92.

Kranzberg, M. (1986). Technology and history: "Kranzberg's Laws". *Technology and Culture, 27*, 544–560.

Kimbell, R., & Stables, K. (2008). *Researching design learning: Issues and findings from two decades of research and development*. Springer.

Kohtala, C., & Hyysalo, S. (2015). Anticipated environmental sustainability of personal fabrication. *Journal of Cleaner Production, 99*, 333–344.

Make: Magazine. (2006). *The maker's bill of rights. Make: Magazine* (Online ed.). Retrieved February 11, 2022, from https://makezine.com/2006/12/01/the-makers-bill-of-rights/

Martinez, S. L., & Stager, G. (2013). *Invent to learn: Making, tinkering, and engineering in the classroom*. Constructing Modern Knowledge Press.

Masschelein, J., & Simons, M. (2013). *In defence of the school: A public issue*. Education, Culture & Society Publishers.

Mersand, S. (2021). The state of makerspace research: A review of the literature. *Techtrends, 65*(2), 174–186.

Next Generation Science Standards. (2013). *Standards for engineering design*. https://www.nextgenscience.org/topic-arrangement/hsengineering-design

Oosterbaan, W. (2021). *Het leven van dingen: Wat wij met dingen doen, en zij met ons*. Atlas Contact.

Papert, S. (1987). A critique of technocentrism in thinking about the school of the future. Retrieved February 11, 2022, from http://www.papert.org/articles/ACritiqueofTechnocentrism.html

Petrina, S. (2020). Philosophy of technology for children and youths. In J. Williams, & D. Barlex (Eds.), *Pedagogy for technology in secondary schools* (pp. 311–323). Springer.

Resnick, M. (2016). Designing for wide walls. Retrieved July 2023, from https://mres.medium.com/designing-for-wide-walls-323bdb4e7277

Rouse, R., & Gillespie Rouse, A. (2022). Taking the maker movement to school: A systematic review of preK-12 school-based makerspace research. *Educational Research Review, 35*, 100413.

Ryan R. M., & Deci, E. L. (2000). Self-determination theory and the facilitation of intrinsic motivation, social development, and well-being. *American Psychologist, 55*(1), 68–78.

Sennet, R. (2008). *The craftsman*. Yale University Press.

Tytler, R. (2012). Socio-scientific issues, sustainability and science education. *Research in Science Education, 42*(1), 155–163.

Van Dijk, G., van der Meij, A., & Savelsbergh, E. (2020). Maker education: Opportunities and threats for engineering and technology education. In P. Williams. & D. Barlex (Eds.), *Pedagogy for technology education in secondary schools: Research informed perspectives* (pp. 83–98). Contemporary Issues in Technology Education. Springer.

Verbeek, P. P. (2005). *What things do*. Pennsylvania State University Press.

Vossoughi, S., Hooper, P. K., & Escudé, M. (2016). Making through the lens of culture and power: Toward transformative visions for educational equity. *Harvard Educational Review, 86*(2), 206–232.

CHAPTER 15

Sustainability of the Case Study Maker Education Initiatives

HildaRuth Beaumont (formerly known as David Barlex)

Abstract

This chapter begins by providing examples of educational reform in order to situate the maker education initiative case studies as exercises in curriculum reform. It derives a framework for scrutinising the studies with regard to their sustainability by using the Danish case study *A participatory Design Approach to Sustaining Maker Space Initiative* (Chapter 3 in this book). Taking the results of this scrutiny along with a definition of sustainability that requires an initiative to become embedded in practice and widespread such that it is seen as the norm and no longer an initiative it questions their sustainability. It identifies three future requirements to be met if these and similar initiative are to become sustainable.

Keywords

curriculum – curriculum reform – maker movement – maker space – sustainability – teachers

1 Introduction

This chapter will scrutinise the case studies about the extent to which the practice described is likely to be sustainable regarding Maker Education activities contributing to the curriculum. It is important to define what such sustainability might entail and identify its key features with regard to educational reform both in general and in technology education in particular. In broad terms sustainability is seen as the ability for a system to maintain itself and endure over time.

The Maker Movement has educational reform intentions. An educational reform initiative will identify a particular feature of education that for a variety of reasons is seen as deficient or even missing and endeavour to rectify the

TABLE 15.1   Examples of educational reform for the UK

Educational reform	Examples from the UK
Complete revision of a national curriculum	In Wales a new curriculum was developed in 2020 with a view to it being implemented in 2022 (Welsh Government 2020)
Reform of an individual subject within a national curriculum	in response to its publication of *Beyond 2000 science education for the future* (Osborne & Millar, 1999) in collaboration with the University of York and the Awarding Organisation OCR, developed the 21st Century Science programme
Improving basic literacy and numeracy for particular age groups	The Primary Framework for literacy and mathematics introduced in England in 2006 (Department for Education and Skills 2006)
Local initiatives at individual school level	The Wreake Valley Science Scheme (Thorburn & Tinbergen, 1976) was written by the science staff at Wreake Valley Community College in the early 1970s. It was one of the first publications to advocate and enable mixed ability science teaching

situation such that the deficiency of a particular feature is overcome, or the missing element is introduced into the curriculum. In most countries there has been a succession of educational reform initiatives at different scales ranging from complete revision of a national curriculum to reform of individual subjects within that curriculum, to improving basic literacy and numeracy for particular age groups, to local initiatives at individual school level. Examples from the UK are given in Table 15.1.

The fact that there has been and continue to be successive educational reform initiatives may be seen to indicate that achieving sustainability is a fool's errand as the requirements of any education system will change as the society in which it is embedded undergoes change and the educational needs of those living in that society will also change. So, in one sense having long-term sustainability as a goal for an individual educational reform initiative is likely to be an impossibility. However, if we consider short-term initiatives in response to current changes in society then their sustainability takes on a different meaning. We can define the success of a reform in terms of immediate impact and the conditions required for this impact to be maintained and extended within the educational system for a limited time until either it becomes embedded in practice and is no longer seen as a reform or is superseded in that better ways of achieving its goals have been devised. For example, the Royal Academy of Engineering in England has been exercised almost since its inception with attracting more young people into the various branches of the engineering professions. Recently they have invested significant effort in the idea of 'engineering habits of mind' and how these may be developed through the study of different school subjects (Lucas, Hanson, & Claxton, 2014). Or, it may be that the teaching goals of a particular subject are no longer relevant to learners in that society. The teaching of technical drawing as a separate subject in secondary schools in England provides an instructive example. Up to the 1970s plans describing the details of artefacts that were to be made were hand drawn and in locations where there were large manufacturing companies schools often taught technical drawing as a separate subject. Young people, usually male, often studied this subject with a view to being employed in a local drawing office. The advent of computer assisted design made the teaching of the subject in schools redundant.

Gerald van Dijk, Elwin Savelsbergh and Arjan van der Meij in their chapter *Maker Education: Opportunities and threats for Engineering and Technology Education* (2020) provide a balanced view of the threats and opportunities afforded for engineering and technology education (ETE) curricula by engaging with maker education. On the one hand there is little doubt that young people involved with their local maker movement experience a rich creative environment and learn to use particular technologies, but on the other hand the informal setting and level of choice they have may preclude the deliberate teaching of previously identified knowledge or skill. This is a particular issue for those educational systems in which there has been a a rise in the interest in and significance of knowledge rich curricula and the importance of teachers identifying and teaching specified substantive and disciplinary knowledge. The serendipity of learning within maker spaces would seem to have little place in this context. The authors use maker education to identify principles for strengthening ETE curricula in what they term a hybridization approach. Within this it is the role of the teacher in the classroom interaction with the students that make use of the approaches developed in maker spacers that is significant. This clearly indicates that in terms of the sustainability of any reform involving adopting Maker practice the involvement of teachers is likely to be crucial.

2   Establishing a Framework for Case Study Scrutiny

The case study *A Participatory Design Approach to Sustaining Makerspace Initiatives* (from Denmark) is presented in Chapter 3 and as the title indicates deals explicitly with sustainability of Makerspace initiatives. Hence it is well suited to providing a framework that can be used to scrutinise the other case studies. The authors of the study argue that the devising of the initiative starts with the involvement of key stakeholders in relevant design decisions from its inception. This participatory design approach prevents a top-down approach in which a few stakeholders make decisions that will affect the roles of other stakeholders and lead to their concerns being marginalized and lessening their commitment to the initiative. Unless all those with a stake in the initiative can work together to develop shared values and a common vision and collaborate in identifying the necessary human and physical resources required then it is unlikely that the initiative will take root and develop beyond a few early adopters. In terms of demonstrating effectiveness the study identified three criteria: ownership, spread and depth with the following features necessary for this:

– Involvement of stakeholders in collaborative practical hands-on activities
– Formal and informal discourse between stakeholders
– Considering Infrastructure as involving not only technical structures but organizational, political and personal structures as well
– Working both horizontally (engaging stakeholders in similar positions) and vertically (engaging with stakeholders at different levels of responsibility)

In this case the breadth of the stakeholders involved in the participatory design was wide and included the following:

– Funding agency
– Project lead
– Director of education
– University researcher
– Makerspace manager
– School principal
– Teachers
– Project partners

The study identified six steps involving some or all of the above that might lead to sustaining makerspace initiatives:

Step 1: Understanding the complexity of a makerspace initiative

This step involved an introduction to the initiative, a tour of a makerspace and a presentation by the makerspace manager with participants able to ask questions followed by the opportunity to meet and talk with teachers and pupils using the facility. It enabled participants to make tentative plans for necessary professional development.

Step 2: Hands-on introduction to makerspace education

This step involved participants in using makerspace facilities to tackle a making activity using digital design and manufacturing tools. This enabled a discussion on teacher – pupil interaction in makerspaces.

Step 3: Establishing the grand narrative of a maker space initiative

This step involved all the participants (including senior leadership) attending a presentation by an acknowledged researcher in the field giving an overview of international research on maker education followed by discussion. This established the dual use of maker spaces – practical activity using digital tools plus raising awareness of the nature and likely impact of digital tools on our society. This gave participants a 'Big Picture' view of maker education.

Step 4: Developing the makerspace initiative within the existing municipality landscape

This step required participants from each district to develop their vision of an ideal makerspace learning environment from a variety of user-centred perspectives. This is important because it avoided a premature focus on technical resources and allowed each district, with the help of a professional facilitator, to develop a detailed diagram of their vision for use in the next step.

Step 5: Confirmation and articulation of management support for the makerspace initiative

In this step participants from each district shared their detailed diagrams with participants from other districts and the directors of education with the directors explaining how the initiative fits into the strategic vision of the district. This enables each district to see the initiative in terms of vertical collaboration and activity.

Step 6: Choosing and purchasing technologies for the maker space

In this final step participants received advice and guidance regarding buying, using and maintaining digital design and fabrication facilities. Participants visit another makerspace, as in Step 1, but now the focus is on the available technology. Participants were able to detail the makerspace technologies they wanted for their individual initiatives.

It is important to note that the context of this case study is Denmark in which there is a very well-established education system with considerable human and physical infrastructure and a well-developed secondary school technology curriculum. The authors note that, "As such, the framework is not a fixed recipe to ensure a sustainable makerspace initiative but a source of inspiration when planning the initial stages of a makerspace initiative based on collaboration and participation among teachers, management and maker-space experts". It is in the spirit of this statement that the remainder of the case studies will be scrutinized. It must be acknowledged that at the time of writing there have been no publications describing how this Participatory Design approach to makerspace initiatives in Denmark has played out, but it has taken every effort to involve all those stakeholders with a vested interest in the success of the initiatives and hence is likely to lead to initiatives that are sustainable. Given that this approach involves teachers, management and makerspace experts and engages them as appropriate in activities that inform them, develop commitment, and lays the ground for implementation that is embedded in the local infrastructure the following questions derived from this study will be used to scrutinise the other studies with a view to exploring their sustainability.

– Who were involved in the initiative?
– Were they able to gain an understanding of the complexity of the initiative?
– Were they able to have a Hands-on introduction to makerspace education?
– Were they able to establish a grand narrative of the initiative?
– Were they able to integrate the initiative within the policy and practice of any local authorities present in the landscape?
– Were they able to confirm and articulate the management support for the initiative?
– Were they able to choose and purchase technologies for the initiative?

3   Scrutinising the Case Studies

We have six studies to scrutinise:
– In Chapter 4. Informal Learning in a Public Library Makerspace for Youth in the Netherlands. (Pijls, Van Eijck, & Bredeweg)
– In Chapter 5. Using "EcoMakerKits" to Stimulate Maker Mindset and Circular Thinking in Mexico. (Núñez-Solís, Madahar, Eskue, & Silva-Ordaz)
– In Chapter 6. Playful learning by design. Remote development of a design education workshop for rural Kenya. (Westerhof, Gielen, van Boeijen, & Jowi)

- In Chapter 7. Connecting Maker Education to Secondary School Technology Education in Korea: A Case of the Technology Teachers' Learning Community in Republic of Korea. (Kwon)
- In Chapter 8. Case Studies of Maker Education in China. (Gu & Yang)
- In Chapter 9. Maker Education in the Applied Physics Bachelor Programme at Delft University of Technology. (Pols & Hut)

3.1   *Scrutiny of Informal Learning in a Public Library Makerspace for Youth*

This study reports on the setting up of a network of makerspaces in Amsterdam Public Library and through eight vignettes highlight particular aspects of the informal learning context and through these identified six critical features of informal makerspaces.

1. The makerspaces provided opportunities for children to develop technological skills and creativity and enhanced their self-efficacy.
2. The after school programs stimulated the children's motivation.
3. The personal guidance was important as it supported children through the inevitable mistakes made in learning through making.
4. The physical embedding of the makerspace in a public library and near other public spaces or shops attracted children from local communities and allowed parents to easily contact the program.
5. Makerspace coaches had to adopt a variety of roles and need continuous professional development especially in pedagogy.
6. Cooperation with maker educators and student teachers from local organizations and institutions and universities stimulated the development of makerspace-coaches.

The intervention was initiated by the Amsterdam Public Library and involved the setting up of makerspaces in ten different libraries and the development of coaches within each makerspace to support the children aged 8–10 who visited the makerspaces. The comments from the coaches indicated that they understood the complexity of the initiative in terms of the different roles required of them. All the coaches received hands-on introductions to makerspace education and saw the initiative as a legitimate part of public library function which inevitably integrated the activity within the policy and practice of the organisation and may be seen as establishing a grand narrative. Given that the coaches received hands-on training and specialist guidance and saw coaching as part of their job working in the public library there was clearly management support for the initiative. In addition to computers each of the makerspaces was equipped with a 3D printer, a laser cutter, a sticker cutter, a sewing machine plus Tinkercad and Inkscape software. The coaches were not involved in choosing and purchasing these resources.

3.2   Scrutiny of Using "EcoMakerKits" to Stimulate Maker Mindset and Circular Thinking

The Mexican electronics recycling company, Recicla Electronicos Mexico S.a de C.V., collects e-waste in order

- to refurbish and resell electronic products,
- to disassemble e-waste to obtain parts that can be resold,
- to utilise parts in the development of new products for sale.

A spin off from the company is a makerspace initiative to engage young people with the idea of a circular economy through the problems of e-waste and give them hands on experience of using e-waste (presented as EcoMaker Kits) to make working products and develop technical skills and understanding alongside the skills of communication and problem solving. The EcoMaker team from within the company supported a small pilot initiative involving four students working with a retired engineer as facilitator. The main protagonists involved in the initiative were the EcoMaker team. From their work within Recicla Electronicos Mexico S.a de C.V. the EcoMaker team understood the enormity of the e-waste problem and the complexity of engaging young learners with possible solutions. The range of resources and activities that the team produced is a clear indication that they understand the complexity of the initiative. Importantly the work of the Recicla Electronicos Mexico S.a de C.V. provided a hands-on introduction to and experience of makerspace education. Through this introduction members of the team were able to produce kits that could be used by teachers in schools and kits for students to use in a summer school. The EcoMaker teams' commitment to solving the e-waste problem both commercially and educationally indicates they have a grand narrative for their initiative. Although lacking a local authority as such in which the initiative was embedded the commercial arena in which Recicla Electronicos Mexico S.a de C.V. operates provides a similar context in which the EcoMaker team are embedded and through this the team receive management support. The activities with young learners taking place in Recicla Electronicos Mexico S.a de C.V. provide examples potentially transferrable to other maker spaces and into schools. The context within which the initiative took place readily made available the technologies the initiative needed.

The scrutiny paints a picture of a successful initiative that is embedded in the commercial activity of Recicla Electronicos Mexico S.a de C.V. Given the enormity of the e-waste problem the continued success of the business seems highly likely and with it the sustainability of the initiative although it is worth noting that the continued goodwill of the CEO Alvaro Nunez will be important. A significant feature of the initiative is that it engages young people with circular economy thinking which will become increasingly important so there is the possibility that the initiative might inform school curricula in Mexico.

3.3   *Scrutiny of Playful Learning by Design Remote Development of a Design Education Workshop for Rural Kenya*

This initiative began with the idea of engaging children in rural Kenya with the designing and making of simple toys as means to develop design related skills through a workshop programme developed by a design academic based in the Netherlands in collaboration with a facilitator working with the children in Kenya. In the light of Covid restrictions, cultural context and the response of the children the workshop program evolved from a 'teaching the children to design' approach to an 'engaging the children in designerly play' approach. The communications between the academic and the facilitator were crucial in enabling the facilitator to capture the children's attention and motivate them to learn through play. The participants in this initiative were the academic in the Netherlands, the facilitator in Kenya and the children taking part in the workshops. The academic and the facilitator were able to develop an understanding of the complexity of the initiative through communication in response to the children's reaction to the workshop. To achieve a hands-on introduction to makerspace education the facilitator a) worked closely with the children using the resources provided by the academic and b) helped with the adaptation of these resources to the local context. A grand narrative of sorts was established at the beginning of the initiative but the way in which the children responded to the workshops caused activities to be altered significantly with the means within the grand narrative changing considerably. The local facilitator integrated the initiative in the context of a local community centre supported by a Kenyan non-profit organisation. Management support for the initiative was confirmed and articulated through the appointment of the local facilitator. The technologies used were to a large extent provided by the children from the local environment. Although in no sense the sort of hi-tech resources usually associated with makerspaces these were very appropriate for the situation.

This initiative is an outlier with regard to conventional makerspace activities but none the less it can be seen to answer the scrutiny questions successfully in terms of its context. However, the continued existence of the initiative is completely dependent on the local facilitator. Through taking part in the initiative under the guidance of the design academic based in the Netherlands the facilitator gained considerable professional expertise but at the moment there appears to be no mechanism to transfer this expertise to others who might become facilitators in similar local situations or replace the existing facilitator should he move away. The non-profit organisation supporting this initiative will need to consider how to use the facilitator to provide professional development for other possible facilitators if this initiative is to become sustainable.

3.4   Scrutiny of Connecting Maker Education to Secondary School Technology Education in the Republic of Korea

The study reports on the use of technology classrooms as maker spaces in response to the Korean Government support for maker education in schools. The participants in this initiative were members of the MAKER group – a voluntary technology teachers' professional community. They gained an understanding of the complexity of the initiative by developing a teaching and learning model for the initiative. At the MAKER group meetings teachers carried out practical projects which provided a hands-on introduction to makerspace education. Members of the Maker group were able to establish a grand narrative of the initiative through their alignment with government initiatives and through their ambition to promote a greater understanding of the nature of technology education and its value to contemporary education. Through alignment with government initiatives and the technology components of the Korean National Curriculum the initiative was able, to some extent, to integrate itself into national policy although the extent to which school practice 'on the ground' aligned itself with these features is unclear. MAKERS is a voluntary organisation existing through the enthusiasm of its members and the study does not reveal the extent to which administrators and senior leadership staff in school supported the aims of MAKERS. The study notes that currently equipment available is limited to '3D modelling, Arduino and coding education'. This indicates that teachers in schools as members of the MAKER group are not able to choose and purchase a wider range of technologies than that already available.

Whilst most elements of the scrutiny have been successfully met it is important to note that this initiative is dependent on the efforts of a group of highly motivated volunteers for its continuation. And although in line with government support for maker education in schools it is unclear as to the extent to which it can become part of regular school practice. The limitation to certain sorts of equipment may build discontent among the participating teachers. So, there is the potential for sustainability, but this would be enhanced if specific links with government agencies were forged to provide explicit support for the maker activities in local secondary schools and garner ring fenced funding.

3.5   Scrutiny of Case studies of Maker Education in China

The Tsinghua Makerspace community, part of the Tsinghua iCenter Project at Tsinghua University, developed a design and make assignment that was carried out by pupils at Tianyi Middle School under the direction of their teacher: the design and creation of a small energy-saving table lamp. The teacher was provided with detailed instructions concerning the resources required, the construction techniques to use, the teaching sequence and product evaluation criteria. In addition to developing technical knowledge and skills it was expected that the nature of the product being designed and made would raise pupils' awareness of energy conservation. The main participants were members of the Tsinghua Makerspace Community (volunteer university students), the middle school teacher and the pupils. The complexity of the initiative was understood by the university students as revealed by their production of detailed instructions and by the participating teacher through his effective use of the instructions. The university students had considerable makerspace education experience prior to the initiative and the teacher acquired this through following the detailed instructions. The work of the Tsinghua iCenter Project and the Tsinghua Makerspace community is underpinned by an appreciation of makerspace education and this established a grand narrative for the initiative. The teaching of the design and make activity in a local middle school was a first step to integrating the initiative into the policy and practice of the local authority. The teacher was able to purchase the items required from the school budget and teach the activity within the school timetable. This indicates management support for the initiative.

Whilst all elements of the scrutiny have been successfully met it is important to note that the initiative is dependent on the guidance provided by the volunteer university students. Given the nature of the Tsinghua iCenter Project it is likely that this guidance will continue. But at the moment the initiative is taking place in just one school. Its continued existence here is dependent on the willingness of the class teacher to continue and is vulnerable to his leaving the area if another teacher cannot be found to continue with the initiative. If the initiative is to become sustainable it is important that efforts are made to recruit and train other schoolteachers to take part in the initiative.

3.6   Scrutiny of Maker Education in the Applied Physics Bachelor Programme at Delft University of Technology

This initiative develops makerspace activity to enable university physics students to develop the practical and intellectual skills to design and make prototype technical equipment. The authors of the study were the main drivers of the initiative but also the students whose took the lab courses Design

Engineering for Physics Students (DEPS), the teachers and teaching assistants of DEPS are significant actors in this initiative. The main drivers of the initiative (the authors of the study) clearly understood the complexity of the initiative from its inception (it was very much their idea) devising suitable lab projects for the students. The teachers and teaching assistants engaged in teaching the lab course became highly involved in the initiative and quickly developed an understanding of the complexity. The structure of the program provided students with a highly hands-on introduction supported strongly by the teachers and teaching assistants. Embedding the DEPS lab course into the degree program in both years 1 and 2 can be seen as establishing a grand narrative assuming that the lab course remains as part of the program. Given that the initiative was conceived as a part of the degree program and introduced as such this indicates integration into the prevailing policy and practice of the content. That the initiative had significant management support is indicated by the physical resources in terms of room and equipment being made available by the university along with funding for student projects. The equipping of three different rooms with appropriate resources indicates that there was autonomy with regard to choosing and purchasing technologies appropriate to the initiative.

Whilst all elements of the scrutiny have been successfully met and the initiative is embedded in a university engineering degree program its short-term future, at least, seems secure. There is little doubt that the enthusiasm of the main drivers is contributing to its current success. If for some reason they moved to another university and the running and maintenance of the initiative was left to those teaching the course, then there is the possibility that it might not be so successful with students becoming less enthusiastic. This might lead to its demise. Strategies to avoid this include induction of those teaching the course into its significance with regard to student experience and professional development to ensure they remain competent in hands-on makerspace activities.

4   Concluding Remarks

There is little doubt that in each of the case studies those involved had clearly identified intentions for their interventions and explicit plans for their implementation. In all cases there is evidence that this combination of intent and implementation led to significant impact. So, from that standpoint these Maker Education initiatives may be seen as successful. However, such success in the short term does not guarantee the sustainability of the initiatives. It is important to be realistic in terms of what is meant by sustainability and for our purpose this might mean that the initiative becomes embedded in practice and widespread such that it is seen as the norm and no longer an initiative. All the case studies reported will have some difficulties in meeting this requirement and these difficulties may be seen to revolve around the following features:

1.   *Continued Perception of Worth by Key Stakeholders:*
Stakeholders who are involved in formulating national or regional educa-tion policy may, for various reasons, decide that such initiatives are no longer worthwhile. If that happens the initiatives will inevitably flounder. Ensuring that this does not happen requires effective political lobbying by those who are convinced of the worth of the initiatives.

If stakeholders who have been responsible for creating and sustaining an initiative as in the Mexican and China case studies lose interest for whatever reason, then the continuance of the initiative will be in doubt. Stakeholders who are involved in implementation, i.e., the teachers and coaches, are crucial to sustainability. If, for any reason, they decide that the initiatives no longer have worth then sustainability will be compromised.

2.   *Continued Funding:*
This is essential to ensure appropriate hardware and software is available not only to enable the continuation of pilot initiatives but for roll out across the educational system.

3.   *Professional Development for Those Responsible for Implementation:*
It is essential to ensure that all the teachers involved are inducted into the culture of the maker movement, experience hands-on makerspace activities and have the opportunity to refresh and enhance this knowledge and skill at regular intervals. This has implications for both initial teacher education and continuing professional development.

References

Department for Education and Skills. (2006). *The Primary Framework for literacy and mathematics.* Crown copyright. http://www.educationengland.org.uk/documents/pdfs/2006-primary-national-strategy.pdf

Lucas, B., Hanson, J., & Claxton, G. (2014, May). *Thinking like an engineer: Implications for the education system.* Royal Academy of Engineering. https://raeng.org.uk/media/brjjknt3/thinking-like-an-engineer-full-report.pdf. Accessed 16 September 2022.

Osborne, J., & Millar, R. (Eds.). (1999). *Beyond 2000: Science education for the future; the report of a seminar series funded by the Nuffield Foundation.* King's College London, School of Education. https://www.nuffieldfoundation.org/project/beyond-2000-science-education-for-the-future

Thorburn, P., & Tinbergen, D. (1976). *Wreake valley science scheme.* Edward Arnold. https://trove.nla.gov.au/work/18912825

van Dijk, G., Savelsbergh, E., & van der Meij, A. (2020). Maker education: Opportunities and threats for engineering and technology education. In P. J. Williams & D. Barlex (Eds.), *Pedagogy for technology education in secondary schools* (pp. 83–98). Springer Nature.

Welsh Government. (2020). *Introduction to Curriculum for Wales guidance.* Retrieved May 6, 2022, from https://hwb.gov.wales/curriculum-for-wales/introduction/

CHAPTER 16

Conclusions

Marc de Vries and Remke Klapwijk

Abstract

In this final chapter we tie together the insights gained in the previous chapters. We discuss how the appreciation for making is related to a worldview in which the materiality of reality and a certain view on mature and humans features. This has consequences for our vision on teaching and learning. We conclude by stating that there is a need for further research into maker Pedagogical Content Knowledge with teachers. With teachers being well equipped to do making activities, there is a lasting value of Maker Education, both in schools and elsewhere.

Keywords

worldview – materiality – science and technology – sustainability – creativity – equality – teaching and learning – educational research

1   'Maker Education': Rich, But Fuzzy

We have made quite a journey along different Maker education examples and reflections. In Chapter 1 we already noted that there is quite a variety of Maker education practices. The term Maker education' seems to be an umbrella term for a great variety of activities of which the main common feature is that artefacts are made. But apart from that, everything seems to vary. The only other limiting feature is perhaps the educational setting – that can be formal, informal or nonformal education, and all cases we have seen are either formal or informal education. Nonformal education settings, such as people having a workshop at home in which they perform do-it-yourself hobby activities do not seem to get the label 'Maker education', at least not as far as the literature goes. The level of education does vary: primary, secondary and tertiary education are all represented in our sample of Maker education cases. We have also seen both high-tech and low-tech practices. The purpose of the Maker activities also varies. The focus can be on the personal acquisition of making skills, but also community building is mentioned as a possible aim of Maker education. The pedagogy that is used also takes different shapes in different situations. It can be more guided and controlled or more open-ended and with lots of room for free creativity.

This complex image of Maker education suggests a certain richness. Apparently making can be used for different purposes in different settings with different means and in different ways. At the same time, this makes the term 'Maker education' rather fuzzy. It can mean almost anything in which making has a place. That makes it difficult to conclude this book with general statements, as there are always examples that do not fit with these conclusions. Yet, we will make an effort to write some general observations having seen the set of cases and the thematic chapters.

2   Worldview

Perhaps it needs a deeper look to see what is really common in the enormous variety of Maker education practices. If making is the one common feature, then where does it come from? Is there, perhaps, a deeper, underlying motive for the focus on making? Is it related to a fundamental view on reality and on people? In other words, is it related to a worldview? The term 'worldview' is used to indicate a coherent set of convictions about what exists, how it came to exist, what it is heading towards, what is right and what is wrong, what we can know about it and how we can act in that reality (Vidal, 2008). Worldviews can be inspired by a religion, but not necessarily so. We all have a worldview, whether we are aware of it or not. Becoming aware of it can help to understand the way we think and act. For the case of Maker education: it can help us understand why making and learning to make is so much valued. In the next sections we will explore some aspects of the worldview that seems to drive Maker education. Most of these aspects have been mentioned in the case descriptions and in the thematic chapters, while some are our own observations.

3   View on Materiality

We live in a world in which virtuality is highly valued. We create a variety of virtual connections between people: the Internet, mobile phone connections, social media, etcetera. On Facebook we have friends that perhaps we have never met in person. Our only connection with those friends is virtual. We create games and other virtual worlds in which we move around without our bodies, only with virtual objects (avatars). Perhaps we make things in such worlds but only with virtual means and virtual resources. Perhaps the rapidly growing popularity of making can be seen as a countermovement for that 'virtualisation' of reality in our current society. After all, we humans are not just brains and minds. We have bodies that are really part of who we are. It is not necessary to fall into the trap of a dual worldview, like Descartes', in which body and mind are separate entities. We have become well aware of how closely they are connected and that leads many people to reduce the world to either the material or the virtual part. But most people intuitively feel that both exist and are not just a matter of appearance. If that is true, then the popularity of Maker education can be explained by a certain feeling that we should do more justice to our materiality in a society that almost overestimates virtuality. After all, one friend that we meet in person may be of more value than a hundred friends that we only know virtually. And likewise: with all the possibilities of creating things in virtual worlds, they do not compensate for a loss of materiality. Having materials in your hands, feeling their surfaces, trying out their bending and twisting strengths, feeling the softness or hardness of their surfaces and sensing if they feel cold or warm is all impossible in a virtual world. That is what Maker education makes valuable in a world in which we already do so many things in virtual ways.

4   View on Science and Technology

Materiality also plays a role in our view on science and technology and their relation. Science is by its very nature an activity that strives for abstract knowledge. In particular the natural sciences do not aim for describing particular situations but for deriving abstract concepts and 'laws' from those particular situations. That way of thinking has proven to be of great value. Science enables us to understand our world in a deep and fundamental way, precisely because of the abstractions it makes. Yet, these insights do not yet change the world. That is what technology is for. Technology does not (only) describe but it aims at changing the world based on ideas about what is 'better' and what is 'progress'. That makes technology a very normative activity, contrary to science that merely describes (although there are of course norms for what we accept as knowledge but the content of that knowledge itself is not normative but only descriptive). But not only differs technology from science in that it is normative and not just descriptive, it also differs in that one cannot get around the concreteness and materiality of reality in technology, whereas in science abstraction is key. Here again Maker education can be seen as a correction for an overestimation of science, as we often see it in our society (for which the term 'scientism' is sometimes used). Making makes us aware that knowing reality becomes even more valuable when we use that knowledge to change the world. It also makes us aware that we do not always need the fundamental and abstract knowledge of science to change the world successfully. The experience of a carpenter is much more helpful in his work than the abstract knowledge from science. Intuition can also be a source of reliable knowledge, just like science can be. Science is certainly a useful source of reliable knowledge but by no means the only one. Making can be based on a variety of different knowledge types, some more abstract and others more concrete. Making can therefore make us aware of the value and the limitations of both science and technology.

5   View on Human Responsibility towards Nature

Making means that we use natural resources that we transform them into something useful or beautiful. Some of these natural resources can be re-used once we no longer use or value what we have made, but others cannot be re-used. Making makes us aware of the fact that there is a limit to the use of natural resources. Thus making can also make us aware of a certain responsibility that we have with respect to natural resources. Of course, we can also develop that awareness through the manifold data and statistics that we read daily in our newspapers and magazines. But what more direct way to become aware of the limits to natural resources than direct experience. Once we have cut a piece of paper or cardboard into parts and pieces, the paper or cardboard cannot again be cut into parts and pieces. Only if the resource is recycled and reworked into cardboard and paper, it becomes again available for our use, be it that we can often see the marks that it is not anymore in its original quality. Maker education is somewhat ambiguous here. It can tempt us to use materials for the fun of the making activity and makes us ignore and overlook the effect our making activities have on the availability of natural resources. At the same time, making is a very direct way to raise an awareness of the limits to natural resource use. Sometimes making activities focus on this, for instance by using recycled materials. Such an activity can show how much value there can be in discarded materials. What is not of use anymore for one person may be of great value for someone else. Using recycled materials contributes to the sustainable availability of natural resources. The issue of sustainability is one that gets increasing attention in education and in society in general. Maker education can clearly play an important role here. This, however, assumes that the making is done in a responsible way without unnecessarily wasting materials (and energy). This is definitely something to keep in mind with the rapidly increasing popularity of 3D-printers. They are easy to make simple products simply for the purpose of having fun when observing the printer put layer onto layer. Often the finished product is thrown away immediately after the printer is finished, as the fun of watching the process is no longer there. This can cost a lot of material and produces a lot of waste, and because plastics are particularly popular for this use, it is also a waste that does not naturally dissolve but requires special processes to become useful again. If making activities are used for contributing to an awareness of the need for sustainable living, this kind of waste of resources has to be avoided.

6 View on Humans

Materiality as part of reality can be part of our worldview, as noted a few sections ago. That includes a view on ourselves as human beings. But there is another aspect of our view on people that is related to making. It has to do with the fact that making requires and develops human creativity. The extent to which it does that depends on the extent to which designing has a role in Maker education. Sometimes pre-made designs are used and Maker education is limited to the making only. However as we saw in the various cases, Maker education is mostly a combination of designing and making. And even when no real design work is included, the making itself also requires some creativity in the use of tools and machines. Maker education therefore supports a worldview in which humans are seen as inherently creative beings. In many worldviews, that will also be seen as something that makes them unique. Although it is more and more claimed that robots and computers can display signs of creativity, such worldviews will claim that robots and computers do not have a 'mind' in the way humans have, and therefore are not creative in the full human sense. In a similar way humans can make in a way that robots cannot. Robots follow a program but humans can deviate from whatever at least partially determines their behavior (and we have become increasingly aware that there are all sorts of biological and social factors that do determine our behavior to a certain extent). If in our worldview creativity is one of those characteristics that makes us unique, then enhancing creativity by making is highly valued. This may well be one of the underlying values that explain the popularity of Maker education. A third element in the view on humans that gets increasing attention nowadays is the equal value of all human individuals and the need to prevent people with certain backgrounds or abilities to be advantaged above others. This is also something that fits well with Maker education due to its accessibility to a wide variety of people. Makerspaces usually do not have high fees (if they have fees at all) and thus do not exclude economically deprived people. Making does not require a high cognitive ability so lower achievers can flourish in Maker education as well as high achievers (what is 'low' and 'high' achievement anyway?). Making can be fun for all genders, depending on what is made and in what context. Making education can thus support a worldview in which all humans are seen as equally valuable and with a right of self-development.

7   View on Teaching and Learning

Related to the previous issue is our view on teaching and learning. If creativity is what makes Maker education valuable, among other things, then a certain view on teaching and learning is also implied. Creativity is not enhanced when learners are told exactly what to do. For a long time our view on teaching and learning was that a learner is an empty vessel that needs to be filled by the teacher. Now we hold a more constructivist view on teaching and learning. This does not necessarily imply that we see knowledge as a social construct only. Realists will maintain the idea that there is an objective reality outside us that determines whether our beliefs are 'true' or 'false', which in epistemology is usually seen as the difference between beliefs and knowledge (problematic as it may be to conceptualize exactly what 'true' and 'false' are, but at least they are somehow related to a reality that exists outside our thinking). This constructivist view on teaching and learning is a most suitable approach for Maker education and thus Maker education can thrive when we see teaching as a process in which we create an environment in which the learner can actively acquire new knowledge and skills. This entails that learning should take place in projects in which the ownership is divided over teacher and learner. The teacher should have some ownership as we know by research that learning does not take place without an active role of the teachers, not to steer but to stimulate. Making also allows for creating communities of learners when the making processes take place in groups of learners. Creating learning communities is also an element in the current dominant view on teaching and learning and Maker education is a suitable context for that, assuming that the making is not only done on an individual basis (which, of course, is always an option in making activities).

8 The Need for Further Educational Research on Maker PCK

The many claims about the values of Maker education and its learning effects are not yet supported by a lot of educational research. The number of references to educational research on Maker education in the book, both in the case studies and in the thematic chapters, is relatively small. Perhaps the fact that Maker education is more associated with informal than with formal education explains that. Measuring learning outcomes is seen as more important in formal education than in informal education because of the allocative function of formal education. Within the small body of research literature on Maker education, the role of teachers is perhaps the smallest issue studied. It would be important, though, to know what Pedagogical Content Knowledge coaches and teachers should have in order to help learners acquire making skills and achieve wider learning goals. Although a certain fuzziness is admitted by most advocates of this concept, Pedagogical Content Knowledge (PCK) is still a term that regularly features in the research literature. One of the unclear elements is the concept of the meaning of the term 'knowledge'. In epistemology the effort has always been to distinguish between beliefs and knowledge. The term 'knowledge' is then reserved for only these beliefs that are in some way or other 'true', as we have remarked earlier in this chapter when we discussed realism versus constructivism. In PCK literature it seems, however, that any belief a teacher may hold is counted as part of her/his PCK. In that respect the term Pedagogical Content Beliefs or PCB would be more appropriate. It must be acknowledged that knowing false beliefs of teachers is no less relevant than knowing true beliefs, but it does not help conceptually to reckon all beliefs as knowledge. In the Maker education literature, research into teachers' beliefs is still scarce, irrespective of whether they are true or false beliefs. Obviously, there is still work to be done here.

9 The Lasting Value of Maker Education

More research support to show that the claims of Maker education do get realized would help enhance the sustainability of Maker education. In the introductory chapter we have already shown what value Maker education can have. One of the issues we discussed there was the relation between Maker education and (Design and) Technology education. Having seen examples of the practice of Maker education as well as theoretical reflections on that practice, we can conclude that both Maker education and (Design and) Technology have their value. Maker education is strong in its emphasis on the pleasure of making. (Design and) Technology education is strong in its embedding of making in a wider curricular context in which relations with design work and concept learning are made. Maker education is strong in its accessibility. (Design and) Technology education is strong in its allocative value (achievement in the subject can open doors to further education). Maker education is very inclusive and learners of all sorts of backgrounds and characteristics can be involved in it. (Design and) Technology education is often taught in settings that fit with a certain type of learner (e.g., more or less cognitively oriented), but it is offered in different ways to different types of learners so that inclusiveness is realized but in a different way. For the future of both, a good cooperation would be helpful. A good relation with formal education could also motivate funding agencies to keep supporting Fablabs and the like in the future. After all, Maker education is often dependent on external funding, whereas for (Design and) Technology education in formal education that support is guaranteed by the government (although the past has shown that the position of this education can be under threat as well).

In summary, there is place for both Maker education and (Design and) Technology education and this book provides knacks as to how they can both flourish and what is needed for the sustainability of both.

Reference

Vidal, C. (2008). What is a worldview. In H. van Belle & J. van der Veken (Eds.), *Nieuwheid denken. De wetenschappen en het creatieve aspect van de werkelijkheid* [Thinking novelty. Sciences and the creative aspect of reality) (pp. 1–12). Acco.

Index